IMPOSSIBLY AMAZING!

IMPOSSIBLY AMAZING!

RIPLEY
PUBLISHING

a Jim Pattison Company

PUBLISHING

Publisher Anne Marshall
Editorial Director Rebecca Miles
Project Editor Charlotte Howell
Editorial Assistant Dominic Lill
Text Geoff Tibballs
Proofreader Judy Barratt
Researchers Charlotte Howell, Dominic Lill, James Proud
Indexer Hilary Bird
Art Director Sam South
Project Designer Rocket Design (East Anglia) Ltd
Cover Design Michelle Foster
Reprographics Juice Creative
Executive Vice President Norm Deska
Vice President, Archives and Exhibits Edward Meyer

PUBLISHER'S NOTE
While every effort has been made to verify the accuracy of the entries in this book, the Publishers cannot be held responsible for any errors contained in the work. They would be glad to receive any information from readers.

WARNING
Some of the stunts and activities in this book are undertaken by experts and should not be attempted by anyone without adequate training and supervision.

Cover image: Maria José Cristerna has transformed herself into Vampire Woman, with numerous tattoos and permanent fangs!

Published by Ripley Publishing 2015

Ripley Entertainment, Suite 188, 7576 Kingspointe Parkway, Orlando, Florida 32819, USA

2 4 6 8 10 9 7 5 3 1

ISBN 978-1-60991-121-8

Some of this material first appeared in *Ripley's Believe It or Not! Download The Weird*

Library of Congress Control Number: 2014953615

Manufactured in China in November/2014
1st printing

First published in Great Britain in 2015 by Random House Books, Random House, 20 Vauxhall Bridge Road, London SW1V 2SA
www.rbooks.co.uk

Addresses for companies within The Random House Group Limited can be found at
www.randomhouse.co.uk/offices/htm

The Random House Group Limited Reg. No. 954009

A CIP catalogue record for this book is available from the British Library

ISBN 9781784751388 (UK)

For information regarding permission, write to VP Intellectual Property, Ripley Entertainment Inc., Suite 188, 7576 Kingspointe Parkway, Orlando, Florida 32819
email publishing@ripleys.com
www.ripleys.com/books

CONTENTS

RIPLEY'S WORLD

Marco Polo, Christopher Columbus, Neil Armstrong... there are few true adventurers that can be compared to such great men—but Robert Ripley just might be one of them! In 1918, considering the limited forms of travel, Ripley's determination to visit countries barely known back home showed a pioneering spirit no less extraordinary than those intrepid explorers.

With style, in bow tie and spats, Ripley traveled to Papua New Guinea, Armenia, China and beyond—his aim was to uncover the world's wonders and weird-ities, miracles and monstrosities and feature them in the Believe It or Not! cartoon he drew daily for *The New York Globe*.

Americans couldn't get enough of Ripley and he rocketed into radio and television—broadcasting from places such as a shark tank! Soon he was said to be more popular than the U.S. President!

By 1933, Ripley had opened an Odditorium (museum) in Chicago to display the artifacts he'd collected. Today, Ripley's is a global empire with 32 Odditoriums, three aquariums, a warehouse packed with artifacts and an archive of more than 25,000 photos and 100,000 cartoons.

Robert Ripley broadcasting from his New York apartment, which was filled with artifacts he had collected on his travels.

Ripley's Believe It or Not! daily cartoon was a huge success and Ripley received millions of pieces of fan mail each year.

Robert Ripley was voted the most popular man in America by the New York Times in 1936, above President Roosevelt.

Here Robert Ripley is being pulled along in a rickshaw by a Zulu warrior in South Africa in 1933. He traveled to 201 countries in his lifetime—and a total distance equal to 18 trips around the world!

RIPLEY'S CARTOONS

The Ripley's Believe It or Not cartoon has been published every day since 1918—making it the longest running cartoon in the world. The cartoon has had just six cartoonists in its history, starting with Robert Ripley himself.

Ripley's early cartoons described the collection of oddities he found on his travels, and were published in a bestselling book in 1929—selling more than two million copies. Ripley signed on as a syndicated cartoonist with King Features that same year and became the first millionaire cartoonist ever—even before Walt Disney!

The cartoon was syndicated in more than 360 newspapers around the world, translated into 17 languages and had an estimated readership of more than 80 million! He was so famous that mailmen delivered letters to him that simply had "To Rip" and "To the World's Biggest Liar" on the envelope—an address wasn't needed. In 1936, a survey found that Ripley's cartoons were the most popular feature in any paper and had more readers than the front-page news!

Ripley with his first ever Believe It or Not! cartoon published in 1918 entitled "Champs and Chumps." He kept this precious cartoon above a fireplace in his mansion on an island in Mamaroneck, New York.

Believe It or Not
By Ripley

Graveyard of the Ages
for All Chinese
SUNDAY, APRIL 7, 1940

RIPLEY's **Believe It or Not!**®

Ripley was just 18 when he first had a cartoon published. It appeared in *LIFE* magazine in June 1908, and he was paid $8!

This cartoon was published in 1930.

Selected cartoons were produced in color from 1933—this cartoon was published in 1940.

A Sunday cartoon published in 1950.

Published in 1946, this cartoon shows Ripley's famous Chinese junk ship the Mon Lei. The ship was built in 1939 for a Chinese warlord and Ripley bought it in 1946!

THE LEGACY LIVES ON

Here at Ripley's, we're inquisitive. Every second of every day, we've got our ears to the ground, eyes peeled and fingers flicking through files and every kind of social media—only stopping short of sniffer dogs—in the pursuit of a barely believable truth, or a person with a life more extraordinary—continuing the legacy of Robert Ripley.

We have researchers, curators, archivists, and model-makers, as well as editors and correspondents, who compile articles and write for the Ripley's Believe It or Not! books. Dedicated and passionate about what we do, we never tire in our mission to research, uncover and preserve the unbelievable side of life.

Robert Ripley always encouraged his dedicated readers to submit material and photographs—a tradition that exists to this day. With a huge computer database of incredible facts, people, and events, a massive photographic archive, and a warehouse stuffed with unique exhibits, Ripley's is able to present a celebration of the amazing diversity of our world, without ever passing judgment.

Today, if all the Believe It or Not! books ever published —well over 200 titles—were stacked one upon another, the total number of books sold would be more than 300 times as tall as New York City's Empire State Building!

Today the cartoon is drawn by Ripley's resident cartoonist, John Graziano.

10

Mateo Blanco, an opera singer from Colombia, South America, created this incredible portrait of the Hulk using only sugar, dyed with food coloring!

Made of Sugar!

Made of toilet paper!

Made of yarn!

Meet the winning dresses of our Cheap Chic Toilet Paper Wedding Dress Contest! Catherine Cox (left) and Kaylee Kehne (right) modeled the wedding dresses made of toilet paper.

A Teenage Mutant Ninja Turtle made of 60 balls of yarn! Created by Mateo Blanco, the same artist that created the Hulk, the figure is over 6 ft (1.8 m) tall!

11

UNUSUAL MAIL

Ripley's has received the strangest mail in the world for nearly a century, so to reward our fans we created the Ripley's Unusual Mail Contest. We asked Ripley's fans from all over the world to send in the weirdest and wackiest items they could find to Ripley's HQ in Orlando, Florida, in 2014.

Hundreds of items were sent into us and the craziest submission received a grand prize of a complete collection of Ripley's Believe It or Not! annuals. The contest had just one rule—the mail couldn't be packaged in any way, no envelope or wrapping or box of any kind could be used, and the stamp and address had to be fixed to the item directly. Every submission received a copy of *Dear Mr. Ripley* and archival photos. We were sent items from across the globe, including a wooden spoon from Australia!

The 2014 winner was Pat Moser from King, North Carolina, who sent in this tree stump! Pat found a horseshoe inside the 75-year-old tree! The item weighed a massive 19 lb (8.6 kg)!

Join our World!

Instagram
instagram.com/ripleysodditorium

Twitter
twitter.com/ripleys

Facebook
facebook.com/RipleysBelieveItorNot

Pinterest
pinterest.com/RipleysBION

The 2014 runner up was Lisa Palmer from Baltimore, Maryland, who sent us this homemade life-size Raggedy Ann doll. It was one of the biggest items we received and cost a whopping $79.96 to mail!

Giant hand-painted fan sent by Lisa Palmer, Baltimore, Maryland.

Mannequin hand from Bev Lambinse, Middlesex, New Jersey.

Inflatable pink flamingo sent by Barry Wood, Vero Beach, Florida.

Beehive from Krisztina Kremenes, Grant, Florida.

Whether it's a giant story or just a tiny nugget of information...CONTACT US! We'd love to hear from you.

SEND US STUFF...
www.ripleys.com/submit

WRITE TO US...
BION Research, Ripley Entertainment Inc., 7576 Kingspointe Parkway, 188, Orlando, Florida 32819, U.S.A.

ON THE WEB...
www.ripleys.com/books

EMAIL US...
bionresearch@ripleys.com

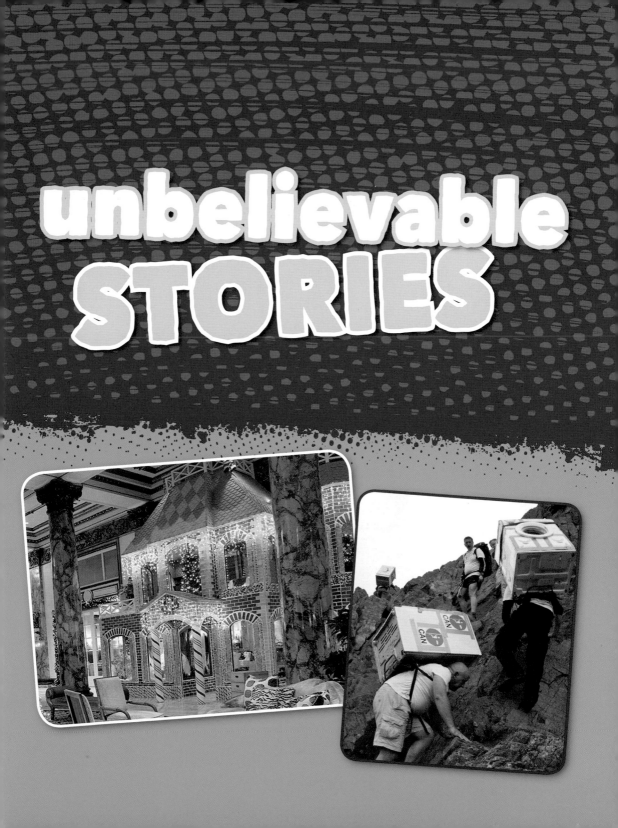

unbelievable STORIES

THE ODD COUPLE

They must be one of the world's oddest couples. He swallows swords, hedge trimmers and umbrella handles, while she hangs upside down and lifts 110-lb (50-kg) lead weights by just her hair.

Meet husband and wife Hannibal Helmurto and Anastasia IV who, since 2005, have performed with the Circus of Horrors.

Hannibal, whose body is covered with over 200 tattoos, used to be a German tax inspector called Helmut Kirchmeier until he went to a circus and was inspired by a sword swallowing act. He can now swallow a blade attached to a revolving electric drill.

Polish-born Anastasia Sawicka ran off to join the circus at 18, and now she specializes in hair hanging. Anastasia can suspend upside down from a rope, and use her hair to lift a 120-lb (54-kg) woman off the ground.

JELLY BRAIN

Online retailer Firebox sells gelatin candies in the shape of human brains. The life-sized Gummi Brain is a little over 7½ in (19.5 cm) long, weighs over 6 lb 10 oz (3 kg), and comes in bubblegum flavor.

Chopstick Trade

A lack of wood in China has led to a U.S. company, Georgia Chopsticks, producing two million pairs of chopsticks a day to export to the country. Until the shortage, manufacturers in China produced 63 billion sets of chopsticks every year.

Acquired Tastes

Exotic snacks offered for sale by vendors on Wangfujing Street, Beijing, China, include dried sea horses, silkworms, sheep's penis, giant grasshoppers, starfish, roasted sparrows, cicadas, and inside-out snakes.

Grub Protein

The European Union is promoting the nutritional benefits of eating low-cholesterol insects in dishes such as scorpion soup and locust salad. Grasshoppers offer 20 percent protein and just 6 percent fat compared to lean ground beef's 24 percent protein and 18 percent fat. Crickets are said to be high in calcium, termites rich in iron, and a single portion of giant silkworm moth larvae provides all our daily copper and riboflavin needs.

Mummified Larva

Mummified caterpillar fungus is served with chicken or pork in soups in China and Tibet to improve the flavor. The Thitarodes caterpillar feeds on the roots of a fungus that grows high up in the Himalayas, but the fungus reacts by invading the caterpillar's entire body, eventually killing and mummifying it.

Bear Feast

On May 10, 2010, the Union Rescue Mission Shelter in L.A., California, served meals of donated game meat including elk, boar, antelope and black bear. The meat was served in tacos and was eaten by hundreds of residents.

Head Waiter

Tokyo, Japan, is gaining a reputation for outlandishly themed restaurants. The Alcatraz ER restaurant is styled after a prison hospital and has drinks served in a life-sized mannequin head.

Metro Ban

The French cheese Epoisses, once a favorite of the emperor Napoleon Bonaparte, has been banned on the Paris Metro because of its strong odor.

Healthy Snacks

Kansas State University nutritionist Dr. Mark Haub lost 27 lb (12.2 kg) in two months on a junk-food diet of chocolate bars, potato chips, cookies, pizza, doughnuts and sugary cereals. Despite his diet of sugary, salty and fatty processed food, his body fat and bad cholesterol levels both fell. He focused on measuring his calorie intake, limiting himself to small portions of the junk food. This way he only consumed 1,600 calories per day, 900 less than the recommended amount.

SUPERMARKET SURPRISE

Tesco, the U.K.'s leading supermarket chain, is opening stores across China, but the stock is a little different from that usually found on its shelves. Its store in Qingdao caters for local tastes by selling such items as chicken's feet, turtles, dried sea horse and whole dried lizard! Rice wine infused wth dried lizard is said to be a fortifying drink.

19

Miss Maple

Using detective skills she had learned at a Junior District Attorney crime-fighting summer camp, 12-year-old Jessica Maple quickly solved a burglary at her late great-grandmother's house in Atlanta, Georgia—a crime that had baffled the police.

Fated to Marry

Amy Singley and Steven Smith of Bushkill Township, Pennsylvania, were born at the same hospital on the same day in 1986—when their mothers shared a hospital room—and on June 12, 2010, the 24-year-olds were married.

Parallel Lives

Graham Comrie, 45, and Graham Cormie, 47, who live just 10 mi (16 km) apart in Scotland, look almost identical, are both professional photographers and married to redheads, and have two daughters, and Lhasa Apso dogs as pets. Both men celebrated their silver wedding anniversaries in 2011. People confuse them for each other all the time, and they get messages from each other's friends on Facebook.

CRASH MAN

Rusty Haight is the human crash-test dummy. As director of the San Diego-based Collision Safety Institute, Rusty has experienced more than 950 violent vehicle crash tests at speeds of up to 54 mph (87 km/h), and taken 140 air bags to the face. A former police traffic officer, Rusty uses his unique car-wreck experience to research automobile safety and investigate and reconstruct collisions.

Birth Pattern

Emily Beard was born in 1997 in Portsmouth, England, at 12 minutes past 12 on the 12th day of the 12th month. Her father David had been born at 40 minutes past four on the fourth day of the fourth month, her mother Helen was born on the tenth day of the tenth month, her brother Harry arrived on the sixth day of the sixth month, and their grandmother Sylvia was born on the 11th of the 11th.

Limped Away

One of South Africa's most wanted criminals—due to stand trial in relation to 35 armed bank robberies—escaped from police custody by simply walking out of a Pretoria courtroom door... on crutches.

Missing Ring

Robert McDuffy, a firefighter from Wareham, Massachusetts, lost his wedding ring while fighting a house fire. However, luckily for Robert, the homeowner found the ring—11 years later—and returned it.

BRAVE HOUND

Vernon Swart from Stellenbosch, South Africa, was horrified when he returned home to find his dog Bella running around with a large knife lodged firmly in her skull. The six-year-old Alsatian terrier crossbreed had suffered the injury as she chased burglars away from the property, but incredibly she did not appear to be in any pain, and later recovered. The veterinarian who eventually removed the knife said the dog had been only a fraction of an inch from death.

MOUTH CAMERA

This photo of young Louis Quinnell was taken with a pinhole camera fitted in the back of his dad's mouth! Justin Quinnell from Bristol, England, positioned the film in his mouth so that his back teeth could keep it stationary, and then held his mouth wide open to take the pictures. He created the pinhole camera by placing tinfoil over a pinprick one-fifth of a millimeter wide on the cartridge, and used it to take unique mouth's-eye pictures of the world around him, including the Sydney Opera House in Australia and more everyday occurrences such as taking a bath. Sometimes he had to stand still with his mouth open in front of his subject for a minute to ensure that the film was properly exposed.

Tiny Camera

U.S. catalog company Hammacher Schlemmer has introduced the world's smallest fully functional digital camera—which is no bigger than a human fingertip. The tiny camera measures just over 1 in (2.5 cm) in all dimensions and weighs only 0.5 oz (14 g).

On Time

All three children born to Lowri Dearsley of Manchester, England, have arrived at precisely the same time, 7.43. Overcoming incredible odds, daughter Ella was born at 7.43 a.m. on October 10, 2005; another daughter, Evie, was born at 7.43 p.m. on December 26, 2007; and a son Harrison was born at 7.43 a.m. on January 20, 2011.

Liver Op

U.S. actor Larry Hagman—famous for playing ruthless oil tycoon J.R. Ewing in *Dallas*—has an artwork containing a collection of 150 silver staples from his 1995 liver transplant.

Waste of Money

The U.S. Bureau of Printing and Engraving produced more than a billion $100 bills for release in 2011 that were rendered worthless when a machine improperly creased the bills during printing.

Toilet Auction

A man who owns a toilet tissue roll that was once rejected by The Beatles has been offered $1,500 for a single sheet. The Liverpool, U.K., band refused to use the paper while recording at London's Abbey Road studios in the 1960s because it was too hard and shiny and had the name of record company EMI stamped on every sheet. The roll was bought at an auction by Beatles fan Barry Thomas for $120 in 1980.

100-ft Geyser

When a car smashed into an L.A., California, fire hydrant in 2011, shearing off the top, the broken hydrant sprayed a fountain of water 100 ft (30 m) into the air, flooding streets and causing people to be evacuated from their homes.

Invisible Beggar

Fed up with being ignored by passersby, street beggar Nemanja Petrovic from Subotica, Serbia, tossed his cap and shoes down on the sidewalk with a handwritten card saying "Invisible Beggar" and abandoned his pitch. He returned to find his cap full of money—so now he puts down the card and a pair of shoes as a prop and goes to a nearby café while the donations pour in.

Beached Whale

A dead 33-ft-long (10-m) whale was found in a field in Yorkshire, England—half a mile from the sea. It became stranded after being carried to shore by an exceptionally high tide while it was hunting.

Banana Attack

A costumed gorilla mascot at a cell-phone store in Strongsville, Ohio, was attacked in July 2011— by a banana. The store manager reported that a boy dressed as a banana emerged from bushes and leaped at the man wearing the gorilla suit. The banana split before police arrived.

Ring Reunited

Joan Spiers was reunited with a diamond ring that she had flushed down the toilet two-and-a-half years earlier. Following the mishap—at a hotel near Gatwick in Surrey, England—she hired a waste firm to search 12,000 gal (54,500 l) of sewage for the ring, but to no avail. Then, by coincidence, an employee from the same firm stumbled across it 30 months later at a sewage works.

Tuna Record

The owner of a chain of sushi restaurants in Tokyo, Japan, paid a record $747,000 for a 593-lb (269-kg) bluefin tuna in January 2012, the equivalent of $106 for each piece of sushi.

Wine Flood

Workers at a liquor store in Sheboygan, Wisconsin, fled for their lives when a 78-ft-long (24-m) shelf collapsed, sending nearly 7,000 bottles of wine crashing to the floor.

Golden Cheese

Cheesemakers in Leicestershire, England, have made a Stilton cheese containing real gold. Clawson Stilton Gold is made from white Stilton infused with a mixture of edible gold leaf and real gold liqueur. The golden cheese sells for about $1,000 per kilo (2.2 lb).

Cupcake Tower

Volunteers in Vereeniging, South Africa, baked 21,000 cupcakes that were then arranged into a vast tower 19 tiers high and 11 ft 9 in (3.6 m) wide.

MONSTER MUSHROOM

Picked from the wild in Shaanxi Province, China, this edible puffball mushroom weighed in at a whopping 10 lb (4.5 kg).

Eggstraordinary

Brian Spotts of Dacono, Colorado, balanced 900 eggs on end on the marble floor of a Hong Kong mall in March 2011. He practices egg balancing for half an hour daily and stresses the need for a light touch and the correct grip with the thumb and forefinger of each hand positioned at the top of each egg as he balances.

Robo-noodle

Robots cook noodles for customers at a restaurant in Nanping, China. The restaurant owner, Fan Ming, paid $1,500 for the robots whose eyes and chest lights flash as they drop the noodles into boiling water.

Longest Log

A team of 80 chefs in Shanghai, China, created the world's longest Christmas yule log, measuring more than 0.6 mi (1 km) long and more than five times the length of the previous record. It took 24 hours to make the log using 904 eggs, 2,304 lb (1,045 kg) of flour, 460 lb (209 kg) of sugar, 884 lb (401 kg) of bitter chocolate, and 75 lb (34 kg) of vanilla.

Stir-fry

On September 5th, 2011, the University of Massachusetts made the world's largest stir-fry at 4,010-lb (1,820 kg). Using a custom-built, 14-ft-wide (4.3-m) frying pan, staff and students at the university prepared the world's largest stir-fry. The meal had 800 lb (363 kg) of chicken, 500 lb (227 kg) of onions, 400 lb (181.5 kg) of carrots and 300 lb (136 kg) of broccoli.

CHINESE TREAT

The slippery sluglike marine creature, the sea cucumber (or sea rat), is a popular delicacy in Chinese cooking. It is considered an aphrodisiac and is used in medicine to treat everything from high blood pressure in humans to joint pain in pot-bellied pigs. The dried ovary of the sea cucumber is eaten in Japan and is called *konoko*.

SNAKE TWIST

For more than 30 years, Liu Fei of Jiangxi Province, China, has been pulling 3-ft-long (0.9-m) snakes through his nose, sometimes even using two snakes simultaneously. His most unnerving moment came when he accidentally swallowed one of the snakes, but luckily for Liu it died in his stomach before it could cause any harm.

Monster Wombat

In 2011, paleontologists in Queensland, Australia, uncovered an almost complete skeleton of a diprotodon, a prehistoric wombat-like creature the size of an SUV car, that was the world's biggest marsupial. The three-ton monster, which had large tusks but a tiny brain, became extinct about 35,000 years ago.

Robot Marathon

At the world's first robot marathon—raced around 423 laps of a track in Osaka, Japan, in February 2011—the winner completed the 26-mi (42-km) course in just over two days at an average speed of 0.48 mph (0.77 km/h). At the finish, the winning robot—16-in-tall (40-cm) Robovie-PC—waved its arms and bowed to the crowd.

Not Again!

Two years after being ticketed for speeding in London, England, a man emigrated to Christchurch, New Zealand, and was again booked for speeding—by the same police officer who had stopped him in England! Like the disbelieving driver, Constable Andy Flitton had recently moved across the globe to New Zealand.

Steel Cage

April Pignatoro and Michael Curry married in Riverhead, New York State, on June 6, 2010, in a steel cage placed underwater in a shark tank.

Human Cow

Scientists in Argentina have created a cow that produces "human" milk. By incorporating two human genes into the cow before birth, scientists from the National Institute of Agribusiness Technology in Buenos Aires have developed an animal that will produce milk similar to that of humans.

Treble Chance

Believe it or not, Jennifer and Driss Allali from Eastbourne, England, have three children with the same birthday—Najla, Adam and Sami were all born on October 7, in 2005, 2007 and 2010 respectively.

Bank Error

While renovating a former bank in Ghent, Belgium, as a base for his accounting firm, Ferhat Kaya opened an old safe that had been left behind by the previous owners and found bags of 20 and 50 euro bills, totaling around $380,000.

Million-dollar Bottle

For the woman who wants to smell like a million dollars, DKNY created a million-dollar bottle of perfume. They created a special bottle of their Golden Delicious fragrance, the bottle was carved from polished 14-carat yellow and white gold. Covered in 2,700 white diamonds and 183 yellow sapphires, it also has a flawless 2.43-carat single diamond in the bottle cap.

Space Lesson

People who spend long periods of time in space have to relearn to place objects down when they return to Earth rather than letting go of them in midair.

Diamond Planet

Astronomers believe they have discovered a planet named 55 Cancri E that contains large amounts of diamond 4,000 light-years away. The planet, which is about 37,000 mi (60,000 km) wide—over five times the diameter of Earth—is thought to be the remains of a once-massive star in the Milky Way. Its high density indicates that it must be made of crystalline carbon—in other words, diamond.

TITANIC

At the time of her launch, the luxury liner *Titanic* was not only the biggest ship in the world, but also the largest movable object ever built. Yet, she made only one voyage, in April 1912, which ended in disaster. More than a hundred years later, the story remains as compelling as it is chilling.

After setting off from Southampton, England, the New York-bound *Titanic* struck an iceberg in the dead of night in the North Atlantic and sank in the early hours of April 15, with the loss of over 1,500 lives. Out of the estimated 1,523 people who perished, only 328 bodies were recovered, of which 128 were unrecognizable. The temperature of the water was only 28°F (−2°C) and most passengers would have died of hypothermia or heart attacks. Over 62 percent of first-class passengers on the *Titanic* were saved, compared with just 25 percent of those who traveled third class.

Although only 12 sq ft (1.1 sq m) of the *Titanic*'s hull was gouged open by the collision, the design of the ship meant that a little over 2½ hours after impact, the supposedly "unsinkable" vessel disappeared beneath the waves.

The last *Titanic* survivor, Millvina Dean, died on May 31, 2009. She was just nine weeks old at the time of the tragedy, the youngest passenger on the ship. Her father died when the boat sank, but her mother and brother survived.

more...

Titanic under construction at the Harland and Wolff shipyard in Belfast, Ireland. The deck sat 60 ft (18 m) above the waterline.

Ship workers in the Belfast shipyard are dwarfed by one of *Titanic*'s three propellers, measuring almost 24 ft (7.3 m) across.

THE FACTS

- It cost $7.5 MILLION to build—the equivalent of $400 million today

- Each of the engines was the size of a THREE-STORY HOUSE

- The FOUR FUNNELS were 62 ft (19 m) high and 22 ft (6.7 m) in diameter, wide enough to drive two trains through

- The hull was constructed with THREE MILLION rivets

- The center anchor weighed 15.5 TONS and needed 20 horses to pull it through Belfast to the shipyard

- The ship contained more than 200 MI (320 km) of electrical wiring

- The ship was lit by 10,000 lightbulbs

- *Titanic*'s whistles could be heard from a distance of 11 MI (18 km) away

- The ship was fitted with 29 boilers and 159 furnaces, and carried more than 8,000 TONS of coal

- 16,800 GAL (63,645 l) of drinking water were consumed on board every day

- If the 882-FT-LONG (269-m) ship had been stood on its end, it would have been taller than any building in the world at that time

- SIXTY chefs and chefs' assistants worked in five kitchens providing food for the passengers

more...

No human remains have ever been discovered on or around the wreck of the *Titanic*. Any bodies that sank with the wreck have been eaten by fish and crustacea. All that remain are the shoes and boots of the victims still lying on the sea floor.

On board were 13 couples celebrating their honeymoons.

The wreck of the *Titanic* was discovered on September 1, 1985, by underwater explorer Robert Ballard. It lay largely intact at a depth of 12,000 ft (3,660 m) below the surface of the Atlantic off the coast of Newfoundland. This depth is six times deeper than a human diver has ever descended, and enough to crush human lungs. Using a small submersible craft, Ballard explored the wreck in 1986, but it wasn't until August 1998 that a section of the hull was hauled to the surface.

Titanic memorabilia, including a pocket watch recovered from the wreck.

LOST PROPERTY

Among passengers' insurance claims submitted to the White Star Line following the sinking were:

- Personal property $177,352.75 **Charlotte Drake Cardeza**
- Oil painting $100,000 **Hakan Bjornstrom-Steffanson**
- Renault 35 hp automobile $5,000 **Billy Carter**
- Signed picture of Garibaldi $3,000 **Emilio Portaluppi**
- Champion French bulldog $750 **Robert W. Daniel**
- Four roosters and hens $207.87 **Ella Holmes**
- Set of bagpipes $50 **Eugene Daly**

SHIP'S STORE

- 75,000 lb (34,000 kg) of fresh meat
- 25,000 lb (11,400 kg) of poultry and game
- 11,000 lb (5,000 kg) of fresh fish
- 40,000 eggs
- 36,000 oranges
- 16,000 lemons
- 20,000 bottles of beer
- 1,500 bottles of wine
- 40 tons of potatoes
- 1,500 gal (5,700 l) of fresh milk
- 12,000 dinner plates
- 8,000 cut-glass tumblers
- 45,000 table napkins
- 15,000 pillow slips
- 25,000 fine towels
- 18,000 bedsheets

Realizing they would not escape, U.S. mining magnate Benjamin Guggenheim and his valet changed into full evening dress, reappearing on deck to declare: "We've dressed up in our best and are prepared to go down like gentlemen."

TRAIN TRACK TREATMENT

A risky remedy has recently grown in popularity in West Java, Indonesia. Locals believe that lying down on active railway tracks will cure various ailments. Participants remain on the tracks for as long as the speeding trains will allow, believing that electrical currents running through the lines are beneficial to their health.

Stones Fan

In October 2010, police in Chennai, India, arrested a man for smuggling more than 2,000 diamonds and precious stones in his stomach.

Wedding Machine

In 2011, Marvin's Marvelous Mechanical Museum in Detroit, Michigan, bought a new vending machine that enables couples to get married for just $1. Devised by British company Concept Shed, the AutoWed has a robotic voice that takes couples through their vows, they can then either press one button for "I do" or another for "Escape." At the end, they get a wedding receipt and two plastic rings.

Shot Ornament

Called to a home in Kansas City, police officers shot an alligator twice in the head before realizing it was a garden ornament. It was lurking next to a pond when officers arrived, and only when the second shot bounced off the alligator did they realize it was made of concrete.

Dig the Bride!

To save money on wedding cars, groom Zhang Zongqiang, who works for a heavy machinery company, used a fleet of six mechanical diggers to transport himself, his bride Ye Yuzi, and their guests to the marriage ceremony in Henan Province, China. The couple stood in the bucket of the lead digger, which was decorated with ribbons and balloons, and tossed candies to well-wishers along the route.

I Dooooooo

Jason Jenkins of Stoke-on-Trent, England, proposed to his girlfriend Melissa Bowen by having her engagement ring delivered by an owl. Carrying a diamond ring in a pink velvet bag on its leg, Zulu the owl swooped from a perch and landed on Jason's arm.

Heavy Load

A truck carrying steel pipes that increased its total weight to 98 tons was so heavy that it fell through a bridge and landed in a river. The truck was being driven across the Dongrong Bridge in Changchun, China, when the road suddenly collapsed beneath it, leaving a truck-sized hole measuring 46 x 16 ft (14 x 5 m).

Floating Van

An amphibious ice-cream van toured Britain's seaside resorts in 2011. Driven by Dave Mountfield from Brighton, Sussex, HMS *Flake 99* had a top speed of five knots and chimed Rod Stewart's "Sailing" as it took to the water.

Cash Jigsaw

After a Taiwanese businessman had inadvertently dropped the equivalent of U.S. $6,000 of banknotes into a shredder, justice ministry worker Liu Hui-fen put them back together in just seven days. The 200 New Taiwan $1,000 bills were each ripped into about 20 pieces, but by locating the Chinese character *guo* (country) on each bill and then working outward, she managed to complete the cash jigsaw.

Double Delight

Shop owner Ron Rea of Belle Vernon, Pennsylvania, sold himself a winning $1.8-million lottery ticket in November 2010—and as the seller of the ticket, he received an extra $10,000!

First-class Male

Chester Arthur Reed, aged 95, of Riverside, California, retired from his job as a U.S. postal worker after 37 years with nearly two years of unused sick time.

SURPRISE CARGO

When police in Bargteheide, Germany, stopped a van that was being driven erratically, they opened the rear doors—and found a car neatly parked on its side in the back. It was the brainchild of two men from Kazakhstan who, after buying a Mazda 626, decided to save on the costs of shipping it home on a trailer by loading it into their van, placing a mattress beneath the car to stop its doors getting scratched on the floor of the van. The police confiscated both the van and the car until the pair found a proper transporter.

Memorable Dates

Tyler Ashton Marx was born in Meridian, Idaho, at 11.11 a.m. on 1/11/11 (January 11, 2011). His older sister was born on September 9, 2009—09/09/09.

Late Delivery

A postcard from a soldier serving in the British Army in World War I was finally delivered in 2010—94 years late. The loving message from 19-year-old Alfred Arthur to his sister Ellen did not reach her address in Norwich, England, until long after both of them had died.

Rich Pickings

Raffi Stepanian, with a pair of tweezers, made $450 a week by searching the pavement cracks of New York City for valuables. The former jewelry setter found diamonds, rubies and even platinum and gold.

Tusks Seized

In January 2011, a court in St. Petersburg, Russia, confiscated 3 tons of mammoth tusks—64 full and 14 reconstructed—from a criminal gang that had been trying to smuggle them out of the country. The tusks came from Siberian mammoths and had survived for thousands of years because of the permafrost that covers most of the region.

HOLD TIGHT!

This brave lamb was snapped hitching a ride on the back of his owner's motorcycle in Havana, Cuba, in early 2011.

Robot Safety

Robot-driven cars created by the software company Google have traveled more than 140,000 mi (224,000 km) on U.S. streets with only a single accident. The cars use artificial-intelligence software that can sense anything near the vehicle and mimic the decisions made by a human driver. Engineers say that robot drivers react faster than humans, have 360-degree perception, and do not get distracted, sleepy or intoxicated.

Ferrari Fan

Jon Ryder of Sheffield, England, loves his yellow 1996 Ferrari 355 Spider so much he parks it in his living room. He drives it through a garage door at the end of the room so he can admire it from his sofa.

Butter Blunder

In May 2011, a visitor to Boijmans van Beuningen museum in Rotterdam, the Netherlands, accidentally trod in an artwork made of peanut butter. He absentmindedly wandered onto Peanut Butter Platform, a piece by Dutch artist Wim T. Schippers that was acquired by the museum in December 2010. It features 290 gal (1,100 l) of peanut butter—enough to fill more than 2,000 regular-sized jars.

Singing Mice

Japanese scientists have created mice that can sing. By tinkering with a mouse's DNA so that it randomly mutated, they have managed to develop more than 100 mice that can chirp like sparrows.

Wrong Turn

A British man and his wife drove their Renault into the side of a church near Immenstadt, Germany, after obeying faulty instructions from their GPS. The couple ended up in the hospital with minor injuries, their car was wrecked, and $30,000 of damage was done to the church—all because the GPS directed them to turn right where there was actually no road.

Keep Turning

California's Ridge Route mountain highway—built in 1915 and linking L.A. to Bakersfield—has 697 turns in just 36 mi (58 km) of road.

METAL MARRIAGE

Elaine Davidson, who has nearly 7,000 body piercings, got married in June 2011 to Douglas Watson... who has none. At her wedding in Edinburgh, Scotland, only her face was visible—and that was painted with bright colors and covered in 192 piercings.

Rice Crazy

There are more than 40,000 different types of rice in the world. The Chinese alone eat 130 million tons of rice every year.

Stinking Bishop

After the highly pungent Stinking Bishop cheese—made on a single farm in Gloucestershire, England—was mentioned briefly in the 2005 Oscar-winning animated movie *Wallace & Gromit: The Curse of the Were-Rabbit*, demand for it rose by 500 percent.

Sausage Addict

David Harding from London, England, has spent nearly £2,000 ($3,230) on counseling and hypnosis to try to beat his addiction for eating an average of 13 sausages a day. He has eaten at least one sausage a day since he was five and spends up to £700 ($1,100) a year on sausages.

"Cashier Number Four, Please"

The voice of Terry Green is heard in the U.K. about 30 million times every month as his is the voice that directs customers at banks and post offices to the next available counter.

Jesus Image

Toby Elles of Salford, England, fell asleep while frying bacon—and woke up to find a lifelike image of Jesus Christ, complete with long hair and beard, burned into the pan.

Dancing Carrots

To pave the way for proposing to his girlfriend, Pang Kun persuaded 48 of his friends to dress up as giant dancing carrots in a shopping mall at Qingdao, China. He spent $15,000 on carrot costumes and they rehearsed their dance routine for two days. The idea was to attract the attention of Zhao Xinyu because orange is her favorite color.

Lucky Find

When Reg Barker of Suffolk, England, bought a box of old postcards at a garage sale, he was amazed to find one of them featured a picture of his mother. He paid $4 for the box stuffed with more than 200 postcards in 2009. When he looked through them, he saw one of crowds celebrating Victory in Europe Day on May 8, 1945. There, dancing with Canadian troops in London's Leicester Square, were his mother and aunt.

No Name

Maximus Julius Pauson of Pasadena, California, wasn't given a name on his birth certificate and went without an official name for 19 years.

Job Search

During 2008 and 2009, a homeless, jobless Californian economics graduate landed 50 jobs in 50 different U.S. states in 50 weeks. In his search for work around the country, former financial analyst Dan Seddiqui became—among other things—a lobster fisherman, a jazz-band conductor, a TV weatherman, a syrup processor, and even a Las Vegas wedding planner! He said that his favorite job was as a bartender in Louisiana during the Mardi Gras festival.

Largest Deck Chair

Visitors to the beach at Bournemouth, England, in 2012 saw the world's largest deck chair—standing 28 ft (8.5 m) tall, 18 ft (5.5 m) wide and weighing six tons. It was built by sculptor Stuart Murdoch whose previous works include spending 512 hours creating a life-sized army tank out of 5,016 egg boxes.

View from inside the house

TASTEFUL HOTEL

During the holiday season in December 2011, the Fairmont Hotel in San Francisco, California, put on display a gingerbread house of epic proportions. Constructed out of 7,500 home-baked gingerbread bricks and 1,200 lb (544 kg) of royal icing, the 23-ft-high (7-m) house was decorated with 650 lb (295 kg) of colorful candies and featured a special room where children could write a letter to Santa—with express delivery to the North Pole.

Ashes Tour

Deb Green from Vancouver, Canada, advertised on the classified ads website craigslist for volunteers to each take a vial of her late parents' ashes around the world and to sprinkle them at major landmarks. As a result, their ashes are now sprinkled, among other places, in a fountain in Las Vegas, Nevada, in a beer garden in Amsterdam, the Netherlands, and at the base of the Eiffel Tower in Paris, France. Deb said Alice and William Green couldn't afford to travel but had always wanted to visit far-flung countries.

Lucky Numbers

Twice in the space of a month in 2010, Israel's biweekly national lottery drew the same six winning numbers—13, 14, 26, 32, 33 and 36.

Married Herself

On November 6, 2010, Chen Wei-yih, a 30-year-old office worker from Taipei, Taiwan, got married to herself. The ceremony was held at a hotel and witnessed by 30 relatives and friends. Her purpose was to show she was confident and happy with who she was.

Premature Aging

To demonstrate their commitment to growing old together, Zhang Jin, 25, and his fiancée Yao Zenni, 26, of Nanjing, China, had pre-wedding photographs taken showing them as an elderly couple battling against the cold. The pair wore makeup and dyed their hair gray to make themselves look 50 years older.

Under-qualified

The Italian government funded a Libyan man to attend a training program in Rome so that he could learn how to be an underwater frogman, only to discover that he couldn't actually swim. It was later revealed that the candidate was the cousin of the official tasked with choosing participants for training programs and had liked the idea of a vacation in Rome.

That's Progress!

It took three years for the first U.S. mint to produce its first million coins. Today, the Philadelphia, Pennsylvania, mint can stamp out a million coins in 30 minutes.

SWEATY ROBOTS

U.K. designer Kevin Grennan has created robots with sweaty armpits. He has augmented three existing robots with "sweat glands" made from Japanese artificial sweat, a product used to test fabrics for sweat stains. In response to a chemical stimulus, each robot targets a specific form of human subconscious behavior—fear, focus and trust—to improve its effectiveness.

LUCKY BREAK

A three-year-old boy had an amazing escape when he fell from the eighth-floor window of an apartment building in Beijing, China, but became wedged behind an air conditioner protruding from a window on the floor below. Trapped between the conditioner and the wall, he was unable to fall any farther and was rescued with nothing worse than a few scratches and bruises.

Poetic Justice

U.K. filmmaker Martin Cassini defended himself on a charge of speeding to overtake a truck by pleading his case to the court in Barnstaple, Devon, in rhyming couplets. Despite his testimony in verse, he was fined £175 ($285).

Mercy Mission

World-War-II German fighter pilot Franz Stigler allowed a heavily damaged American B-17 bomber to escape during a 1943 mission—and 46 years later he became good friends with Charlie Brown, the bomber's pilot.

Beginner's Luck

Just minutes into his first attempt at metal detecting, three-year-old James Hyatt, of Billericay, England, struck gold—in the form of a 16th-century religious locket valued at nearly $4 million.

BIZARRE BIKERS

If you see a watermelon riding a bike, it's almost certainly the result of a Kazakhstan company that has designed a range of weird motorcycle crash helmets in such styles as a brain, a tennis ball, a cracked walnut and a watermelon.

Underpants Run

On September 24, 2011, thousands of people stripped down to their underwear and ran through Salt Lake City in protest at what they considered the strict laws of Utah.

Florida Tattoo

A burglary suspect in Tampa, Florida, was arrested after his alleged victims recognized him from a facial tattoo on his left cheek—an outline of the state of Florida.

Home Lover

A couple from Mestre, Italy, took legal action in a desperate attempt to force their 41-year-old son to leave home. The parents said their son had a well-paid job but refused to move out, preferring to have his clothes laundered and his meals cooked by his mother. Forty-eight percent of Italians between the ages of 18 and 39 still live at home.

Food Tattoos

Chef Lauren Wilton of Toronto, Canada, has decorated her body in food-related tattoos, including a whisk, a fork and spoon, two garlic heads, dandelion greens, and a boar's head on a platter.

False Freckles

Scottish prosthetic technology company Touch Bionics has introduced a highly realistic range of false limbs that feature freckles, hairs and even tattoos.

Cushioned Fall

In January 2011, a woman survived falling 23 stories from a hotel rooftop in Buenos Aires, Argentina, after she landed on the roof of a taxi, which broke her fall.

Married on the Run

A couple from Houston, Texas, got married during the 2011 city marathon. David Upton and Molly Johnston started the race as boyfriend and girlfriend but crossed the finish line as husband and wife after pausing briefly at the 16-mi (26-km) mark to exchange their marriage vows in front of friends. The bride complemented her running cap with a small white veil.

Micro Brewery

Bragdy Gwynant, a brewery in Capel Bangor, Wales, is located in a former outhouse and is only 25 sq ft (2.3 sq m) in size. It brews ale for just one customer—the Tynllidiart Arms inn next door.

Two-toed Tribe

Many of the Vadoma people, a reclusive tribe in western Zimbabwe, have only two toes on each foot.

Clever Feller

In May 2010, a man lost in the wilderness of Northern Saskatchewan, Canada, signaled for help by chopping down electrical poles. He was rescued when the power company came out to investigate the downed lines.

Grave Vows

In May 2011, two couples held their weddings in a Chinese cemetery, exchanging their vows among the gravestones. Wu Di and his bride Yang Xi and Wei Jian and his bride Liu Ling, all of whom work at the cemetery, chose the unusual venue as a declaration of their intention to be together until death. The wedding procession to Yong'an Cemetery in Tianjin consisted of 26 decorated cemetery carts.

Wheelchair Robber

Peter Lawrence, 71, robbed a San Diego, California, bank of more than $2,000 while in a wheelchair.

Nonprofit Cafe

In 2010, the Panera Bread Company opened a nonprofit café in Clayton, Missouri, where customers pay just what they can afford and those who are unable to pay can volunteer their time instead.

Price of Bread

At the height of Zimbabwe's economic collapse in 2008, it cost 700 million Zimbabwean dollars to buy a single loaf of bread. Thus, 200 million Zimbabwean dollars was equivalent to $1!

Taco Line

As part of the 2011 Phoenix Phestival in Oregon, a group of taco engineers took just 15 minutes to build a line of tacos measuring 177 ft (53.9 m) long.

Shrimp Cocktail

More than 80 chefs in Mazatlán, Mexico, joined forces to concoct the world's largest shrimp cocktail, weighing 1,187 lb (538.5 kg). It was served in a dip containing 127 lb (58 kg) of ketchup and 22 lb (10 kg) of lemon juice.

RAVISHING RATS

Finger-licking-good rats are rounded up and sold at almost $1.70 a pound ($3.80/kg) in the markets of Canh Nau, Vietnam. Formerly a food eaten through necessity in times of poverty, the rodents are now a popular, local specialty.

FOWL FOOD

Grilled, stewed or fried, a plate of duck tongues is considered one of the most luxurious snacks in parts of the Far East. Devotees of the dish say it's the faint hint of meat, the paper-thin layers of cartilage, and the pockets of fat that make the tongues so delicious! The taste of the tongues, barely 2 in (5 cm) long, is like no other duck meat, and the texture is much more creamy. Those who need further convincing might try this recipe for duck tongues—fried.

Vegetable King

Gardener Peter Glazebrook from Nottinghamshire, England, set a new record for the world's heaviest onion when he exhibited a monster weighing just under 18 lb (8.1 kg) at the Harrogate Flower Show in 2011.

Red Hot Chili

Chili grower Nick Woods of Grantham, England, has grown a new chili, Infinity, with a heat that measures 1.17 million on the Scoville Scale that grades chili heat. That's 300 times hotter than Tabasco sauce, and so hot it carries a health warning. When he first tasted the chili raw, he was unable to speak or stand up, shook uncontrollably, and he felt physically sick.

Perfect Pie

A £3,000 ($5,000) mince pie—the most expensive in the world—went on display in London, England, in 2011. Made by chef Andrew Stellitano from a 17th-century recipe, the mince pie included high-grade platinum leaf, holy water from Lourdes to bind the pastry, vanilla beans and cinnamon from Eastern spice markets, and ambergris sugar harvested from the secretions of sperm whales.

Prize Puff

At the 2011 Wisconsin State Fair, a team of bakers created a cream puff that weighed a whopping 125.6 lb (57 kg). The prize puff measured 7½ in (19 cm) high and 38 in (96 cm) wide.

PICTURE ROOM

Dutch artist Erik Kessels filled a room with photos after downloading and printing every picture uploaded to the photo-sharing website Flickr in a 24-hour period—that's over one million images.

Twitter Winner

Actor Charlie Sheen collected one million Twitter followers in just over a day when he signed up to the site in March 2011, becoming the fastest tweeter to reach seven figures. Sheen gained 60,000 followers before even posting his first tweet; he now has more than 10 million, but that isn't even enough to place him inside the top 20 celebrity tweeters.

Safety Bowl

The Longxiang Public Bus Company in Changsha, China, uses a hanging bowl of water in its buses as a visual reminder for bus drivers to drive calmly and carefully.

Wall Vaulter

The U.S. military's research arm has devised a robot the size of a shoebox that can jump over walls 25 ft (7.5 m) high. The Precision Urban Hopper is a four-wheeled, GPS-guided remote-control car fitted with a piston leg that can propel it over obstacles up to 60 times its own size.

Rare Malt

A rare 3-pt (1.5-l) bottle of single malt Scotch whisky sold for $460,000 at an auction in New York in November 2010. The 64-year-old Macallan malt had been bottled in a one-of-a-kind, handcrafted crystal Lalique decanter.

Virtual Shopping

The world's first virtual retail store opened in a busy subway station in Seoul, South Korea, where all the goods on display are just pictures. Choosing from over 500 items, ranging from food to electrical goods, smartphone users download an app and take photos of the barcodes to make purchases. They can order goods on their way into work and have them delivered when they get home.

Tight Squeeze

In December 2010, 26 members of the New York City-based Pilobolus Dance Company squeezed their bodies into a standard MINI car.

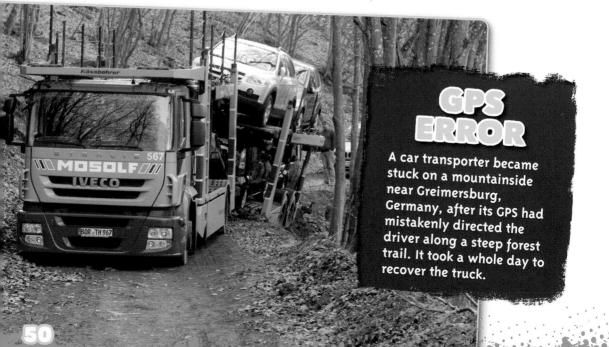

GPS ERROR

A car transporter became stuck on a mountainside near Greimersburg, Germany, after its GPS had mistakenly directed the driver along a steep forest trail. It took a whole day to recover the truck.

Where the Streets have no Name

About 100 street signs mysteriously disappeared from the town of Northborough, Massachusetts, in the first six months of 2011.

Paper Plane

In October 2010, near Madrid, Spain, a paper airplane fitted with a tiny camera was launched into space to photograph its descent to Earth. For Operation PARIS (Paper Aircraft Released Into Space), it was attached to a weather balloon. When the balloon burst 17 mi (27 km) up, the plane began to fall, taking pictures on its way.

Jail Break

On August 22, 2011, exactly 25 years after he first performed the stunt of escaping from Waushara County Jail, Wisconsin, Anthony Martin, the "King of Escapists," repeated the feat—and in almost half the time. Despite being placed in a straitjacket, strapped to a ladder and locked behind four steel doors, he was able to complete his escape in just 2 minutes 50 seconds—nearly two minutes faster than his first attempt in 1986.

OVER-THE-TOP

Arturas Zuokas, mayor of Lithuania's capital city, Vilnius, surprised bystanders when he drove over an illegally parked vehicle in a Russian armored personnel carrier, crushing the vehicle beyond repair. The elaborate stunt was a headline-grabbing response to luxury cars being parked illegally in the capital.

Longest Interview

Australian radio presenter Richard Glover set a world record for the longest-ever radio or TV interview when he talked to journalist and author Peter FitzSimons for 24 hours in a Sydney studio.

Strange Hybrid

Motorbike-crazy Markus Sell, from Jonschwil, Switzerland, welded the rear half of a Renault Clio car onto the front half of a motorbike. But, as he roared along at 70 mph (115 km/h), police stopped him and claimed the vehicle was unsafe.

Mini Mini

Retired mechanic Lester Atherfold from Napier, New Zealand, trimmed over 2 ft (60 cm) off his 1964 MINI car so that it could fit into the trunk of his motor home. He reduced the 10-ft-long (3-m) MINI to a mere 7 ft 10 in (2.4 m) by slicing a chunk from the middle, narrowing the chassis, and fitting a new sub-frame, transmission, clutch and dashboard.

Armored Car

The "Popemobile," the Roman Catholic Pope's touring car, is armored with 3-in (8-cm) blast-resistant glass panels and has its own internal air supply for protection against a chemical or biological attack.

Quick Thinking

Duane Innes of Kent, Washington State, deliberately crashed into a truck driven by 80-year-old Bill Pace. The crash stopped Pace's truck, saving his life after he had passed out behind the wheel.

Wooden Scooter

Carlos Alberto, a carpenter from Portugal, built a functioning replica of a Vespa motor scooter almost entirely from wood.

Gears

Exhaust pipes

ALIEN BIKE

It looks like an alien monster, but it's really a motorbike. This stunning creation was assembled by artist Roongrojna Sangwongprisarn at his workshops in Bangkok, Thailand. Roongrojna builds crazy-looking motorbikes from the recycled spare parts of cars, motorcycles and bicycles—and his awesome metal sculptures can actually be ridden.

Bike chain

Bike chains

Springs and cables

Bank Party

On June 2, 2011, June Gregg celebrated her 100th birthday with a party at the Huntington National Bank branch in Chillicothe, Ohio—where she still held the same savings account her father opened for her in 1913.

TONGUE TWISTER

China's Li Jinlong used his mouth to balance a tower of three plastic bottles, 12 wine glasses, five glass plates and 16 soccer balls, and then made the entire tower spin using only his tongue. His tongue had to support and spin a total weight of 33 lb (15 kg).

Toilet Museum

In Wiesbaden, Germany, toilet fan Michael Berger has opened a museum devoted exclusively to the lavatory. The unusual attraction contains his personal collection of toilet brushes, toilet roll holders and toilet seats. Among the extraordinary artifacts are a "Mona Lisa" toilet roll holder, a Virgin Mary toilet brush holder, and a urinal with Adolf Hitler's face on the inside, which was designed after World War II to show disapproval of the Nazi regime.

Channel Swim

At the age of 70 years 4 months, Roger Allsopp, a retired surgeon from Guernsey in the Channel Islands, U.K., became the oldest person to swim the English Channel when he completed the 24-mi (39-km) crossing from Dover, England, to northern France in 17 hours 51 minutes on August 30, 2011.

Snake Challenge

In 2010, David Jones, a 44-year-old carpenter from Crawley, England, spent four months locked in a room with 40 poisonous snakes, including cobras, black mambas and puff adders, in Johannesburg, South Africa.

Movie Statues

Dave Bailey of Middlesex, England, has collected Star Wars memorabilia for over 30 years. His £60,000 hoard includes full-sized statues of all the main characters, including a 7-ft-tall (2.1-m) Darth Vader.

Delayed Diploma

Eighty-six-year-old James Livingston from Savannah, Georgia, graduated from Screven County High, and was awarded his high-school diploma, on May 28, 2010. His parents had allowed him to leave high school in 1942 to help fight World War II on condition that he earned his diploma when he got back.

Island Swim

Julie Bradshaw, a sports coach from Loughborough, England, swam the 28.5 mi (45.9 km) around New York's Manhattan Island in 9 hours 28 minutes, using only the butterfly stroke.

Wing Walk

On November 15, 2010, pensioner Tom Lackey from Birmingham, England, broke his own record as the world's oldest wing walker—at the age of 90. He was strapped to the 32-ft-long (9.7-m) wing of a plane and flown 500 ft (152 m) above the ground in Gloucestershire.

Bike Leap

Chilean base-jumper Julio Munoz roared off a massive cliff in the Andes on his motorbike, free-falling around 3,000 ft (915 m) before opening his parachute. It took him three years to plan the spectacular stunt, during the jump he had several cameras attached to his body so that he could film the stunt from different angles.

Family Run

Competing in the London Marathon on April 17, 2011, 52-year-old Kelvin Amos and his son Shane, 31, from Stoke-on-Trent, England, finished in a combined time of 6 hours 3 minutes 7 seconds—the fastest-ever father-and-son team to run a marathon.

HEAVY LOADS

On August 27, 2011, 11 former U.K. servicemen climbed England's highest peak with 100-lb (45-kg) tumble driers or washing machines on their backs. It took the ex-marines and paratroopers eight hours to climb up and down the 3,209-ft-high (978-m) Scafell Pike.

Weed Wheels

We could soon be driving cars or riding bicycles with tires made from weeds. A species of dandelion—*Taraxacum kok-saghyz* (TKS)—produces molecules of rubber in its sap, and scientists at Ohio State University are conducting crossbreeding experiments in the hope of increasing the rubber yield from the plant so that it can be used commercially.

Microscopic Frog

A computer sciences professor at a university in Nanchang, China, has artificially bred a tiny species of frog that can be seen clearly only through a magnifying glass. Hu Gansheng's frogs are just 0.2 in (0.5 cm) long but can leap 4 in (10 cm)—20 times their body length.

Red Roses

Xiao Wang, a happy groom in Qingzhen, China, spent a year's salary buying 99,999 red roses for his wedding to Xiao Liu—because in China the number nine is considered lucky. The flowers had to be flown in from the other side of the country and were delivered to the wedding in a fleet of 30 cars.

Explosive Fish

Walu—or Hawaiian butterfish—contains a high level of waxy compounds in its tissue, which when eaten in large amounts can cause severe diarrhea. Native Hawaiians called the fish Maku'u, or exploding intestines. It is banned in Japan and Italy.

Artificial Brain

Scientists at the University of Pittsburgh, Pennsylvania, created a tiny artificial brain that demonstrated 12 seconds of short-term memory. The microbrain was derived from rat brain cells and grown in a petri dish.

Breaking the Mold

To mark its centenary in 2011, U.K. chocolate manufacturer Thorntons created the world's biggest chocolate bar at its factory in Derbyshire. The giant bar weighed 12,770 lb (5,792 kg)—around six tons—and measured 172 sq ft (16 sq m). The mold for the bar was set up in the company's parking lot and it took more than 50 bucket-carrying workers ten hours to fill it with liquid chocolate and then three days for it to cool off and solidify.

Ancient Soup

Archeologists in China have discovered what they think is a 2,400-year-old pot of soup. The liquid and bones were in a sealed, bronze cooking vessel near the city of Xian, which was China's capital for more than 1,100 years.

Shared Husband

Undecided whether to marry for love or proceed with an arranged marriage to a bride chosen by his family, Azhar Haidri found a solution by marrying both women in the space of 24 hours at Multan, Pakistan, in October 2010. Both brides—21-year-old Rumana Aslam, and his family's choice, 28-year-old Humaira Qasim—were equally happy to marry the same man.

Bacon Clock

California-based inventor Matty Sallin has devised an alarm clock that wakes you up with the smell of bacon. Wake n'Bacon turns on ten minutes before you are due to wake up and slowly sizzles frozen slices of bacon beneath two halogen lightbulbs. Its built-in fan then wafts the aroma of cooking bacon around the room to wake you up gently.

BLADE RUNNER

On March 23, 2011, a man in Chongqing, China, set a record for the highest broadsword ladder climb by scaling a ladder 94 ft 6 in high (28.8 m) built with 168 razor-sharp broadsword rungs... in bare feet.

crazy
ANIMALS

TWO-FACED CAT

Despite being born with two faces, two mouths, two noses and three eyes, Frank and Louie, a cat owned by Marty Stevens of Worcester, Massachusetts, has set a world record by living to the age of 12.

Most Janus cats—named after a Roman god with two faces—fail to survive, often because their two mouths cause them to choke. However, although both of Frank and Louie's noses work, only one mouth does. The nonfunctioning mouth isn't connected to his sole esophagus, meaning that he can't eat with it. Frank and Louie has a single brain, meaning both faces react simultaneously in the same way.

Missing arm!

HAPPY SNAPPERS

Brutus, an 18-ft-long (5.5-m), two-ton saltwater crocodile on the Adelaide River in Australia's Northern Territory, has a fearsome reputation. The 80-year-old monster, who can be lured out of the water by dangling kangaroo meat from a pole to allow riverboat tourists to take frightening close-up photos, has such powerful jaws that he once bit a log cutter's noisy chainsaw in half... while the log cutter hid up a tree. Brutus is not invincible, however, having lost his right front leg during a fight with a shark in the river estuary.

Long Cat

Stewie, a five-year-old Maine Coon cat owned by Robin Hendrickson and Erik Brandsness of Reno, Nevada, measures more than 4 ft (1.2 m) long from the tip of his nose to the tip of his tail.

Pooped Park

A campground in Cornwall, England, faced a $15,000 clean-up bill in February 2011 after a huge flock comprising tens of thousands of starlings covered it in a layer of bird droppings that was 7 in (18 cm) deep in places.

Confused Cat

Overcoming her natural tendencies, a female cat named Niu Niu acted as a mother to 30 newborn chicks. Her owner, farmer Lao Yang of Suibin County, China, was amazed to see the cat licking, embracing and playing with the chicks, who responded by following her everywhere.

Best Friends

A mynah bird and a dog have become so inseparable that their owner has built a special perch for the bird that can be attached to the dog and enables them to go for walks together. Qiao Yu of Shandong Province, China, says the mynah combs the dog's fur and plucks fleas off it, while the dog responds by barking loudly whenever someone goes near the bird.

Uninvited Guest

After floodwaters receded from her home in Parauapebas, Brazil, in February 2011, a woman was shocked to find an alligator behind the couch in the living room—and her three-year-old son happily patting the 5-ft-long (1.5-m) reptile on the head.

RAINBOW CHICKS

Chickens are dyed with artificial coloring to make them more appealing to buyers at a market in Semarang, Central Java, Indonesia.

Spin Cycle

An eight-week-old kitten named Princess survived an hour-long spin in a washing machine after creeping unnoticed into the drum. It was only when her owner, Susan Gordon of Aberdeen, Scotland, was removing the clean items from the machine that she spotted the sodden kitten.

Bunny Cart

The O'Rourke family of Tucson, Arizona, discovered an abandoned baby rabbit in their garden that could not use his hind legs. They built a little cart on wheels and strapped it to the rabbit's rear so that he no longer had to drag his legs behind him.

Rotten Look

Nimbochromis livingstonii, a fish found in Africa's Lake Malawi, has the blotchy appearance of a rotting fish and lies motionless on the lakebed to attract the scavengers on which it preys.

Rescue Center

Ha Wenjin gave up her job and sold her house, car and jewelry to adopt more than 1,500 stray dogs at her rescue center in Nanjing, China. She employs 12 people to care for the dogs and to look after 200 adopted cats at a second center nearby.

SLEEPY BIRD

After eating a hearty meal of ants, a green woodpecker appears to have been caught dozing against the branch of this tree in Worcestershire, England.

Show-jumping Cow

Regina Mayer from Laufen, Germany, has trained a cow on the family farm to jump fences like a horse. Denied a horse by her parents, teen Regina fulfilled her riding ambitions by spending hours training Luna the cow to get accustomed to having a rider on her back and to wearing a halter and saddle. Luna now understands commands such as "go," "stand" and "gallop."

Vulture Arrested

Finding a griffon vulture in Hyaal, Saudi Arabia, carrying a GPS transmitter and a tag from Tel Aviv University, Saudi security services held the bird in custody on suspicion of spying for the Israeli intelligence agency Mossad. However, wildlife experts pointed out that the vulture was simply part of a migration study and the bird was eventually released without charge.

WILD WOOD

In 2010, spiders in Pakistan's Sindh province were forced from the ground by floodwaters. The arachnids took shelter in thousands of trees and stayed for months because the water did not recede. Eventually their new homes became entirely cocooned in thick webs, which according to locals helped control the number of malaria-carrying mosquitoes in the stagnant waters.

PUGS MIGHT FLY

On August 15, 2011, in the skies above California, Otis the skydiving pug made his 64th jump with his master, veteran skydiver Will DaSilva. Otis has been skydiving in a special tandem harness with his owner for more than nine years and seems to love every minute of the ride.

Diving Gear

Gannets dive headfirst into the sea at speeds of up to 90 mph (145 km/h) and can reach depths of 30 ft (9 m) below the water surface. To withstand the impact as they hit the water, the birds have an extra-thick skull that acts as a crash helmet, as well as a throat pouch that inflates like a little airbag to protect their body.

Keep Away

Mandrill monkeys learned how to perform sign language to tell other group members to keep away. They place one hand loosely over their eyes, but with their fingers parted slightly so that they can still see. While the hand is in place, the other mandrills at Colchester Zoo, England, keep their distance.

Clean Sweep

A golden retriever uses a specially made small broom to sweep the streets of Changchun, Jilin Province, China, while walking with his owner Xu Ming. The dog takes the broom everywhere and, under Xu's instructions, runs in a zigzag pattern to sweep away dust and debris. He became a viral sensation in China after he was photographed in Changchun with his broom.

Natural Daredevils

To avoid predators, barnacle geese build nests high on mountain cliffs—and at just three days old, the tiny goslings must jump from nests as far up as 300 ft (90 m) to reach food on the ground.

Working Monkeys

Two baby monkeys, Nehime and Rakan, work as station masters at Hojomachi station on the Hojo railway line in Japan's Hyogo Prefecture in an attempt to boost visitors to the rail line. The monkeys wear special blue uniforms and miniature hats.

Nose for Wine

With a nose that is 2,000 times more sensitive than a human's, bloodhound Louisa Bella has been trained as a wine tester by her owners. Wine label proprietors Michelle Edwards and Daniel Fischl of Melbourne, Australia, found that after just two weeks of training, she could sniff out a tainted wine cork within 30 seconds.

Terrier Terror

Sucked up by a twister raging through Birmingham, Alabama, Mason, a terrier mongrel, managed to crawl back to his owners' home three weeks later despite suffering two broken front legs.

Prize Piglet

A court in Primorye, Russia, seized a woman's piglet to pay her overdue debt after it was judged that the animal was her most valuable possession.

TOMBSTONING MONKEYS

Mimicking the human tombstoning craze of jumping from great heights into water, these thrill-seeking macaques in Jaipur, India, climb a 12-ft-high (3.6-m) lamppost and then hurl themselves into a shallow trough of water—apparently just for fun. Even a ring of barbed wire around the lamppost could not stop their crazy antics. Macaques have also been seen jumping from 9-ft (2.7-m) rocks into the sea off Thailand and are one of the few primates that are not scared of water.

Dancing Dolphins

Wild dolphins are teaching themselves to "walk" using their tails on the ocean surface. Researchers in Australia say dolphins have developed the art of tail-walking, which seems to have no practical use and has been compared to dancing in humans.

Gator Snatch

After a 6-ft-long (1.8-m) alligator snatched his Jack Russell terrier Lizabeth while walking along the Hillsborough River in Tampa, Florida, Tom Martino fired shots into the water to force the reptile to release the dog. He then performed CPR on Lizabeth until she breathed again.

Double Trouble

Oscar the Labrador and his 53-year-old master both survived with just broken bones after plunging 200 ft (60 m) over the edge of a cliff in North Yorkshire, England. After Oscar fell off the cliff, his owner was desperately trying to work out how to reach his pet when a strong gust of wind blew him over the edge, too.

Dangerous Dance

As part of their courtship ritual, pairs of bald eagles perform a cartwheel dance, soaring high into the air, locking their talons together, then spinning out of control toward the ground, breaking off at the very last second to fly upward again.

Versatile Swimmer

The black ghost knifefish, found in the rivers of South America, is able to swim forward or backward equally well and navigates by emitting a small electric charge.

Mail Misery

Toby, a Jack Russell terrier belonging to Gill Bird of Hampshire, England, chewed up his owner's mail—and the combination of the envelope glue and wet paper fixed his mouth shut.

Tail Force

Thresher sharks have a tail that can grow as long as the rest of their body. They use it to smack and stun their prey.

CAT IN A VAT

Ksyusha, a white-haired Himalayan kitten, can somehow squeeze herself into a small glass jar. Her owner, Yuriy Korotun of Moscow, Russia, says the kitten—nicknamed Mewdini—loves to curl up in confined spaces but always manages to escape unharmed.

GIANT CROC

A huge saltwater crocodile weighing more than a ton is thought to be the largest specimen ever captured. The 21-ft-long (6.4-m) monster weighed 2,370 lb (1,075 kg), that's well over a ton, and had been hunted by villagers in the Philippines for nearly a month following a spate of attacks on humans and animals. It may have eaten a farmer who went missing in July 2011, along with several water buffaloes near the town of Bunawan, where the head of a 12-year-old girl was also bitten off by a crocodile in 2009. The record-breaking croc was so big that it took 30 local men to capture it, and it could fit three men inside it at once. Sadly, the croc died at an ecotourism park in 2013.

Fish out of Water

A 1-ft-long (30-cm) sturgeon dropped at night from the sky (probably by a heron) on a lawn in Worcester, England, was found the following morning, having survived thanks to the moisture on the grass.

Dolphin Scan
Tapeko, a female bottlenose dolphin, had her pregnancy confirmed by undergoing a human-style ultrasound scan at Brookfield Zoo, Illinois. The dolphin was happy to float belly-up for the scan—in return for a fish reward.

Natural Prawn Killers
The Mantis shrimp of the Indian and Pacific oceans has a sting as powerful as a shot from a .22-caliber bullet. The shrimp kill prey by dismembering or spearing it with their claws, but can also stun it with their fearsome sting.

Jury Service
Tabby Sal the cat was summoned to do jury service in Boston, Massachusetts, even after his owner Anna Esposito told the court he was "unable to speak and understand English" and was "a domestic short-haired neutered feline."

Skinny Scavengers

Hagfish are primitive, tubelike scavengers that eat using their skin. On finding a carcass on the ocean floor, the hagfish burrows into the dead body, where it not only uses its mouth to eat, but also absorbs nutrients through its gills and skin.

Self-Sufficient

The spiny-shelled species of deep-sea snail, *Alviniconcha hessleri*, lives near geothermal vents and gets its food from bacteria that live within its own gills.

Blind Sheepdog

Liz Edwards, a farmer in Cheshire, England, bought Jack, a sheepdog that was so good at his job it took several months for her to realize the dog had gone blind. "He's such an inspiration," she said. "He carried on as if nothing had happened. He must have had our farm mapped out in his head. He knows exactly where everything is." She discovered he had lost vision in both eyes only when he ran straight into a wooden peg sticking out of the ground.

Savior Lilly

After suffering a bad epileptic fit, Nathan Cooper of Bournemouth, England, came close to death—but was saved by his cat Lilly, who alerted Nathan's parents. She can detect the weekly fits her owner experiences before they happen, and once resuscitated him by licking his mouth. Experts think cats' and dogs' acute sense of smell helps them detect minute chemical changes within the human body prior to a fit.

PANDA SUITS

To prepare captive-born giant panda cubs for life in the wild, keepers at the panda conservation centers in western China dress up in fluffy black-and-white panda costumes. They wear the suits whenever approaching the cubs so that the pandas have only minimum contact with humans. Here, baby panda Tao Tao is being transferred to a large wilderness area where it is planned he and his captive-bred mother, Cao Cao, will start their reintegration into the wild.

JELLYFISH SURVIVOR

Ten-year-old Rachael Shardlow is the first person known to have survived an extensive sting from a box jellyfish—one of the world's most venomous creatures. She was stung while swimming in the Calliope River, Queensland, Australia, and after her brother pulled her from the water, she fell unconscious with the jellyfish's tentacles still strapped to her limbs. Rachael spent six weeks in the hospital before being allowed home.

Gator Drag

Ten-year-old Michael Dasher of Rockledge, Florida, dragged a live alligator, measuring 5 ft 9 in (1.75 m) in length, home from a nearby canal. The boy was fishing with friends when the alligator snapped at the line and ran at him. He hit it with sticks and jumped on its back before dragging it home, suffering just minor scratches on his arms and hands.

Snake Island

Although Shedao Island, China, covers only 180 acres (73 ha), it is home to over 15,000 poisonous pit vipers.

Long-Distance Swim

A migrating humpback whale swam 6,200 mi (10,000 km) from Brazil to Madagascar—a quarter of the way around the world. She was spotted off the coast of Brazil in 1999 and just over two years later, identified by the distinctive markings on her tail, she was seen in the Indian Ocean off the east coast of Madagascar.

Secret Drinker

After checking the plumbing of hot tubs that appeared to have been leaking water, workers at the Etali Safari Lodge in North West Province, South Africa, discovered the culprit wasn't in fact a water leak—but actually a thirsty elephant. They nicknamed the elephant Troublesome.

GARGANTUA THE GREAT

Gargantua the Great was billed as "the world's most terrifying living creature" and was described by noted journalist Heywood Broun as "the fiercest looking thing I have ever seen on two legs."

An African lowland gorilla, he was said to be the largest gorilla ever exhibited, weighing some 600 lb (272 kg)—a whopping 160 lb (72 kg) heavier than the average lowland gorilla.

Gargantua was captured as a baby in the Belgian Congo in the late 1920s and given to a sea captain as a pet. He traveled with the captain and was popular with the crew until a drunken sailor threw acid in his face. He was left scarred and became increasingly aggressive.

Unable to cope with him, the captain presented the young gorilla to Gertrude Lintz who cared for sick creatures in Brooklyn, New York, and she named him Buddy. One night a thunderstorm panicked Buddy, who smashed his way out of his cage. By then he weighed about 460 lb (209 kg), so Mrs. Lintz sold him to the Ringling Bros. and Barnum & Bailey Circus for $10,000 in 1938.

At the circus Buddy was renamed Gargantua the Great on account of his size and mean disposition and went on to become its star attraction. Gargantua died of pneumonia in 1949, at the age of 20.

RINGLING BROS AND **BARNUM & BAILEY** COMBINED SHOWS

THE LARGEST GORILLA EVER EXHIBITED—

THE WORLD'S MOST TERRIFYING LIVING CREATURE!

GARGANTUA The Great

A circus poster advertising the spectacle of the enormous gorilla.

Gargantua the Gorilla, with his trademark sneer, which was the result of plastic surgery to repair acid-burn scars on his face.

Rain Allergy

Researchers in the remote mountain forests of Burma have discovered a species of snub-nosed monkey that sneezes whenever it rains. To avoid getting rainwater in its upturned nose, the monkey spends wet days sitting with its head between its knees.

Mucus Cocoon

Some species of parrotfish spend up to an hour each night preparing a cocoon of mucus, which they wrap around themselves like a sleeping bag.

Titanium Teeth

Axel, a prison guard dog from Melbourne, Australia, was fitted with titanium teeth after losing his real ones when they shattered as he bit into a bed board.

High Life

During construction of the Shard skyscraper in London, England, a fox was found living on the 72nd floor—944 ft (290 m) above the ground. The animal entered the building through a central stairwell before climbing to the top, where for over two weeks it lived on scraps that construction workers left behind.

Big Mouth

Owing to its loosely hinged mouth, a gulper eel can swallow prey with a volume ten times the size of its own body.

Smoking Chimp

A chimpanzee that became addicted to smoking cigarettes died in 2010 at age 52—ten years longer than the life expectancy of an average chimp. Charlie the Smoking Chimp picked up the unhealthy habit from visitors to Manguang Zoo, near Bloemfontein, South Africa, who threw him lit cigarettes through the bars of his enclosure.

Rabbit Heating

Up to 6,000 nuisance rabbits in Stockholm, Sweden, are culled each year and taken to an incinerator in Karlskoga where their carcasses are burned and processed for biofuel to heat nearby homes.

Mini Marvel

Weighing just 2½ lb (1.1 kg), Nancy the Chihuahua has a natural talent for herding sheep several times her size. Owner Ali Taylor says that Britain's tiniest sheep dog learned her trade from watching border collies in action.

Chatty Chimp

Kanzi, a mature bonobo ape, has a vocabulary of around 450 words, up to 40 of which he uses daily. Dr. Sue Savage-Rumbaugh of Des Moines, Iowa, has taught Kanzi to "speak" by pointing at different symbols on a computer.

Four-footed Duck

A duck born in China's Guangxi Province had three legs and four feet. Behind its normal two legs, the duckling had a third leg with two feet, probably the result of a genetic mutation.

New Eyes

When seeing-eye dog Edward lost his eyesight, he got his own seeing-eye dog! Edward the Labrador had helped partially sighted Graham Waspe of Suffolk, England, for six years but then suffered glaucoma and had to have both eyes removed. So another dog, two-year-old Opal, joined the family and now helps both Graham and Edward to get around.

Wide Wings

Queen Alexandra's Birdwing—a butterfly found only in Papua New Guinea—can grow to have a 1-ft-long (30-cm) wingspan.

TWO-HEADED SNAKE

Beating odds of more than 10,000 to one, a two-headed albino Honduran milk snake was hatched by a Florida conservation group. A few days later, the snake's right head ate its first meal—a small mouse—while the left head watched.

X-ray showing where the snake's spines are fused together

HAIR LIP

Alfie, a black shire-horse cross from Bristol, England, has a 7-in-long (18-cm) blond mustache. While most horses with mustaches have them trimmed every six months, Alfie's has been growing for more than five years because he refuses to let the stable hands get close enough to shave it off.

Speeding Horse

A police roadside camera designed to catch speeding drivers in Meppen, Germany, caught something different on film in July 2011—a runaway horse. The horse had escaped from a paddock and galloped off down a busy main road into the town. The speeding driver who triggered the picture pleaded to be excused the automatic fine because he claimed he was simply trying to get away from the horse.

Bird Rescue

When his pet dog carried a limp goose that had been hit by a car into the yard of his home in Urumchi, China, Yu Yanping thought the dog would eat it. Instead, the dog licked the bird until it recovered, and the two went on to become inseparable, feeding from the same bowl and even sharing the dog's kennel.

Stowaway Kitten

Amy Bindman of Calgary, Canada, found a kitten in a shipping container sent from China. It had survived being sealed away without food or water for nearly 45 days.

Robbers Attacked

Two armed robbers who held up a tobacco store in Altadena, California, fled after being attacked by the owner's pet Chihuahua. Little Paco refused to be intimidated even when one of the robbers pointed a shotgun at him, and chased the men out of the shop and down the street.

Short Legs

The Munchkin breed of cats has a mutation that gives it short legs and a stature similar to dachshund or corgi dogs. Although short-legged cats were known in the early 20th century, the breed was not rediscovered until 1983 when Louisiana music teacher Sandra Hochenedel found two pregnant cats. Half of the kittens in one litter were short-legged, and today's Munchkin cats are descended from that line.

Horse Fall

A horse stumbled through an open window and landed in the basement of her owners' home in Elbert County, Colorado. It took rescue teams four hours to get the mare—named Summer—out of the house.

Sweet Revenge

Oystercatcher birds have bladelike beaks for prying open shellfish—but sometimes their prey does get the better of them, holding their beaks in place until the birds drown.

CYCLOPS

A fisherman in Mexico landed what might well be a one of a kind—an albino baby shark with just one eye, located centrally above the mouth. He actually caught the mother, a 286-lb (130-kg) bull shark, but when she was filleted, ten pups were found inside, including her Cyclops offspring.

One beady eye!

LONG TAIL

A calf born on Jennifer Showalter's farm in Fairfield, Virginia, on September 15, 2011, had a tail that was 60 in (1.5 m) long! Calves' tails are usually between just 5 and 8 in (13 and 20 cm) long.

Escaped Croc

A 6-ft-long (1.8-m) crocodile that was taken by its owner, a photographer, to Lake Shira, Siberia, to pose for pictures with tourists caused panic when it escaped into the water, terrifying hundreds of swimmers. The reptile bolted for freedom while the photographer was haggling with tourists over the price of a souvenir photo.

Two-headed Tortoise

Magdalena, a tortoise owned by Roman Gresak from Zilina, Slovakia, has two heads and five legs. Each of the heads has its own nerve system and the tortoise has two brains, which work independently of each other, meaning that sometimes one head wants to go in a different direction to the other.

Orange Flock

After losing 200 of his sheep to rustlers, farmer John Heard from Devon, England, took drastic action—he painted his entire flock orange. The harmless dip of orange dye made the sheep so visible that thieves left them alone.

Horse Artist

A nine-year-old, 1,500-lb (681-kg) Friesian horse named Justin has produced a series of paintings, which have been exhibited in art galleries and have sold for hundreds of dollars. His owner, Adonna Combs of Columbus, Indiana, first spotted his talent when he used her whip to draw patterns in the sand. Encouraged with carrots—he goes through 5 lb (2.2 kg) per painting—he holds the brush in his mouth and daubs non-toxic paint onto the canvas. He even signs each artwork by stepping onto the canvas wearing a painted horseshoe.

Five Ears

A cat named Luntya, found in the streets of Voronezh, Russia, has five ears. She has two normal ears, two extra ears turned at an angle of 180 degrees, and a tiny fifth ear.

Small Cow

Swallow, an 11-year-old cow owned by Caroline Ryder of West Yorkshire, England, stands only 33 in (84 cm) tall at the shoulder, making her shorter than most sheep.

ORANGE CROC

Snappy, an 8-ft-long (2.4-m) saltwater crocodile that lives in captivity in Geelong, Australia, suddenly turned orange. He chewed water pipes in his tank, damaging the filter, which caused pH levels in the water to rise and red algae to form. The combination of the two prompted his startling change in color. He is expected to return to a more crocodilian green over time. Tracey Sandstrom, Snappy's keeper, said, "There's no change in his behavior, his aggression, or his territorialism. He's still a really nasty crocodile."

Noisy Bug

Although just 0.08 in (2 mm) long, the lesser water boatman, a pond insect that swims upside down using two long legs as paddles, produces 99.2 decibels of noise—louder than any other animal relative to its body size, and the equivalent of listening to an orchestra playing at full volume from the front row.

Train Crash

On April 27, 2011, termites chewed through a tree branch that then fell onto train tracks, causing a crash in Taiwan that killed five people and injured around a hundred others.

Army of Clones

Every insect in a nest of *Mycocepurus smithii* ants from Latin America is a clone of the queen. The species reproduces asexually from a single parent and is entirely male-free, which removes the stress of finding a mate.

Mice Crossing

A council in South Wales spent £190,000 on building bridges for dormice. The three overhead walkways were put up so that the little rodents could cross a busy road safely.

Death March

Army ants that begin marching in a circle can end up marching endlessly by the thousands in the same circle until they all die from exhaustion or starvation.

Monster Molars

In proportion to its body size, the deep-sea fangtooth fish has the largest teeth of any sea creature—its skull has special sockets to hold the teeth and allow it to close its mouth. The fish itself is only 6 in (15 cm) long, but its teeth can reach nearly ¾ in (2 cm) in length. If these proportions were replicated in a great white shark, it would have teeth 2 ft 6 in (76 cm) long.

Belly Flop

New Zealand's Maud Island frogs don't croak and they don't have webbed feet. When they hop they land on their belly instead of their feet.

Light Meal

Atolla wyvillei, a deep-sea species of jellyfish, starts glowing brightly when being attacked by its prey in an attempt to attract other predators that will attack its assailant. Its glow is so bright it can be seen from 300 ft (90 m) away.

Speed Bug

The fastest species of tiger beetle can run at 5.6 mph (9 km/h), which, relative to its body length, is the equivalent of a human running at 480 mph (770 km/h)—about 17 times the speed of Usain Bolt. The beetles move so quickly that their eyes and brain are unable to process vision in sync with their movement and they momentarily go blind, needing to stop and start several times while in hot pursuit of prey.

Hiss-terical

A snake spent six months in a wall cavity behind the toilet in a woman's apartment in Allschwil, Switzerland. After escaping from the flat above, the 27-in-long (70-cm) corn snake slithered down into Anika Bauer's home where it hid until she discovered it on a trip to the bathroom.

Sticky Problem

An estimated 14 million bees got loose in July 2011 after a delivery truck carrying more than 400 hive boxes and honey overturned on a highway in Fremont County, Idaho. Trying to avoid being stung, crews worked throughout the day to remove all the honey from the road.

BAT KILLER

The Amazonian giant centipede is so powerful and agile that it can catch and eat bats. An adult centipede reaches 14 in (35 cm) long—the length of a man's forearm—and is able to climb the walls of caves. BBC cameraman Tim Green spent two weeks in a cave in Venezuela waiting to film this unique event. Eventually, he witnessed this fearsome beast hang down from the cave ceiling, grab a passing bat with some of its 46 legs, and kill it with its venom. It then devoured every piece of bat flesh over the next hour.

Day Trip

Frankie, a six-year-old Jack Russell terrier, walked 2 mi (3.2 km) from his home in Gravesend, Kent, England, to the nearest train station and then boarded a train for a 30-minute journey to London. When he arrived in London, he was detained by station staff until his owners caught a train up from Kent to collect him.

Constant Companions

Jane Hartley of Loughborough, England, loves her pet parrots Fiz and Buzz so much that she takes them shopping, cycling, walking and even skiing. The small birds sit on her hand while she cycles, and nestle in her pocket as she hurtles down Alpine mountains during her skiing vacations.

RAINBOW ANTS

Dr. Mohamed Babu of Mysore, India, set up this eye-catching experiment whereby ants turned different colors after drinking sugar drops mixed with edible red, green, blue and yellow coloring. As the ant's abdomen is semi-transparent, they absorb the colors as they sip the liquid. His wife gave him the idea after showing him how ants turned white after drinking spilt milk.

No Contest
In 2010, a 150-lb (68-kg) mountain lion was chased up a tree in South Dakota by Chad Strenge's Jack Russell terrier, Jack, who weighed just 17 lb (7.7 kg).

Fox Thief
Anna Clark, of Sussex, England, was horrified when a fox brazenly ran off with her handbag in a car park—and amazed when a few minutes later the animal suddenly reappeared and dropped the bag meekly at her feet.

Mixed Litter
A female Dalmatian dog in Meridiano, Brazil, adopted a piglet and a baby goat and allowed them to suckle her alongside her puppies. The puppies accepted the newcomers, both of which were also black and white.

Color Change
Rhacophorus penanorum, a species of tiny frog that lives on the island of Borneo, has bright green skin at night but changes color to brown by day—and its eyes match it by changing color, too.

Cat Call

While James Cocksedge was out at work, his inquisitive pedigree Singapura kitten, Bruce, pawed at telephone buttons and called 999, the number for the U.K. emergency services. Tracing the silent call, police officers rushed round to the London flat and smashed down the front door, leaving Bruce's owner with a bill for several hundred pounds.

Wonder Web

The newly discovered Darwin's bark spider of Madagascar builds webs that cover an area of 30 sq ft (2.8 sq m) and span gaps over 80 ft (25 m) across.

Cow Beds

Dairy farmers in Norway are required by law to provide a place for their cows to lie down—such as on a rubber mattress.

DOGS IN DISGUISE

Canine competitors were participants in a creative dog-grooming competition in Pasadena, California. Creative grooming events are hugely popular in the U.S. Owners trim their poodles to resemble zebras, lions, ponies, snails and American footballers or movie characters such as Captain Jack Sparrow from *Pirates of the Caribbean.*

Pop Star

Anastasia, a Jack Russell terrier owned by Doree Sitterly of southern California, can pop 100 balloons in 44.49 seconds—that's faster than two balloons per second.

Canine Mayor

Lucy Lou, a border collie, was elected mayor of Rabbit Hash, Kentucky, in 2008, defeating rival political candidates that included a cat, a jackass, an opossum and several other dogs.

Tiny Police Dog

A long-haired Chihuahua has been accepted as a police dog in Japan's Nara prefecture. Momo, who weighs just 6 lb 10 oz (3 kg), passed a search-and-rescue test by finding a person in five minutes after merely sniffing their cap. Momo specializes in rescue operations following disasters such as earthquakes, where she can squeeze her tiny body into places too small for normally sized rescue dogs.

Thick Fur

The furry chinchillas of South America have fur so dense that 50 hairs grow out of a single hair follicle.

Wife Attacks Tiger

A man who was attacked by a tiger while hunting squirrels near his home in Malaysia was saved when his 55-year-old wife began hitting the big cat over the head with a wooden soup ladle. Han Besau ran to the rescue of Tambun Gediu after hearing his screams and instinctively beat the tiger with the ladle, causing it to flee.

A Helping Paw

Sandie, a Sheltie-collie and Staffordshire bull terrier cross, has performed countless jobs for her disabled owner Sue Line of Coventry, England, including doing the shopping, the laundry, and paying for the groceries. On trips to the store, Sandie puts the shopping in a bag, which she carries in her mouth, and at the checkout she can take money from Sue's purse and hand it to the sales clerk. Sandie loads the washing machine, separating the dirty clothes into light and dark piles, and locks the machine door before the cycle begins. She has also learned how to unlock the kitchen door to let herself out to go to the toilet—and always remembers to close it behind her on her way back.

Tortoise Wheel

A tortoise that lost a front leg after it was severed by a rat while she was hibernating can now outrace other tortoises thanks to a toy tractor wheel being fitted in place of the missing limb. Philip Chubb of Norwich, England, made a brace out of metal and velcro strips to fasten the wheel to the shell of Tuly the tortoise.

Canine Couple

Louise Harris of Essex, England, spent more than £20,000 on an elaborate wedding ceremony, complete with outdoor marquee, for her Yorkshire terrier Lola, and Mugly, a Chinese crested dog. On her special day, Lola wore a £1,000 wedding dress customized with 1,800 Swarovski crystals. Her outfit was adorned with a £400 pearl necklace, £250 Swarovski crystal leg cuffs, and a £350 Swarovski crystal leash. The groom looked resplendent in a tuxedo before the happy couple and their canine guests wolfed down a buffet of dog-friendly cupcakes.

Blood Popsicles

To keep its tigers cool during the scorching April of 2011, London Zoo gave them special popsicles made with blood.

SWIMMING WITH BEARS

Children at the Cochrane Polar Bear Habitat in Ontario, Canada, look to be swimming right next to the most feared predators on Earth, but what you can't see is a 10-in-thick (25-cm) plexiglass barrier that separates the humans from the bears, allowing the children to swim in safety.

87

Ancient Tortoise

Jonathan, a giant tortoise on the South Atlantic island of St. Helena, is at least 178 years old. His life has spanned eight British monarchs and 37 U.S. Presidents, yet he still has the energy to mate with three younger females. The St. Helena five-pence coin has a picture of Jonathan on its reverse.

Hidden Menace

People swam about in a public pool in Darwin, Australia, unaware that a 20-in (50-cm) baby saltwater crocodile was lurking in the deep end. The reptile, which was thought to be a rubber toy until it tried to bite a handler, was rescued and released back into the wild.

Fishy Tale

Two goldfish survived 134 days without food or electricity to power their tank filter following the 2011 earthquake in Christchurch, New Zealand. Shaggy and Daphne—named after Scooby Doo characters—spent over four months left unattended in an accountants' reception area, but pulled through by eating algae growing on the side of the tank.

KEYCHAIN CREATURES

Live fish, tiny tortoises and young giant salamanders, all sealed in plastic pouches, are sold as keychains at a roadside stall in Beijing, China. The vendor says that a special liquid inside the pouches provides all the necessary oxygen and nutrients for the creatures.

WEALTH

HAPPINESS

TATTOOED FISH

Tattooed goldfish are sold at a pet market in Changchun, China, for around $12 each. Laser-inscribed decorations on the fish include flowery patterns and the Chinese characters for sentiments such as "wealth," "longevity" and "happiness." Personalized messages were also available.

Drunken Owl

A brown owl was spotted sitting by the side of a busy road in Pforzheim, Germany, seemingly oblivious to passing traffic. The feathery friend did not appear to be injured, but one of its eyelids was drooping noticeably. Looking around, police found two empty bottles of Schnapps nearby and realized that in fact the bird was drunk. So the police took the owl into custody and gave it plenty of water until it sobered up.

Reindeer Reflections

In an attempt to reduce the number of car crashes that kill around 500 reindeer each year in Norway, 2,000 of the animals were fitted with reflective yellow collars or small antler tags, making them more visible in the dark.

Cracking Crows

Crows in Japan have been seen placing walnuts on roads, waiting for cars to drive over them to crack open the shells, and then flying back to feast on the nuts' contents.

Copycat Squirrel

Jim Watkins of Carthage, Mississippi, rescued a stranded baby squirrel that his pet cat and her kittens then adopted. The squirrel soon learned how to purr for affection like a cat.

DIVING CHAMPIONS

Wildlife photographer Charlie Hamilton James has spent thousands of hours taking pictures of kingfishers from a hideout attached to his riverside cottage near Bristol, England. This stunning photograph captures a kingfisher as a vibrant flash of blue as the bird dives into the water to catch a fish. When they dive, kingfishers tuck in their wings and hit the surface of the water at speeds of up to 25 mph (40 km/h), like darts.

Tight Spot

A black bear was released back into a forest near Newport, Tennessee, after spending at least three weeks with a plastic jar stuck on its head. Before being removed by state wildlife officers, the jar had hindered the bear's attempts to feed, as a result of which the animal weighed only 115 lb (52 kg), barely half its healthy weight.

Extra Ears

Shun Shun, a dog in Xinjiang Province, China, has four ears. The extra ears started to grow behind the main pair when the animal was only a puppy, but are now more than 4 in (10 cm) long, making them bigger than his original ears.

Big Bird

The Newby family from Essex, England, share their home with a 6-ft-tall (1.8-m) pet emu named Beaky. The 196-lb (89-kg) bird was hatched from an egg by dad Iain, who works at an animal rescue center, and Beaky has become so much part of the family that she watches TV with them. She eats 14 lb (6.4 kg) of corn a week, 5 lb (2.3 kg) of fruit and vegetables, plus anything else she can find, including keys, sponges and drill bits.

New Mom

A wild lynx kitten that had been abandoned by its mother was adopted by a spaniel at a wildlife park in Kadzidlowo, Poland. Kraska the spaniel, who had just given birth to a litter of puppies, readily accepted six-month-old Mis the lynx as one of her own.

Goose Patrol

A Canada goose and her goslings were given a police escort on a Washington State highway in June 2011. Three police cars closed two lanes of traffic on the busy Seattle highway during morning rush hour while they guided the geese to the nearest exit.

Hostile Home

The most heavily armed border zone in the world—between North and South Korea—has become a refuge for the red-crowned crane, one of the rarest birds on the planet. This is because it is such a restricted area that there is very little human activity to disturb the birds.

Albino Actors

Showbiz manager Tom Beser has set up the world's first acting agency for albino animals. From his base in Rheinfelden, Germany, he leases his collection of albino creatures—including lizards, minks and a raccoon—to moviemakers for films and TV commercials.

Gold Fish

Curt Carish of Kaua'i, Hawaii, caught a fish that had swallowed a gold watch—and the watch was still ticking and keeping correct time.

Fighting Spurs

Several species of South American birds called screamers have spurs on their wings that they use for fighting. The spurs can break off in another bird's body, but will grow back.

Screaming Tadpoles

Scientists in Argentina have discovered tadpoles that can scream. The larvae of the Argentine horned frog, which are carnivorous and eat other species of tadpole, emit a short, audible "metallic-like" sound.

Mimicking Mom

A keeper at China's Wuhan Zoo has to wear a black-and-white-striped T-shirt every day to persuade a newborn, orphaned zebra that he is its mother. Chen Nong realized that whenever he wore black and white the baby zebra became excited, and soon it would take milk from him only if he wore that zebralike shirt.

No Eyes

Rowan, a German Spitz dog owned by Sam Orchard of Bedfordshire, England, was born without eyes but is able to navigate its way around by echolocation, using its barks.

Rare Fly

The Terrible Hairy Fly is a flightless species of fly that breeds in bat feces and has only been found in a single Kenyan cave. A specimen collected in 2010 was the first to be tracked down since 1948.

MONKEY BUSINESS

For Connie Tibbs, her five pet macaque monkeys are part of the family. They play on the trampoline in the back garden of the family home in Pekin, Illinois, join her three children in the swimming pool, and even go horseback riding. One monkey is so skilled that it can ride a horse unaided. Connie also takes one of the monkeys—dressed in pajamas—to bed every night, much to the amusement of her husband Steve.

Connie is so devoted to her pet monkeys that she even takes them out shopping.

Eel Power

Finland's Helsinki Sea Life Center found an environmentally friendly way of powering its Christmas lights—by using an electric eel. Four plastic-encased steel probes were built to capture the eel's 650-volt discharge and filter it through to the lights, which shone particularly brightly at the eel's feeding time.

Bear Necessity

Scientists working north of Alaska tracked a polar bear that swam for nine days straight, 426 mi (687 km) across the Beaufort Sea to an ice floe. That's the equivalent to the distance between Washington, D.C., and Boston, Massachusetts. Polar bears have been forced to swim longer distances to reach land in areas where the sea ice is shrinking.

Underwear Thief

Benji the pet kangaroo escaped from his owner's home in Prague, Czech Republic, and hopped through neighboring gardens collecting women's underwear from washing lines as he did so. He was caught after one victim saw him escaping with her panties.

Cold Comfort

When the Arctic ground squirrel goes into hibernation during long Arctic winters, its body temperature drops below the freezing point of water to 26.4°F (−3°C). Scientists have yet to discover another mammal that survives with such a low body temperature.

Beavering Away

Beavers within Wood Buffalo National Park in Alberta, Canada, have spent decades building and maintaining a massive dam, a combination of two original dams, that measures a staggering 1/2 mile (0.8 km) long.

Octopus Spray

A common octopus at an aquarium in England has been called Squirt because he deliberately aims a jet of water at visitors. The inquisitive octopus learned to lift the top part of his body above the water in his tank so that he could look around and then realized that if he breathed out while he was doing it, he could fire a stream of water like a hose. Octopuses draw water into their body to absorb the oxygen from it and then pass it out again through special tubes alongside their beak.

Hero Husky

Nanook, a Siberian Husky cross, instinctively knew that her owner Coleen Kilby from St. Catharines, Ontario, was about to suffer a heart attack in the middle of the night. The dog started howling, barking, and licking her face, and on waking up, Coleen felt chest pains and was rushed to hospital. If the heart attack had occurred while she was asleep, it could have been fatal.

Jaws Beach

In September 2010, a fisherman caught a tiger shark off Jaws Beach in the Bahamas and a human left leg fell from its mouth. When the shark's belly was slit open, police found a right leg, two arms and a torso, and were able to use fingerprints to identify the victim as a missing sailor. The beach was used as the location for the 1987 shark movie *Jaws: The Revenge*.

Hound Hotel

Alongside its normal rooms for human guests, the Riverside Hotel in Evesham, England, has three dog suites that provide luxury accommodation for pets. Dogs staying there can feast from a special canine menu, swim in a spa pool, and have their portrait done.

Bird's-Eye View

In a case of real life imitating art, Bobby Haas took a stunning aerial photograph of a colony of hundreds of flamingoes off the coast of the Yucatán Peninsula, Mexico, that had arranged themselves into the shape of a giant flamingo.

Guard Goat

Zhao Huaiyun of Sichuan Province, China, has trained his pet goat to act as a guard dog. As well as warding off stray dogs from his owner's property, the goat makes sure Zhao answers his cell phone, if he hasn't heard it, by running up to him, putting its forelegs on his arms, and baaing nonstop.

Agile Goat

When Yang Yang the goat was born without hind legs in Liaoning Province, China, farmer Lu Shanlu trained the unfortunate animal to walk on its forelegs. Within three months, Yang Yang could run around his yard several times on two legs without stopping.

Rodent Couture

In May 2011, New York City staged a fashion show with a difference—the models were all rats. The sociable rodents, which became popular pets, showed their loveable side, dressed in miniature tutus, wedding dresses and other flattering outfits.

Feathered Fiend

Shanna Sexton of Devon, England, became so annoyed by what she thought was a faulty smoke alarm sounding nonstop for seven days that she called in workmen to try to locate the problem. Then she discovered the culprit was an African gray parrot named Sammi, who had escaped from a neighbor's house and spent the week hidden in Shanna's garden mimicking the beeping sound of an alarm.

Hasty Hippos

With a top speed of around 25 mph (40 km/h), an adult hippo can outrun a person in a short sprint. Hippos keep fit by walking up to 6 mi (10 km) a night foraging for food.

RARE BABY

A farmer in Hebron, Palestine, feeds milk to a newborn goat with two heads. The extremely rare condition, in which animals are born with more than one head, is called polycephaly.

MASTER OF DISGUISE

The Satanic leaf-tailed gecko is a lizard with a devilish disguise that enables it to adjust its body color to blend in with its surroundings. With its coiled shape, its camouflage is so effective that it is barely visible against these dead leaves in a national park in Madagascar.

Monkey Bounty

In October 2010, Yuki Yoneyama of Mishima, Japan, claimed a 200,000-yen ($2,600) bounty for capturing a wild macaque monkey that had bitten more than 100 people.

Toxic Mud

The bearded goby fish of coastal Africa thrives in toxic mud, can live for hours without oxygen, and eats jellyfish.

Light Swarm

A worker honeybee weighs about 1/300 oz (90 mg), meaning that a swarm of 50,000 bees weighs only 10 lb (4.5 kg).

Big School

Schools of Atlantic herring can stretch for more than 25 mi (40 km) and number millions of individual fish.

Daisy
the dog

TOWER

JUL 29 NITTY GRITTY BAND
OCT 12 CHINESE ACROBATS
OCT 27 MILES DAVIS TRIBUTE

TOWER MEMBERS
TAKE 20% OFF
2011 2012 SERIES

PILOT POOCH

Is it a bird? Is it a plane? No, it's the spectacular flying Chihuahua. Photographer James Holmdahl of Bend, Oregon, attached his 5-lb (2.3-kg) dog named Daisy to a cluster of helium balloons and watched her soar into the skies at a Fourth of July Parade.

Missing Mate

Pei Pei, a male orangutan at China's Yunnan Wild Animal Park, was so distraught when his mate La Tewhen was moved to an adjoining enclosure while she was pregnant that he started digging a tunnel in the hope of being reunited with her.

Long Journey

Four months after disappearing from her home in Cornwall, England, a collie named Lucy mysteriously turned up 500 mi (800 km) away in a garden in Edinburgh, Scotland. Her owners, Sonya and Billy McKerron, made a 20-hour round trip to collect her.

Poop for Gold

Dog owners in New Taipei City, Taiwan, were given the chance to turn their pets' poop into gold. In an attempt to clean up the streets, anyone handing in a bag of dog poop was entered into a lucky draw. The top prize in the draw was $2,100 in gold bars.

Rolling Toads

Venezuela's pebble toad flees predators by rolling like a ball down the rocky inclines of its mountainous home—without coming to any harm, and as their name suggests, looking like a pebble. Pebble toads breed communally, and a single nest has been found to contain 103 toads and 321 eggs.

Sea Dog

Just Nuisance, a Great Dane from Simon's Town, South Africa, was inducted into the British Royal Navy in 1939. He never went to sea, but as an official Able Seaman he performed a number of promotional duties ashore and was once taken up in a plane to look for submarines. He was buried with full military honors in 1944 and a statue was erected in his memory. Since 2000, there has been an annual parade of Great Danes in Simon's Town from which the best look-alike is chosen.

MUTTON BUSTIN'

Budding rodeo riders typically under the age of six and weighing no more than 60 lb (27 kg) try to hold on to a 180-lb (81-kg) ewe for six seconds in the sport of Mutton Bustin' that is sweeping the U.S.A. To prevent injury, the riders wear ice-hockey helmets, face guards and protective vests.

TIGHT FIT

A bullock in Ayrshire, Scotland, was rescued by animal charity officers after getting its head stuck between the rungs of a ladder in its field. The Belgian blue bull was returned to its herd unharmed after the unfortunate incident.

$1.5 Million Puppy

A red Tibetan mastiff puppy named Hong Dong was sold for $1.5 million in 2011. Tibetan mastiffs are fierce guard dogs and are rarely found outside Tibet, which makes them highly exclusive and sought-after. Hong Dong was bred in Qingdao, China, and weighed more than 180 lb (82 kg) at 11 months old.

Tree-eating Fish

A newly discovered species of armored catfish in the Amazon chews on the wood of fallen trees. Whereas other types of catfish use their teeth to scrape organic matter from the surfaces of submerged wood, this species actually ingests wood. The wood is subsequently expelled as waste, passing through the fish's body in less than four hours.

Piranha Terror

More than 15 people swimming off a popular tourist river beach in Cáceres, Brazil, lost toes and chunks of their legs and ankles in November 2011 after thousands of flesh-eating piranhas flooded the river. Piranhas are common in rivers on the outskirts of Cáceres, but this was the first time they had infiltrated the city itself.

DOUBLE LUCK

This double-footed horse belonging to R. van Wert of Cincinnati, Ohio, was photographed in 1930. You wouldn't want that hoof standing on your foot!

Walking Upright

Treasure, a one-year-old poodle, prefers to walk upright on his hind legs rather than on all four. His owner, Dou Xianhui of Jilin City, China, briefly trained Treasure to walk on two legs when he was a puppy—but now he walks like that for up to 30 minutes at a time.

Hippo Hygiene

At China's Shanghai Zoo, keepers use giant toothbrushes to clean the teeth of hippos. The hippos, whose mouths measure up to 4 ft (1.2 m) wide, are fed on fruit and vegetables, which would clog up their teeth if they weren't brushed three times a week.

incredible WORLD

FULL HOUSE

Ziona Chana, 67, is head of the world's largest family—consisting of 39 wives, 94 children, 33 grandchildren and 14 daughters-in-law. They all live in a rambling four-story house in a hill village in the Indian state of Mizoram, where Ziona is head of a religious sect that allows members to take as many wives as they want.

While he has his own double bed, his wives sleep in giant communal dormitories, the youngest women sleeping closest to his bedroom. His oldest wife, Zathiangi, organizes the other wives to carry out the daily household chores so that the compound is run with military precision. The house even has its own school and a vegetable garden that grows enough produce to feed the entire family.

The 100-room mansion where the family all live.

CASTLE CLIMB

Ma Jei climbed the 70-ft-high (21-m) wall of Zhonghua Gate Castle, China—without a rope or safety equipment—just so that she could avoid paying the $3.75 admission fee. When other visitors tried to follow her example, two fell and broke their legs, and three others had to be rescued.

Siesta Time

Spain's first National Siesta Championship took place in Madrid in 2010 to help revive the tradition of taking a short sleep after lunch. Competitors were monitored as they tried to doze for 20 minutes on sofas in the middle of a shopping mall. The highest points were awarded to people who managed to sleep for the full 20 minutes, but marks were also awarded for inventive sleeping positions, distinctive outfits and the loudest snore.

China Census

China, the world's most populated country, employed six million people—more than the entire population of Denmark—simply to administer its 2010 population census.

First Snow

In August 2011, a cold blast from the Antarctic brought snow to Auckland, New Zealand, for the first time in 35 years—snow was last seen there in the 1970s. The unusual weather created such excitement that people rushed to post pictures and videos online of the snow as it fell in the city.

Mystery Fireball

When Croatians spotted a mysterious ball of fire dart through the sky over Bjelovar in February 2011, many thought it was a comet or even an alien attack. Instead, it turned out to be nothing more than a patch of burning grass caught by the wind. Local farmer Marin Kiselic had decided that, with no time to mow his fields, it was cheaper to set them on fire.

Undersea Volcanoes

A chain of 12 huge, underwater volcanoes has been found in the icy waters of the Southern Ocean. The volcanoes—some of which are active—are dotted over an area the size of Britain and several are around 2 mi (3 km) high, making them nearly four times higher than the world's tallest building, Dubai's Burj Khalifa.

Somali Split

When Somalia's dictator, Siad Barre, was overthrown in 1991, the northwestern part of the country seceded and declared independence as Somaliland. They have a currency, a police force and democratic elections but no other country in the world recognizes them.

Tearful Brides

The Tujia people in Central China maintain an ancient tradition of "crying marriages." Brides begin daily crying a month before the wedding, with female friends eventually joining in so they can weep together.

Cardboard Boats

The Cardboard Boat Museum in New Richmond, Ohio, displays some of the weird and wonderful craft that have competed in 20 years of the annual cardboard boat race on the Ohio River. The race draws about 50 boats each year and thousands of spectators.

FINGER OF FATE

This cloud in the shape of an arm and a hand was photographed pointing from the sky over Tenerife, Canary Islands, by a British couple on holiday there.

$10-million Tree

For Christmas 2010, the Emirates Palace Hotel in Abu Dhabi displayed a jewel-encrusted Christmas tree worth more than $10 million. The tree's branches were draped in bracelets, necklaces and watches containing diamonds, pearls, emeralds, sapphires and other precious stones.

Fairy Rock

A builder was forced to redesign a luxury housing estate in Perthshire, Scotland, around a rock as local people said fairies lived under it and would be upset if it were moved.

Santa Pentathlon

The 54th World Santa Claus Congress, held near Denmark's capital, Copenhagen, in 2011, featured a Santa pentathlon— a five-discipline event between two teams of Santas, one from Denmark and one from the rest of the world, including the U.S.A., Sweden, Russia and Germany. The fitness contest required the Santas to throw gifts, fire cannonballs, ride bumper cars, race over an obstacle course and compete in a horse-race game.

Glowing Lakes

Gippsland Lakes in Victoria, Australia, glow in the dark— owing to a combination of fires, floods and algae. The fires of 2006 were followed by severe floods, which washed ash and nitrogen-rich soil into the lakes. When temperatures warmed up in the summer, blue-green algae feeding on the high level of nutrients, appeared across great areas of the water. When the organisms were disturbed, they created a chemical reaction called bioluminescence, which emitted an eerie blue light, making the lake glow at night.

BULL PLUNGE

At the annual Bous a la Mar (Bulls-to-the-Sea) festival in Denia, Spain, young bulls run down a street to the harbor chasing revelers who jump into the sea, hotly pursued by the bulls, which are then brought back to land by boat.

Longest Reign

The 76th Maharana of Udaipur, India, is part of the longest ruling dynasty in the world. His family has ruled there since AD 566—that's an unbroken run of nearly 1,450 years.

Fossil Find

While working 700 ft (210 m) underground at a coalmine in Webster County, Kentucky, miner Jay Wright discovered a 300-million-year-old shark jawbone. He noticed the fossil after a rock fell from the roof—he found three pieces of the shark's jaw bone.

Closed Windows

To ensure that the exterior of Buckingham Palace, the home of Queen Elizabeth II in London, England, maintains a unified appearance, none of the front windows are ever opened.

PIG PARADE

At the Lechon (roasted) Pig Parade in La Loma, Philippines, shop proprietors dress up roasted pigs to advertise their businesses—in guises including a singer, a racing driver and even characters from the movie *Matrix Reloaded*.

Duct Tape Festival

Since 2004, the town of Avon, Ohio, has held an annual festival celebrating duct tape, complete with artistic exhibits made from the tape.

Junk Windmill

In 2002, the village of Masitala in Malawi had electricity for the first time when local resident, William Kamkwamba, built a windmill from junk and spare parts to generate power.

Feet of Liberty

The feet on the Statue of Liberty are 25 ft (7.6 m) long and would require U.S. woman's size 879 shoes. They help support her 305 ft (93 m) height and 200 tons of weight, as well as anyone who is visiting at the time!

Dutch Share

Dutch student Ruben Schalk found an early share of the Dutch East India Company in the archives of Hoorn, the Netherlands. The company was disbanded more than 200 years ago, but the share is still worth over $750,000 to collectors.

Hopping Procession

Echternach, Luxembourg, hosts an annual hopping procession. Up to 9,000 men, women and children—linked by a chain of handkerchiefs—hop through the streets in celebration of a local saint, St. Willibrord.

Great Wall

Following in the footsteps of the country's ancient emperors, in January 2011. wealthy residents of Aodi, Zhejiang Province, China, built a 23-ft-high (7-m) wall around their village for protection. They created the 28-in-thick (70-cm) wall from more than 70,000 adobe bricks. The only entrance to the village is via a huge iron gate.

HIGH RISK

Thousands of feet above the ground, at the top of a sheer drop, with no safety precautions, and working on an area no wider than a dinner table, a worker takes his life in his hands to transport building materials for a wooden plank road on Shifou Mountain in China's Hunan Province.

TREE CHAPEL

An 800-year-old oak tree in the French village of Allouville-Bellefosse has two chapels in its hollow trunk. They were built in the late 1600s, along with an exterior spiral staircase, after lightning burned through the tree. Each year, on August 15, a religious pilgrimage is made to the Chapel Oak.

Lightning Strike

A single lightning bolt at a military base in Hattiesburg, Mississippi, in June 2011 struck an entire troop of cadets, sending no fewer than 77 of them to hospital.

Fought Tsunami

While most of the 3,500 people on the Japanese island of Oshima ran to the hills on hearing the March 2011 tsunami warning, 64-year-old Susumu Sugawara took his fishing boat out to sea and rode out a succession of 60-ft-high (18-m) waves. When the tsunami abated, his was the only boat from the island that had not been destroyed.

CLEVER CAMOUFLAGE

After the catastrophic raid on Pearl Harbor on December 7, 1941, the Army Corps of Engineers raced to hide the Lockheed Burbank Aircraft Plant in California to protect it from a possible aircraft attack.

This was no time for half measures—the Corps opted for deception on the grandest scale, covering every inch of the plant with camouflage netting to make it look like a rural subdivision from the air.

Aircraft hangers, factory buildings, runways, planes, as well as the accommodation and everyday comings and goings of the 90,000 employees, took cover beneath the netting. On top, to create a countryside illusion, neighborhood scenes were painted on canvas, fake houses and hundreds of imitation shrubs and trees were built, and rubber automobiles were strategically placed. The canopy was even strong enough to support people hired to ride bicycles randomly.

Life continued as normal beneath the huge canopy, with workers having space to park their cars and able to hold mass meetings.

To an enemy pilot the scene would have seemed perfectly authentic. Below cover, the plant's vital wartime role carried on as normal.

Uncovered

Hidden

LIVING BRIDGE

In the Indian state of Meghalaya, ancient tree vines and roots are trained to stretch horizontally across rivers in order to create latticework structures that are solid enough to be used as bridges. Some of these living bridges are 100 ft (30 m) long and can support the weight of 50 people at the same time.

Sea of Corn

In November 2010, a grain silo collapsed in Norwalk, Ohio, spilling more than 100,000 bushels of corn and creating a "sea of corn" 12 ft (3.6 m) deep that knocked a nearby home from its foundation.

Bad Singing

The Philippines House of Representatives passed a law in October 2010 making it a crime to sing the country's national anthem poorly. A guilty singer could get up to two years in jail.

Population Center

Mongolia covers more than 600,000 sq mi (1.5 million sq km)—about four times the size of Germany—but nearly half its citizens live in one city, its capital Ulan Bator.

Hydrant Toss

Sherrodsville, Ohio, has an annual fire-hydrant tossing contest. Participants hurl heavy 113-lb (51-kg) hydrants distances of over 20 ft (6 m). A women's competition uses lighter 40-lb (18-kg) hydrants.

Pumpkin Race

Each year Ludwigsburg Castle in Germany stages a pumpkin festival, the highlight of which is a giant pumpkin boat race in the former royal palace's massive fountain. The pumpkins can weigh more than 200 lb (90 kg) before their tops are cut off and their flesh scooped out to turn them into paddleboats. The 2010 festival also featured a giant statue of a seahorse made out of pumpkins.

Giant Tree

Since 1981, the Italian town of Gubbio has created an illumination in the shape of the "biggest Christmas tree in the world" on a mountainside above the town. The spectacle boasts more than 800 lights, and uses nearly 8 mi (13 km) of cables and thousands of plugs to create a tree that stretches over 2,600 ft (795 m) tall.

Driftwood Museum

Bandon, Oregon, has a museum dedicated solely to driftwood, displaying weird and natural shapes from gnarled root balls to whole tree trunks.

Long Street

A single street in central Brazil stretches for 311 mi (501 km). Lined with houses, it is the equivalent to a street running all the way from San Francisco to L.A.

SUCKLING COW

A young Cambodian boy feeds himself daily by suckling directly from a cow. The boy had watched a calf nurse from its mother and instinctively did the same thing.

Totem Pole

Over a three-month period, a 40-ft-tall (12.1-m) redwood tree at Confusion Hill, Piercy, California, was carved by chainsaw into a gigantic totem pole. The pole is the largest free-standing redwood chainsaw carving in the world.

Giant Fungus

A enormous fungus found in China is 33 ft (10 m) long, 2 ft 7 in (80 cm) wide, and 2¼ in (5.5 cm) thick—and it weighs half a ton. It was discovered living under a fallen tree and is estimated to hold 450 million spores.

Old-style Holidays

Hotel Morava in Tatranska Lomnica, Slovakia, hosts vacations in the style of the former Communist worker holidays—complete with strict 7 a.m. wake-up calls, compulsory morning exercises, and even a re-enactment of a May Day rally.

Small Cemetery

Ocracoke Island in North Carolina is home to a cemetery owned by Britain that has only four graves. All four souls were washed ashore from a capsized British trawler in 1942.

Bedroom Sinkhole

A sinkhole 40 ft (12 m) deep and 2 ft 7 in (80 cm) in diameter suddenly appeared overnight beneath the bed of a woman's home in Guatemala City in July 2011. Guatemala City is prone to sinkholes because it is built on volcanic deposits and experiences abnormally high rainfall.

Drive-thru Mortuary

There is a drive-thru mortuary in Compton, California. The Robert L. Adams Mortuary has a drive-thru viewing option where mourners can see the open casket of a dead relative displayed behind a long bulletproof glass window without getting out of their car.

Cave School

Until 2011, a school in a remote mountain community in Guizhou Province, China, had all its classrooms and its playground in a cave. The 186 pupils at the Getu Village Cave Primary School took their lessons in a vast cave the size of an aircraft hangar, surrounded by bats and lizards. The acoustics helped the school to have the best choir in the area.

FIERY RIDER

Believe it or not, this rider from Kyrgyzstan set light to his back during a spectacular fiery stunt at the Lake Son-Kul folk festival in the north of the country.

DRIVEN CRAZY!

HARD LUCK

Making a sudden U-turn in an attempt to get out of heavy traffic, a driver in Houston, Texas, found herself in a lane of freshly laid cement. Stuck fast, she had no choice but to sit there in her $70,000 Lexus, and wait for help.

WATER RIDE

In Monterey, California, the driver of this BMW sports car escaped serious injury after accidentally propelling the vehicle off the edge of a parking lot, over a sun deck and through a fence, before flipping into the pool below. It's thought that the driver pressed the accelerator by mistake. Fortunately, the deck and the pool were empty at the time.

MIND THE GAP

Driving at night along a country road in Arnsberg, Germany, this motorist failed to spot that the road ahead had collapsed. Her car fell headlong into the gap, but she escaped unhurt.

BUMPY RIDE

Following a wrongly positioned sign to the parking lot in a shopping mall in Liuzhou, China, Xiang Zhen drove her car down a staircase, where it got stuck. As startled shoppers fled, Xiang abandoned her car and phoned a tow-truck company to winch it back up to the street.

Sacred Bell

A Buddhist temple bell in Liuzhou, China, weighs 120 tons, stands 30 ft (9 m) tall, measures 20 ft (6 m) in diameter at its widest point, and is engraved with 92,306 sacred Chinese characters.

Prize Crash

Truck driver David Dopp of Santaquin, Utah, won a $380,000 Lamborghini sports car in a competition in October 2011, but within six hours of driving it away, he crashed it.

Military Past

The MV Liemba, a ferry that runs across Africa's Lake Tanganyika, was originally built in 1913 as a warship for Imperial Germany.

Shocking Shower

Lightning can strike twice! Twelve-year-old Alice Svensson of Gothenburg, Sweden, was struck by lightning twice as it traveled through water pipes while she showered. Although badly shocked, she was unharmed.

Rig Pods

Visitors to Den Haag, the Netherlands, can pay $75 a night to stay in hotel rooms that have been transformed from oil rig survival capsules. One of the bright orange pods has even been given a James Bond theme, with silk sheets on the bed, champagne and a vodka martini bar. Another just has a hammock made from fishing nets.

Starting out
In Prudhoe Bay—June 2008

Southern Bolivia
"We took a 400-mile detour up and over the Andes."

AMERICAN ODYSSEY

For nearly three years from June 2008 to March 2011, John and Nancy Vogel and their twin sons Daryl and Davy of Boise, Idaho, cycled the entire length of the Pan-American Highway from Alaska to the tip of Tierra del Fuego, Argentina—a pedaling distance of 17,300 mi (27,850 km). The boys were just ten years old when they set off, making them the youngest people to cycle the length of the Americas.

Endless roads
"In Argentina, I never thought we would reach the end of the road!"

In the Colombian Andes
"The Andes took us by surprise with their long, steep climbs."

Village in South America
"We were either on the open road or in small villages."

Arriving at the end of the world
Ushuaia, Argentina—March 2011

121

KILLER PLANT

A carnivorous pitcher plant at a garden nursery in Somerset, England, killed and ate a great tit—only the second documented case in the world of a pitcher plant eating a bird. The plant's inner wall secretes a nectarlike substance to attract insects, and the bird probably leaned in too far to catch a bug and became trapped by the plant's slippery, waxy surface. It then fell into the pool of enzymes and acid that is housed at the base of the pitcher. Large pitcher plants often eat rats and frogs, and can completely devour a piece of meat in just a few days.

Eaten great tit!

Doomsday Vault

Millions of seeds taken from more than 500,000 different crop varieties are stored in a special vault situated 425 ft (130 m) inside a frozen mountain on a remote Norwegian island near the Arctic Ocean. The location for the Doomsday Vault, as it is known, was chosen because it is thought to be about the safest place on the planet to protect the world's seed collections from nuclear war or other disasters.

Plant Life

The South Atlantic's arid and volcanic Ascension Island received its diverse plant species in the 1850s when the British Royal Navy populated it with annual shipments of plants from around the world.

Orange Goo

A strange, sticky, orange goo made up from millions of rust fungal spores washed ashore near Kivalina, Alaska, in 2011.

Skeleton View

A five-bedroom house in Visby on the Swedish island of Gotland has a medieval tomb and skeleton in the cellar. The house was built in 1750 on the foundations of a Russian church. The kitchen rests on the presbytery, and the tomb containing the skeleton of a Russian man who died about 800 years ago is visible through a glass panel.

Wild Orchid

A single Lady's Slipper orchid growing on the Silverdale Golf Course in Carnforth, Lancashire, England, is the last of its kind growing wild in all of Britain and is protected by police patrols. The orchid, which is more than 100 years old, attracts hundreds of visitors each year, with people traveling over 200 mi (320 km) just to see it.

Waterproof Vault

The Crypt of Civilization— a waterproof vault beneath Oglethorpe University in Atlanta, Georgia—was sealed in 1940 and contains objects and information of the day. Its stainless steel receptacles are filled with inert gases and so are designed to last 6,000 years.

LONG AND WINDING ROAD

Drivers compete on the twisty 24 Crankle Stilwell Road (also known as the Burma Road) during a hill-climb rally in Guizhou Province, China. The road is 717 mi (1,154 km) long and runs from Yunnan Province, China, to Burma. Over 2,300 laborers lost their lives while building the Chinese section of the road in 1938.

Whistling Language

The whistling language of Silbo Gomero has only four vowels and four consonants, and its speakers can easily converse while standing 2 mi (3 km) apart. It is used only by inhabitants of La Gomera in the Canary Islands and is communicated by whistling at different tones.

Undersea River

Differences in temperature and salt content cause water from the Mediterranean to flow into the Black Sea as an underwater river, complete with waterfalls and a riverbed on the sea floor.

No Doors

The homes in the village of Siala in Orissa, India, have no doors. Residents believe a goddess watches over their village, protecting it from theft.

Holy Stalagmite

India's ice "Shiva Lingam," a stalagmite that is worshiped by Hindus, began melting in August 2011 because of warmer weather and a record number of vistors generating too much body heat. Over a 40-day period that summer, 620,000 people went to see the holy stalagmite at Amarnath caves in Kashmir.

Statues Stolen

The Dutch city of Nijmegen removed ten large bronze statues from the streets in November 2010 after four of them had been ripped from their foundations, probably stolen to be sold as scrap metal.

War Tours

A Swiss travel agency offers vacations in the world's most dangerous war zones. Babel Travel's catalog has package tours for Iraq, Sudan and Somalia, as well as giving tourists the chance to spend Christmas in Afghanistan or enjoy a New Year's party in Iran. A 45-day vacation in Afghanistan costs more than $30,000—and that's without adding in the cost of travel insurance.

Longest Constitution

With 444 articles, 12 schedules and 98 amendments totaling more than 117,000 words, India's Constitution is the longest written constitution of any independent country in the world. By contrast, the U.S. Constitution is the shortest, with just seven articles and 27 amendments, giving a total of only 4,400 words.

BUDDHIST BODY

Inside a large pot at a temple in Fujian Province, China, construction workers found the body of a Buddhist nun that had been buried for 32 years. Although Chen Zhu's corpse had not been embalmed, it was so well preserved that it has now been wrapped in gauze and coated in black lacquer and gold foil to make a human body statue. Buddhists say the nun's vegetarian diet kept her body in a good state.

GLASS BEACH

The Glass Beach is a beach in Fort Bragg, California, that is completely covered with stone-sized pieces of natural glass in different colors. The beach was used as a public dump during the 1950s and 1960s, which included a lot of glass that ended up in the ocean. The glass has since been deposited back on the beach over a number of years, after the harsh waves and cold waters of the North Pacific Ocean have softened and polished the pieces.

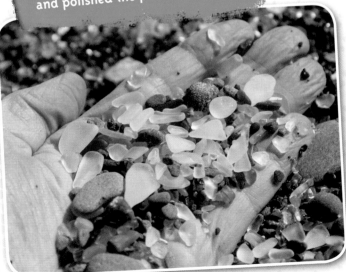

Snake Village

Just over 25 years ago, the 160 families in China's Zisiqiao village farmed the land and raised livestock—now they breed more than three million snakes every year for food and use in traditional medicine. The "snake village" was started by a single local farmer, who began by catching wild snakes to sell, and then bred them at home. His practices soon caught on and farming snakes has since brought millions of dollars to what was once a poor village.

Ancient Inn

The Keiunkan Inn in Hayakawa, Yamanashi Prefecture, Japan, has operated continuously for more than 1,300 years. The hotel boasts a hot spring 2,913 ft (888 m) underground that produces 358 gal (1,630 l) of water at a temperature of 126°F (52°C) every minute.

Toxic Tree

The milky white sap of the manchineel tree, native to Florida, the Caribbean and Central America, is so toxic that just standing underneath it during a rainstorm can cause skin and eye irritation. Burning the tree may cause temporary blindness if the smoke reaches the eyes.

MEXICO STONE

This house in Mascota, Mexico, is entirely covered in rocks! The house, which is also a museum, was decorated with rocks of different sizes by the owner after his wife passed away. They are everywhere, even on the picture frames, the television and flower pots!

VOODOO BELIEFS

Visitors to Akodessewa Fetish Market can buy all manner of medicinal skulls, including crocodile heads, vultures, owls, dogs, turtles, rodents and mummified bats.

Voodoo is a traditional religion from West Africa. It is based on a belief that animals and inanimate objects, known as fetishes, have spiritual powers.

These fetishes are used in voodoo rituals. Powders made from various animal parts are administered by voodoo priests, or bokors, which can seemingly send people into a trance.

Traditional West African voodoo was transported to Haiti in the Caribbean and to the southern U.S.A., particularly Louisiana, where it mixed with Catholicism.

Voodoo healers claim to be able to cure a vast range of sicknesses. Akodessewa Fetish Market in Togo, West Africa, is a voodoo supermarket— an outdoor pharmacy where thousands of animal body parts, including crocodile heads, monkey testicles, snake skin and elephants' feet, take the place of conventional medicine.

The heads of dead leopards are used by voodoo priests to make a powdered medicine to cure human head and brain conditions.

Cats with their stomach ripped open line the market stalls at Lomé, Togo. The stench from the market is described as foul.

In Haiti, voodoo dolls, or fetishes, can be seen in graveyards. Some believe they act as messengers to the spirit world, and to help contact loved ones. This doll, found in the national cemetery in Port-au-Prince, belongs to a voodoo priest who practices in the graveyard.

A voodoo priest caked in mud in Port-au-Prince, Haiti. Haitian voodoo believers bathe in sacred mud pools and sacrifice animals as part of an annual voodoo festival in Plaine du Nord, in the north of the country.

CROOKED FOREST

The town of New Czarnowo, Poland, is home to a bizarre forest near the Odra River, where hundreds of pine trees display large bends in the bottom of their trunk, before growing vertically as normal. Surrounding trees are completely straight. The reason behind their deformity is a mystery, and explanations range from man-made techniques used to shape the wood for use in furniture or boats, to extreme environmental conditions when the trees were young.

Tornado Record

On April 27, 2011, a record-breaking 312 tornadoes were recorded over the U.S.'s southern States in a 24-hour period starting at 8 a.m.—more than double the previous record of 148 twisters in a single day in 1974. Four of the April 2011 tornadoes achieved the most powerful ranking possible— EF5 on the Enhanced Fujita Scale—whereas normally such destructive twisters are recorded only once a year or less.

Tsar Bell

The bronze Tsar Bell, which sits in the grounds of the Kremlin, Moscow, Russia, weighs over 200 tons, stands more than 200 ft (6 m) high, has a diameter of 21 ft 8 in (6.6 m), and is 2 ft (60 cm) thick. Cast in 1735, the bell— the biggest in the world—was damaged two years later by fire, the heat from which caused a 12-ton piece to shatter. The bell has been used as a chapel, with people entering and exiting via the broken area.

BIRD BRAINED

Sally Arnold from Kendal, England, returned home one day to find a perfect imprint of an owl on her window. The bird had flown into the window and left behind the eerie image—complete with eyes, beak and feathers—before flying off. The silhouette was made by the bird's powder down, a substance that protects its growing feathers.

World Sign

A famous signpost in Lynchville, Maine, displays the distances to Paris (15 mi/24 km), Denmark (23 mi/37 km), Sweden (25 mi/40 km), Peru (46 mi/ 74 km) and China (94 mi/ 151 km), all of which are the names of genuine towns in the state.

Tree Home

After graduating from college and with his parents moving to Hawaii, Corbin Dunn built a tree house when he was 20 years old and lived in it for five years. Located 40 ft (12 m) above ground at the back of the family home in Santa Cruz, California, the tree house had electricity and boasted a fully functional shower and toilet.

New Islands

New islands regularly appear and disappear off the coast of Pakistan near the Makran Desert over a matter of months. They are created by volcanoes of mud that erupt from deep within the Earth.

Popular President

Indonesian President Susilo Bambang Yudhoyono was re-elected with nearly 74 million votes cast for him in 2009—the most votes ever received by a democratically elected official anywhere in the world.

Gladiator Fight

In August 2011, undercover police officers in Rome, Italy, dressed up as gladiators—complete with togas and capes—to prevent the escalation of a turf war between Italian gladiator impersonators who prey on tourists outside the Colosseum and other city landmarks. When the officers impersonating gladiators came under attack from the regular gladiator impersonators, they were rescued by other undercover officers dressed as garbage collectors and tourists!

Speed Chase

Female police officers in Chengdu, China, patrol the city's Tianfu Square on rollerblades so that they can pursue criminals at speed—giving chase at speeds of up to 25 mph (40 km/h).

Blues Brother

Bill Smith-Eccles (a.k.a. Jake Blues) of Derbyshire, England, is such a fan of the 1980 cult movie The Blues Brothers that he wears sunglasses all the time—even on his driver's license photo, making him the only person in the U.K. that has been allowed to do so.

High Fire

Germany's Paris Gun, a World War I artillery cannon, could bombard the French capital from 70 mi (112 km) away and could be fired so high that the rotation of the Earth affected its trajectory.

Pants Cargo

A man was arrested at Miami International Airport as he tried to board a flight for Brazil—with seven exotic snakes and three tortoises stuffed down his pants.

LEAP OF FAITH

At the annual Goat Jump Festival in the village of Manganeses de la Polvorosa in northern Spain, a goat is thrown from the 50-ft-high (15-m) church bell tower and safely caught by villagers holding a large tarpaulin. The festival is based on a local legend about a priest who owned a special goat, whose milk helped him to administer to the poor. One day the hapless goat wandered into the church belfry and jumped off the ledge in fright when the bells rang for Sunday mass. The goat was luckily caught in a blanket and saved.

Icelandic Festival

The town of Gimli in Manitoba, Canada, holds an annual festival that celebrates all things Icelandic. Since 1890, the Icelandic Festival of Manitoba—or *Islendingadagurinn*—has been crowning a Fjallkona (maid of the mountain) and reenacting Viking warfare tactics.

National Perfume

Lithuania has launched its own national perfume—a blend of sandalwood, cedar and musk designed to convey the Indo-European origins of the Lithuanian language as well as strength of character. Samples of the perfume were sent to Lithuanian embassies, hotels and airports and to the country's soldiers deployed in Afghanistan.

Tree House

Farmer Xiong Yuhu from Xingping, Hunan Province, China, has built a house—with a kitchen, bathroom, bedroom and lounge—at the top of a 50-ft-high (15-m) tree. Inspired by the Bird's Nest Olympic Stadium in Beijing, this luxury tree house is reached by a long wooden staircase. The structure is so solid that 18 adults have stood in the house together.

Underground Hospital

Ukraine's Solotvyno salt mine has a subterranean hospital ward for convalescing asthmatics and people with other respiratory problems. Its salty air is said to have created a unique microclimate that helps people who suffer from breathing difficulties.

Hidden Tunnels

In May 2010, police searched the residence of a man in East Austin, Texas, and discovered he had dug a three-story network of tunnels beneath his home. The tunnels went as far as 35 ft (11 m) deep and in several places were big enough to allow an adult to stand up.

Silver Lady

The Silver Queen, a 19th-century hotel in Virginia City, Nevada, has a 15-ft-tall (4.6-m) painting of a lady in an evening gown adorned with 3,261 real silver coins. Her belt is made from 28 gold coins and her choker and bracelets are made from dimes.

Tree branches, metal skewers and needles are just some of the implements used for piercing at Phuket's Vegetarian Festival.

GETTING THE NEEDLE

At the Phuket Vegetarian Festival in Thailand, devotees self-mutilate by piercing their face and body with dozens of needles. Ritual vegetarianism in Phuket dates back to the early 19th century and participants at the nine-day festival perform acts of body piercing to purge others of evil spirits and bring good luck to the community.

REDNECK GAMES

When people joked that the 1996 Atlanta Olympics would be staged by a bunch of rednecks, local radio station manager Mac Davis decided to reinforce the stereotype by organizing an alternative Redneck Games in East Dublin, Georgia.

About 500 people were expected to attend; instead 5,000 showed up. The Summer Redneck Games was up and running... and hurling... and spitting.

Since then, the one-day Games has grown into a major annual event, showcasing such traditional redneck pastimes as hubcap hurling, watermelon seed spitting and throwing toilet seats.

In one event, the armpit serenade, competitors cup their hands under their armpits to make farting noises or tunes.

There is no financial reward for the event winners—just a trophy. In this case, the trophy is a half-crushed, empty, mounted beer can.

Another competitor makes a splash and gets down and dirty in the mud pit belly flop—for many people the blue riband event of the Redneck Games. Self-proclaimed redneck grandma Barbara Bailey has won the special event on several occasions.

Caitlin Craft plunges face first into a trough of water and uses her mouth to grab a frozen pig's trotter during the bobbin' for pigs' feet contest. Whoever retrieves the most feet in the allotted time wins the coveted beer-can trophy.

A medal-winning contestant in the toilet seat throwing contest (redneck horseshoes) hurls away.

137

ROCK FACE

Photographer Peter Bardsley of Cumbria, England, spotted this creepy face formed by the reflection of a cave in the Hodge Close Quarry, in the Lake District. The skull cave (best seen when the picture is turned through 90 degrees, see right) can be seen only by abseiling 100 ft (30 m) down an unstable cliff, or wading through a 260-ft (80-m) mine tunnel. The quarry has not been used for decades, and its flooded tunnels and caves are popular with divers.

Talbot Society

The Talbot Society holds gatherings for people named Talbot. They drive to Port Talbot, South Wales, in their Talbot cars, stopping en route at hotels and inns called the Talbot.

Free Flags

Flags that fly over the Canadian Parliament's Peace Tower are free to residents who request one—but there is a 27-year waiting list to receive one.

Door to Hell

The Door to Hell near Darvaza, Turkmenistan, is a crater—200 ft (60 m) in diameter and 65 ft (20 m) deep—that is filled with burning gas. Geologists ignited it more than 35 years ago so that no poisonous gas could escape from the hole, and it has been burning ever since.

Sea Bridge

China's Qingdao Haiwan Bridge, which spans the waters of Jiaozhou Bay, is 26.4 miles (42.2 km) long—approximately the length of a marathon. The bridge, which carries an average of 30,000 cars every day, is supported by more than 5,000 pillars. It was built using enough steel to build 65 Eiffel Towers, and enough concrete to fill 3,800 Olympic-sized swimming pools. More than 10,000 workers helped with its construction.

Toddler Trip

In April 2012, two-year-old Noah Joel pedaled his small bicycle over 3 mi (4.8 km) across the busy town of Hamelin, Germany, to visit his grandmother in the hospital, while his mother thought he was playing in his room.

Snake Wedding

Nearly 1,000 people converged on a village in Kandal Province, Cambodia, in January 2011 to witness the marriage of two pythons. Locals hoped that the snake wedding would bring good luck.

Flying High

The city of Calipatria, California, sits at an altitude of negative 184 ft (56 m), but its flagpole is just high enough for the U.S. flag to fly right at sea level.

Colossal Cave

At more than 650 ft (198 m) high and almost 500 ft (152 m) wide, Hang Song Doong, a cave in Vietnam, is large enough to contain several 40-story buildings.

Connecticut Corner

If you travel directly north, south, east or west from the city of Stamford, Connecticut, you will enter the state of New York.

Chain Whipping

The Festival of Ashura is celebrated by some Shia Muslims with flagellation ceremonies where participants cut their own scalp with knives or whip their chest and back with chains.

Lost Copy

During its 40th anniversary of independence from Britain, the island nation of Fiji announced that it had lost its copy of the 1970 Independence Order, which granted the country self-rule.

Earth on Earth

There is a place on Earth called Earth—in Lamb County, Texas—with a population of around 1,000. Founded in 1924, it was originally named Fairlawn until it emerged the following year that there was already a town in Texas with that name. The postmaster chose Earth as the new name supposedly because a sandstorm was blowing when he had to fill out a form for the postal authorities in Washington, D.C.

On the Edge

Groups of up to six people who enjoy living on the edge can pay $175 per person to walk hands-free for 30 minutes around a high, narrow ledge on the outside of the CN Tower in Toronto, Ontario—attached only by a cable. The ledge is just 5 ft (1.5 m) wide, has no guardrail, and is 1,168 ft (356 m) above ground, but offers exhilarating views of the city and Lake Ontario.

Hobbit Hotel

Fans of *The Lord of the Rings* can stay in an underground hobbit hotel in Trout Creek, Montana. Steve Michaels has built the 1,000-sq-ft (93-sq-m) Hobbit House of Montana into a hill and designed it so that it looks just like Middle Earth from the outside, but has modern comforts such as HD Blu-Ray TV and WiFi access on the inside.

Underwater Suite

To celebrate its fifth anniversary, the Conrad Maldives Rangali Island Hotel converted its famous underwater restaurant into a honeymoon suite beneath the waves, complete with a double bed, complimentary champagne breakfast, and uninterrupted views of exotic sea life.

Twin Town

About 1.5 percent of all human births are twins—but they are over three times more common in the town of Igbo-Ora, Nigeria. The reason for the high level of multiple births is a mystery, but some doctors believe it could be linked to the large amount of the tuberous vegetable yam eaten by the local people.

Huge Hailstones

More than 20 people were injured when hailstones the size of chicken's eggs hit the Siberian city of Mezhdurechensk on August 14, 2012.

Signpost Forest

The Signpost Forest, near Watson Lake, Yukon, Canada, displays more than 65,000 city limits signs that have been collected from around the world. The collection was started in 1942 after a homesick G.I., Private Carl K. Lindley, accidentally drove a bulldozer into the original sign that pointed out the distances to various locations along the Alaska Highway. While carrying out repairs following the accident, Private Lindley added a sign pointing to his hometown of Danville, Illinois. Each year up to 4,000 new signs are added by tourists and visitors as they pass through Watson Lake, so that the Signpost Forest now occupies a couple of acres.

Class of their Own

A 2011–12 freshman class at Maine South High School, Park Ridge, Illinois, contained 16 sets of twins and three sets of triplets.

Turn, Turn, Turn

Rongorongo—a system of writing in Easter Island—consists of about 120 symbols (including birds, fish, plants and gods) and is read by turning the text 180 degrees at the end of each line.

Out with a Bang

Following his death in 2009, the ashes of Alfonse Kennedy Goss, a keen member of New Zealand's Wellington Cannon Society, were fired from a cannon over the city harbor.

Blind Ambition

Pete Golsby from Suffolk, England, spent nearly five years building a sports car from scratch—even though he is blind and cannot drive it. He put it together using an engine from an old motorbike, piping from a shower, and car parts donated by friends.

Speed Message

To encourage drivers to slow down on country roads, the Australian town of Speed (population 45) renamed itself Speedkills for the month of March 2011. For the campaign, local sheep farmer Phil Down even agreed to change his name to Phil Slow Down.

FINGER FUNERAL

The Dani tribe from the island of New Guinea had an unusual method of mourning their dead relatives. It was customary for females to have one or two fingers chopped off at the first joint when a family member died, eventually leaving some with only shortened stumps. Observers have reported that a tribal elder would numb the arm by knocking the elbow, and then remove the digits with one blow of a stone axe. The finger-cutting ritual has been banned, but you can still see older Dani women bearing the results of the practice.

remarkable FEATS

SUPER STOMACH

Louis Cole from London, England, has an appetite that defies belief.

The daring digester has eaten some of the most disgusting things imaginable for his Internet videos, including 21 live locusts, over 600 wriggling mealworms in one sitting, and one large and lively scorpion—the creature's stinger was sensibly left on the plate.

Louis Cole's Monstrous Menu

- Live May bug
- Live house spider
- 21 live locusts
- Raw sheep brain
- Entire bottle of wasabi sauce
- 3 live cockroaches
- 10 mice liquefied in a blender
- Decomposing frog
- Live giant scorpion
- 660 live mealworms
- Live wasp

ST COUNT: 21

WHAT A MOUTHFUL!

On July 4, 2011, Dinesh Shivnath Upadhyaya, a teacher from Mumbai, India, set a new world record by fitting 800 drinking straws into his mouth at the same time and keeping them there for 30 seconds.

Largest Kilt

Ordering 170 sq yd (142 sq m) of material, Steve Campbell, a Scotsman living in the U.S.A., made the world's largest kilt and used it to dress the 80-ft-tall (24-m) Golden Driller statue in Tulsa, Oklahoma, for the 2011 Oklahoma Scottish Festival. The kilt was 25 ft (7.6 m) long and had a waist measuring 48 ft (14.6 m), nearly 14 times bigger than a U.S. extra-large size.

Underwater Escape

U.S. entertainer Thomas Blacke escaped from a pair of handcuffs underwater in a world record time of 8.34 seconds on October 27, 2010, in Yarmouth, Massachusetts.

1,000 Flavors

Matt and Mike Casarez sold over 1,000 different flavors of ice cream at Crook's Palace, Black Hawk, Colorado. Their more unusual varieties included "Wasabi Sesame," "Popcorn" and "Sweet Pea."

800 straws!

92 pencils!

Wet Guests

Eva and Pavel Jaworzno got engaged and married underwater. Their August 2011 wedding ceremony took place in a flooded open-pit mine in southern Poland, diving with 275 guests, making it the world's largest underwater wedding.

Jackpot Joy

Four workers from the Bell Canada call center in Scarborough, Ontario, who were members of a syndicate that won a $50-million Lotto Max draw in January 2011, were also part of a group of Bell employees who won $1 million in 2007.

Wonder Wheel

On June 18, 2011, the Lilly fireworks factory in Mqabba, Malta, lit the world's biggest pinwheel (Catherine Wheel) firework. With a diameter of 105 ft (32 m), it was 45 times the size of the average car wheel.

Lotta Bottles

Over a 25-year period, Steve Wheeler has collected more than 17,500 milk bottles in different shapes and sizes, some from the 19th century. He has built a giant shed to house the collection, which weighs 15 tons, behind his home in Malvern, England. Ironically, Steve doesn't even like milk!

Army Medic

At 76 years old, U.S. Army medic Dr. John Burson, an ear, nose and throat specialist from Villa Rica, Georgia, was posted to Afghanistan to take his fourth tour of duty in war zones since 2005.

Canadian Crossing

In 2011, Kevin Robins of Fort McMurray, Alberta, Canada, cycled across Canada from Vancouver, British Columbia, to St. John's, Newfoundland, in just over 22 days, beating the previous record by a day and a half. He covered a total of 4,500 mi (7,200 km), clocking up an average pace of 200 mi (323 km) a day.

5 golf balls!

6 table tennis balls!

147

Oldest Ranger

Betty Reid Soskin is still an active ranger in the U.S. National Park Service—at the age of 90. She works at Rosie the Riveter National Historic Park in Richmond, California, six hours a day, five days a week.

Gum Collector

Sarah Maughan of Idaho Falls, Idaho, has collected over 1,400 different packages of gum. She began collecting gum in 1948, beginning with a pack of Popeye bubble gum, and has been adding new types and flavors for more than 60 years.

Loose Change

Craig Davidson of Phoenix, Arizona, spent over 30 years collecting loose change that he found on his morning jogs. He never missed a day running and found more than $8,400 in dropped coins.

Route 66

Andy McMenemy from Harrogate, England, ran 66 ultramarathons—each 31 mi (50 km) long—on 66 consecutive days in 66 different cities in the U.K.

Polar First

Taking advantage of seasonal melting ice caps in August 2011, a team of six British explorers—Jock Wishart, David Mans, Billy Gammon, Mark Delstanche, Mark Beaumont and Rob Sleep—became the first people to row to the magnetic North Pole in a specially designed boat. During their 450-mi (720-km), month-long voyage through Arctic waters, they encountered polar bears and collided with icebergs, and Wishart was bitten by a seal.

WALKING ON WATER

Polish kiteboarder Maciek Kozierski temporarily defied the laws of physics by walking on water—on Israel's Sea of Galilee where Jesus is said to have walked on water in the New Testament. After more than 50 unsuccessful attempts in awkward wind conditions over four days, Kozierski finally used his kite to accelerate to maximum speed, then let go of the kite and ran off his board so that he was miraculously walking on water for a few steps.

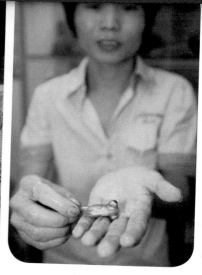

HARD TO SWALLOW

Liang Yuxin from Xia Mei, China, can regurgitate live goldfish, coins and even a 50-in-long (127-cm) chain. He discovered his unusual talent as a boy after accidentally swallowing a ball and finding that he could bring it back up at will.

Scuba Dive

Diver and scuba instructor Allen Sherrod of Groveland, Florida, spent more than five days 20 ft (6 m) underwater in Lake David to complete the longest ever freshwater dive. He surfaced on September 16, 2011, after 120 hours 14 minutes 32 seconds in the lake, during which time he entertained himself with a waterproof keyboard and monitor that enabled him to watch movies and check Facebook.

Flamingo Fan

Sherry Knight of Lecanto, Florida, loves flamingos so much that years ago she started collecting flamingo-related items—and now has over 619 pieces of flamingo memorabilia.

Lost Leg

A year after losing his leg in a climbing accident, Hungarian climber Zsolt Eross scaled the world's fourth-highest mountain—the 27,940-ft (8,516-m) peak of Lhotse in the Himalayas—wearing his replacement prosthetic leg.

LIZARDMAN

Performance artist Erik "The Lizardman" Sprague, from Austin, Texas, has spent years transforming himself into a reptile-man hybrid.

Since 1994, he has undergone almost 700 hours of tattooing in order to achieve a full head and body of green scales. To complete his unique look, four of his teeth have been filed into sharp crocodile-like fangs, he has had his tongue bifurcated, and five Teflon horns have been subdermally implanted above each eye to form horned ridges.

During Erik's act, he inserts razor-sharp scissor blades in the fork of his tongue and through his nostrils, threads a metal corkscrew through his nose and mouth, and sticks a running power drill up his nostrils. He also swallows swords, eats and breathes fire, and acts as a human dartboard.

Erik, who has a degree in Philosophy, estimates that it would cost around $250,000 for anyone wanting to achieve the same unbelievable look as The Lizardman.

As a young boy

As Best Man

Wedding day

The wire carefully goes right into his nasal passage! He corkscrews through his nose, out of his mouth, and then through his ear!

151

BEE SUIT

In May 2011, Zhang Wei from Zizhou County, China, wore a suit of bees weighing a staggering 184 lb (83.5 kg)—that's approximately the weight of an adult American man. Wearing a pair of goggles, but leaving his face and hands unprotected and holding a tube in his mouth for breathing, he sat in a foliage-covered frame as thousands of bees were released next to him.

WHERE'S WALDO?

More than 3,500 people dressed in red-and-white striped costumes and black-rimmed spectacles assembled in a square in Dublin, Ireland, in June 2011 for a mass gathering of the Waldo character from the popular *Where's Waldo?* children's books. Some dogs even turned up dressed as Waldo.

Pogo Hops

Chef Ben Hoyle who comes from Sudbury, England, completed 75 successive pogo hops on the back wheel of his trail bike in September 2011.

500-Mile Crawl

In 2010, two Buddhist monks crawled 500 mi (800 km) on their knees to visit a statue in China's Putuo Mountains—a journey that took them a total of two months.

Beer Labels

Since 1955, Charles Johnson of Cuyahoga Falls, Ohio, has collected more than 108,000 beer-bottle labels from all over the world.

SKYSCRAPER CLIMB

In a six-hour climb, Alain Robert, or "Spiderman," the French freestyle skyscraper climber, scaled the 2,717-ft-high (828-m) Burj Khalifa building in Dubai, United Arab Emirates, in March 2011. He has climbed over 70 of the world's tallest buildings, including New York's Empire State Building and Chicago's Willis Tower.

World Walk

Jean Béliveau of Montréal, Canada, walked around the world for 11 years. He set off on his 45th birthday and traveled 46,940 mi (75,543 km) through 64 countries, wearing out 53 pairs of shoes on the longest-ever uninterrupted world walk. He ate insects in Africa, dog in South Korea, and snake in China, and carried his sleeping bag, clothes and a first-aid kit in a three-wheel stroller.

Ice Ordeal

Two Chinese men stood encased in ice for two hours in Zhangjiajie, Hunan Province, in 2011, wearing only their swimming trunks. Chen Kecai, 52, and Jin Songhao, 54, lasted 118 and 120 minutes respectively standing in transparent boxes with ice right up to their necks. Jin was even able to write Chinese calligraphy during the challenge.

Swallowed Saw

On November 14, 2010, U.S. sword swallower Dan Meyer swallowed a 100-year-old handsaw, which belonged to the Bruce Museum in Greenwich, Connecticut, during a presentation on the history of sword swallowing.

Careful Climb

In December 2010, the Czech Republic's Anatol Stykan climbed the 235 steps leading up to the famous Sacre Coeur church in Paris, France, while balancing his partner Monika on his head.

Star Swimmer

Four-year-old Tae Smith from Poole, England, swam 101 lengths of a pool (1¼ mi/ 2,000 m) just five months after learning to swim. She was meant to swim 30 lengths, but kept going until she had swum more than triple the distance.

Carton Regatta

Thirty-six teams used 45,000 empty milk cartons to make rowboats to take part in the 2011 milk carton boat regatta over a 165-ft-long (50-m) course on Latvia's Lielupe River.

Rocket Racer

Students at the Joseph Leckie Community Technology College in Walsall, England, developed a rocket-powered scale model car that reached a speed of 88.92 mph (143.1 km/h)—that's an equivalent speed of 259 mph (417 km/h) in a regular-sized car. The 21-in (53-cm) car was fitted with D-Class Estes rocket motors and fired 328 ft (100 m) along a high tensile wire.

Haircut Tour

Hair salon owner Patrick Lomantini from Wichita, Kansas, did at least 50 free haircuts a day, in all 50 U.S. states in 50 days in 2011—a total of more than 2,500 haircuts. Visiting a different state each day, the former personal trainer, traveled between states overnight and cut hair all day.

Delayed Graduation

Leo Plass of Redmond, Oregon, dropped out of college in 1932 to take up a job in logging when he was less than one semester away from graduating—but in 2011 he finally received his diploma from Eastern Oregon University at the age of 99.

Iron Man

Seventy-year-old pastor Bob Kurtz—known as "Golf's Iron Man"—completed 1,850 holes of golf over a seven-day period at Quail Creek Golf Resort, Hartselle, Alabama, in June 2011. Despite playing for 16 hours a day in temperatures touching 100°F (38°C), he still shot an average score of just 74 (par for the course is 72), and shot better than his age four times.

DANCING BALLOON

Australian entertainer Bruce Airhead uses a voice-activated vacuum cleaner to inflate a 6-ft (1.8-m) balloon—and then he slides his entire body inside, bit by bit, and starts dancing. As a final twist, although he enters the balloon wearing only Lycra® shorts, he emerges through the burst balloon fully dressed as Elvis.

DOUBLE MUSCLE

Strongman pastor Kevin Fast enlisted the help of his 18-year-old son Jacob to pull two fire trucks 100 ft (30 m) down the street in their hometown of Cobourg, Ontario, in June 2011. Combined, the trucks weighed a massive 153,780 lb (69,755 kg). The event was the latest in a long line of strength feats for Kevin. He has also pulled an entire house and a giant CC-177 Globemaster III airplane weighing 208 tons.

Easy Catch

Jason Kresse of Freeport, Texas, was out fishing for red snapper in the Gulf of Mexico in March 2011 when a 375-lb (170-kg) mako shark leaped into his boat without provocation, thrashing about and damaging the vessel before dying hours later.

Gold Coin

Australia's Perth Mint unveiled the world's largest gold coin in 2011, weighing 2,205 lb (1,000 kg) and measuring 31½ in (80 cm) in diameter and more than 4¾ in (12 cm) thick. Made of 99.99 percent pure gold, the supersized coin bears an image of Queen Elizabeth II on one side and a leaping kangaroo on the other, and is worth more than $50 million.

Mountain Jump

In September 2011, stuntman Jeb Corliss of Malibu, California, flew from the 5,000-ft-high (1,524-m) summit of China's Tianmen Mountain wearing a wingsuit—which has extra fabric between the legs and under the arms to help with lift. He glided like a bird down the mountain and across surrounding valleys before landing safely by parachute on a mountain road.

Brave Swimmer

Despite losing nearly half his body in China's 2008 Sichuan earthquake, Dai Guohong has become one of his country's top swimmers. He lost both legs when they were crushed under tons of rubble after the roof of his Beichuan school collapsed, killing 26 of his classmates.

One-track Mind

A collector of rare vintage toy trains for 50 years, Jerry Greene amassed over 35,000 items, worth a total of more than $50 million. He kept them in the basement of his home in Philadelphia, Pennsylvania. He had about 1,700 locomotives and cars, 700 stations and thousands of accessories. When he decided to sell the collection, it took his family three weeks to unpack just 5,000 of the pieces for display.

Living with Lions

Ukrainian private zoo owner Alexander Pylyshenko lived for 36 days in a cage with a lioness and her two cubs. He slept on hay on the floor and ate food that was passed through the bars. He installed a toilet and shower inside the cage for personal hygiene, but had to avoid using shampoos and deodorants in case they irritated the lions. An artist by profession, he spent much of his time in the cage painting portraits of his roommates.

Top Dog

On July 23, 2011, the Brockton Rox baseball team of Massachusetts created the world's most expensive hot dog, selling for $80.

GOLF HANDICAP

Carbrook Golf Club in Brisbane, Australia, has some unique obstacles on its course—sharks. A dozen or so bull sharks circle the waters in the lake, their fins poking through the water. The 9-ft-long (2.7-m), 330-lb (150-kg) man-eaters spilled into the lake during a flood from nearby rivers, some 5 mi (8 km) away—and have bred in the lake's waters.

Pier Pressure

Harnessing winds of more than 60 mph (96 km/h) on November 11, 2010, kiteboarder Lewis Crathern of Worthing, England, became the first person to jump clean over Brighton Pier. He navigated the waves for about two hours before finally finding one big enough to launch him on his death-defying leap over the 50-ft-high (15-m) structure.

Kiteboard Crossing

Russian extreme sport enthusiasts Yevgeny Novozheev and Konstantin Aksyonov became the first people to cross the 60-mi (97-km) Bering Strait from Russia to Alaska by kiteboard. During their seven-hour journey, they survived water temperatures of 34°F (1°C), a fierce storm, and a collision with a whale.

Rock Star

Alex Honnold of Sacramento, California, climbs some of the most daunting cliff faces in the world—without a safety rope. The free-climber scaled the notorious 2,000-ft (610-m) northwest face of the Half Dome in Yosemite National Park, California, solo in only 2 hours 50 minutes—an ascent that can take some climbers up to five days to complete.

Solo Pilot

On June 4, 2011, nine-year-old Bobby Bradley of Albuquerque, New Mexico, became the youngest solo hot-air balloon pilot when he flew a balloon for 26 minutes over his home state before making a perfect landing. Bobby already had 30 hours' flying experience with his parents—both keen balloonists—and started taking control of the burner when he was just four.

Double Ace

Golfer Adam Smith from Aberdeenshire, Scotland, beat odds of 67 million to one by getting two holes-in-one in the space of seven holes during a round of golf at nearby Stonehaven in January 2011.

Tied Finish

Five runners—Brad Weiss, Chris Solarz, Terence Gerchberg, Stephen England and Francis Laros—finished the 2011 God's Country Marathon in Coudersport, Pennsylvania, in 3 hours 26 minutes—while tethered together.

Bottle-cap Chain

Students and teachers at Seaview Elementary School in Linwood, New Jersey, created a chain from 10,714 bottle caps.

NEAR MISS

Raimana Van Bastolaer nearly lost his head in a surfing contest. Surfers are towed out by Jet Ski, but Raimana's friend, Reef McIntosh, lost control of the machine, which was pulled over the lip of the 12-ft (3.6-m) wave, missing the surfer's head by inches.

STEVE'S WEIRD HOUSE

Steve Bard's rambling Victorian home in Seattle, Washington, has every room crammed from floor to ceiling with hundreds of thousands of curiosities, ranging from an 8-ft-tall (2.4-m) human skeleton to two-headed animals and a collection of 100-year-old pickled human fetuses in jars.

He started out collecting books, but as he picked up oddities and old sideshow artifacts on eBay and from various other sources, his collection spread out from the library to fill the entire house and garden.

Live birds reside in the kitchen, but everything else is dead. There are stuffed gazelles, bears, monkeys and a tiger, as well as preserved curiosities such as conjoined weasels, two-headed kittens, two-headed chicks and a two-headed calf. Many of his exhibits are stored in jars, including one containing a human finger lost in an accident in the 1950s.

Paintings line every wall of the house, and Steve also has hundreds of kinetic art objects and art deco statues.

Adjoining the library is a "Devil Room" devoted to all things Satanic, and the basement has been converted to a glow-in-the-dark "Future Room," decorated in the style of The Jetsons and Barbarella.

This shrine of creepy curiosities extends outside, where Steve has set up a Minotaur Garden in his backyard. For all the weirdness that surrounds him, Steve claims the weirdest thing of all was the one question that a lady visitor to his house wanted to ask: "How do you dust?"

more...

Every inch of Steve Bard's house is filled with old sideshow artifacts and weird human and animal curiosities. The narrow paths that wind from room to room are just wide enough for a person to walk through. Yet it remains a functional house. The kitchen boasts a microwave, a refrigerator and a burner, all cleverly concealed by human skulls, figures, severed heads and other oddities. The house is not open to the general public, but Steve does sometimes give private tours to those who share his eclectic taste in the freaky and the creepy.

WEIRDEST OF THE WEIRD

•Feejee-type mermaid	staircase
•Elephant skull ridden by a skeleton	living room
•Ancient mummy	living room
•Alligator/fish hybrid	dining room
•Chandelier decorated with human skulls	dining room
•Stuffed bear	parlor
•Two-headed calf	parlor
•Antique toaster collection	kitchen
•8-ft-tall (2.4-m) human skeleton	library
•Pickled human fetuses in jars	bedroom
•Sensory-deprivation tank	basement
•13-ft-tall (4-m) Minotaur bust	garden

MONSTER WAVE

On November 1, 2011, American surfer Garrett McNamara set a new world record by riding a 90-ft (27-m) wave off the coast of Portugal. Towed by jet ski out to the freak swell, which was created by a 1,000-ft-deep (300-m) underwater canyon in the area, he managed to catch a lift on a moving wall of water, which was the height of a nine-story building.

Endurance Race

The 2011 Hoka Hey Motorcycle Challenge traveled through 48 U.S. states and part of Canada, from Mesa, Arizona, to Sydney, Nova Scotia—a journey of over 14,000 mi (22,530 km). Entry is limited to Harley-Davidson bikers, and during the event riders must never sleep more than 10 ft (3 m) away from their bike, which rules out nights in hotels. The race was won for the second successive year by Florida's Will Barclay, who completed the course in just two weeks.

Unbroken Run

From 1992 to 2010, National Football League quarterback Brett Favre started in 297 consecutive games.

NAILED IT!

Xu Tiancheng can do a headstand on a nail for 30 minutes—and he has the dent in the top of his head to prove it! The 56-year-old performs his unusual ritual as part of his daily morning exercise routine at a park in Changsha, China—a pain-defying display of endurance that attracts large crowds.

Crossing America

In 2010, six British and U.S. servicemen ran 3,530 mi (5,648 km) from New York to Santa Monica, California, on a Gumpathon, named after the movie Forrest Gump in which the hero runs across the U.S.A. Their eight-week journey took them through three deserts, four time zones, ten mountain ranges, 16 states and 789 towns. Among the team, which ran in relays, was British Royal Marine Mark Ormrod, a triple amputee who lost both legs and one arm when he stepped on a land mine in Afghanistan on Christmas Eve 2007.

Bunny Hops

Polish stunt cyclist Krystian Herba bunny-hopped his way up the 48 flights of the 656-ft-high (200-m) Millennium Tower in Vienna, Austria, in 18 minutes 9 seconds.

Knife Exercise

Xie Guanghai, a 57-year-old physics professor in Luoyang, China, does 4,000 push-ups a day—on upturned chopping knives. By developing thick calluses on his palms, he feels no pain from the blades of the knives, which are held in place on a wooden board.

Bungee Jumps

Scott Huntly from Edinburgh, Scotland, made 107 bungee jumps in just nine hours from a bridge 702 ft (214 m) above the Bloukrans River in the Western Cape region of South Africa.

Yo-Yo Hero

James Buffington, founder of the Chicago Yo-Yo Club, has built a working yo-yo with a string length of 39 ft 9 in (12.1 m). He demonstrated it from the roof of a store in the city, where it hung down over three stories.

Wild Walk

In windy conditions in August 2011, Austrian daredevil Michael Kemeter completed a death-defying walk for 148 ft (45 m) along a ¾-in-wide (2-cm) slackline at an altitude of 2,600 ft (793 m) on Austria's highest mountain, the Grossglockner. He had a safety rope but wore no shoes and despite the cold went topless to reduce wind resistance. A week earlier, he crossed a 525-ft-long (160-m) slackline—the longest in the world—over the Gruenen See in Styria, Austria. In slacklining, the thin nylon line is anchored between two points, but unlike a tightrope it is not taut.

Sock Line

As part of National Red Sock Day—in memory of yachtsman Sir Peter Blake who used to wear red socks for good luck— New Zealanders donated more than 30,000 socks, which, when stretched out on a line, extended for more than 1.8 mi (3 km).

Wire Ball

Starting in 2001, landscaper Rick Fortin of New Boston, New Hampshire, has created a copper wire ball that now measures over 3 ft (0.9 m) in diameter and weighs more than 922 lb (418 kg).

Large Leaf

On his way home, nine-year-old Joseph Donato from Pickering, Canada, picked up a maple leaf that, without the stem, measured 13½ x 11½ in (34 x 29 cm)—that's bigger than most serving platters.

Pole Position

Israeli stuntman Hezi Dean stood on a small platform on top of a nine-story-high pole in Tel Aviv for more than 35 hours in May 2011. A crane hoisted him to the top of the pole and he descended at the end of the endurance test by jumping into a pile of cardboard boxes.

PLANE SWAP

In an incredible midair stunt, Austrian skydiver Paul Steiner climbed from one glider to another 6,560 ft (2,000 m) up in the air while both planes were traveling at 100 mph (160 km/h). He climbed out of the cockpit, crawled along the wing, somersaulted under the wing, and then stepped onto the wing of the second glider flying below. Then, while the first glider turned upside down and flew overhead, Steiner reached up to form a human link between the two planes.

Seven Summits

At just 16 years old, George Atkinson from London, England, reached the summit of the world's highest mountain, 29,029-ft (8,848-m) Mount Everest, and in doing so completed his challenge of conquering mountaineering's famous Seven Summits. Despite his young age, he had previously climbed Tanzania's Mount Kilimanjaro, Russia's Mount Elbrus, Indonesia's Carstensz Pyramid, Argentina's Mount Aconcagua, the U.S.A.'s Mount McKinley and Antarctica's Mount Vinson.

Epic Flight

Paraplegic pilot Dave Sykes of Dewsbury, England, flew an ultralight aircraft 13,480 mi (21,700 km) from the U.K. to Sydney, Australia. Sykes, who lost the use of his legs in a motorbike accident in 1993, battled through dust storms, thunder and lightning, and baking heat on his three-month solo flight over 20 countries.

High Basket

From the top of a light tower that was almost 220 ft (67 m) above the ground, basketball stunt team How Ridiculous (comprising Derek Herron, Brett Stanford, Scott Gaunson and Kyle Nebel) sank an incredible basket at the Western Australia Cricket Association Ground in Perth in 2011.

Underwater Cards

A group of 16 German SCUBA divers played a card game underwater for 36 hours in March 2011. The divers sat on the bottom of a pool in Geiselhoering, playing a traditional Bavarian card game called "Sheep's Head."

Daily Ascent

Matt Loughrey climbed Croagh Patrick, a 2,507-ft-high (764-m) mountain in Ireland, every day for a year between June 2010 and June 2011.

Bird Watch

British birdwatcher Chris Gooddie took just 12 months to find and photograph all 32 species of one of the world's most elusive birds, the pitta. He gave up a well-paid job as a sales director in London to travel 130,500 mi (210,000 km) around the world by plane, truck, motorbike, taxi, canoe and motorboat to find the rare and secretive birds, which live in the rainforests of Africa, India, Southeast Asia and Australia.

Hat Mosaic

The New Era Cap Company of Buffalo, New York State, created a hat mosaic made up of 1,875 official Major League Baseball caps.

Senior Skydiver

In March 2011, Fred Mack of Newtown Square, Pennsylvania, celebrated his 100th birthday by performing a tandem skydive at an altitude of 13,000 ft (3,960 m) in the skies over New Jersey. He made his first skydiving jump aged 95 and vowed to repeat the feat if he lived to be 100.

BALL BOY

Benji Williams of L.A., California, has been making rubber-band balls since he was six. Here he is standing next to the world's biggest rubber-band ball, made by Joel Waul and weighing 9,432 lb (4,282 kg). Benji's ball is already well over 100 lb (45 kg)—and growing fast.

I SPY WITH MY LITTLE EYE...

Ali vs. Liston on the head of a pin

Willard Wigan, a sculptor from Birmingham, England, makes amazingly detailed microscopic sculptures, some of which measure just 0.0002 in (0.005 mm) tall—more than three times smaller than the period at the end of this sentence.

His figures can be viewed only under a microscope and magnified 400 times. They can fit on a single grain of sand or on the head of a pin, and he has even managed to fit nine camels into the eye of a needle.

As a child with undiagnosed dyslexia, Willard had an unhappy time at school and sought refuge in local woods, where he watched ants running about the floor of a shed. "I was four or five," he recalls, "and I thought the ants must be homeless, so I built them houses from splinters of wood. Then I thought the ants needed furniture, so I made little chairs and tables that could fit inside the tiny houses."

Each nano-sculpture takes up to three months to create. His homemade carving tools consist of tiny shards of diamond attached to a needle, as well as filed-down acupuncture needles. He uses one of his own eyelashes or a hair plucked from the back of a housefly as a paintbrush. To keep his hands still, he enters a meditative state and works in the 1.5-second space between heartbeats.

His work is mentally and physically draining, but he strives to get smaller still. Referring to the nine camels in the eye of a needle, he says: "One day, I'll get 20 in there. It'll probably drive me nuts, but I will do it."

Betty Boop in the eye of a needle

Titanic on the tip of a crystal

Nine camels in the eye of a needle

Hairy biker on the head of a pin

Rugby player on a pinhead scoring goal through the eye of a needle

CHIN UP

Farmer Zhu Baobing is capable of carrying great weights on his chin. Known locally in Guli, China, as "China's First Chin," he successfully held aloft a 90-lb (40-kg) child while filming a TV program in Jiangsu Province in May 2011.

Chopstick Champ

Ma Deqi, a farmer from Yuzhou, China, can catch 40 ping pong balls with a pair of chopsticks in one minute.

Two-day Kiss

Husband and wife Ekkachai and Laksana Tiranarat kissed nonstop for 46 hours 24 minutes to celebrate Valentine's Day in Pattaya, Thailand, in 2011.

Hot Wheels

Driving down a ramp ten stories high and designed to look like a Hot Wheels toy ramp, Hollywood stuntman Tanner Foust jumped his car across a world-record-breaking 332-ft (101-m) gap before the running of the Indianapolis 500 in May 2011.

Senior Worker

Hedda Bolgar Bekker, who runs her own psychotherapy clinic in L.A., California, still works at age 102, giving lectures and seeing patients for up to 20 hours a week.

Eye Run

Noel Bresland from Manchester, England, ran 26 mi (42 km)—the equivalent of a marathon—on a treadmill inside a capsule of the giant wheel, the London Eye, in 3 hours 51 minutes in London, England, in April 2011.

Duck Line

Families from Seattle, Washington State, joined forces to create a record-breaking line of 17,782 yellow rubber ducks that stretched a mile long at the city's Warren G. Magnuson Park.

EGGSERCISE

Darryl Learie of Alberta, Canada, is able to complete one-armed push-ups on the top of a raw egg, without smashing it. Incredibly, Darryl's record stands at 11 repetitions before the egg finally gave way. Darryl explains that the arched top and bottom of the shell enable the egg to withstand the forces he exerts when performing the feat.

Stilt Walk

Wearing specially made 2-ft-high (60-cm) aluminum stilts, Samati Yiming, a 33-year-old physics teacher, walked 65 ft (20 m) on a high wire that was suspended 70 ft (21 m) above the ground at a park in Xinjiang, China. Samati, who has been stilt walking for over 15 years, did not even use a safety rope. In 2004, he walked for eight days on stilts, covering 180 mi (290 km), and the following year he walked for 49 steps on stilts that were an incredible 52 ft (16 m) high.

Stunning Stogie

In 2011, Cuba's José Castelar "Cueto" Cairo rolled a massive cigar that measured over 268 ft (81.8 m) long.

Magic Number

Indian businessman Mohammed Farooque Dhanani from Mumbai, has collected more than 31,000 currency notes from across the world—all ending with the serial number 786. The number has no significance—he simply started collecting it over a decade ago as a unique hobby. His since then found that the serial number on his new credit card ended in 786.

Blowing Bubbles

In 2011, British professional bubble-maker Samsam Bubbleman (real name Sam Heath) created a large bubble, 19 in (48 cm) in diameter, with 56 smaller bubbles inside. It took him over two hours to blow and required conditions of low wind, low humidity, and no rain. He has been making amazing bubbles since 1989, and once fit 50 people inside a giant bubble.

Scissor Happy

Barber Nabi Salehi of London, England, cut the hair of 526 customers in just 24 hours on June 3, 2011. He raised over £2,344 ($3,793) and donated all of the money to charity.

Mountain Walk

In 2009, 34-year-old Buddhist monk Endo Mitsunaga completed the "Sennichi Kaihogyo"—1,000 days of meditation and walking around Mount Hiei, Japan. During this time he walked 26 mi (42 km) a day, for periods of 100 or 200 days in a row.

OPTICAL EXTRUSION

Kung fu expert Dong Changsheng performed an incredible feat at a festival in Hubei Province, China. Reports claim that he swallowed two metal ball bearings, before executing several martial arts moves to move the balls up into the back of his mouth. He then proceeded to force the balls out of one of his eyes, with the help of a chopstick!

Kung Fu Granny

Zhao Yufang, an 82-year-old grandmother from Beijing, China, is a master in Shaolin kung fu. She had wanted to learn kung fu as a girl, but her local master would not teach her. So she taught herself, went back to the school, and defeated the master, forcing him to apologize.

Football on Wheels

Founded in 2008 in San Marcos, Texas, the Unicycle Football League features teams playing American football while balancing atop unicycles. Players wear bike helmets but no shoulder pads.

10th Dan

Standing only 4 ft 10 in (1.47 m) tall and weighing just 100 lb (45.4 kg), Sensei Keiko Fukuda of San Francisco, California, became the first woman in history to reach the highest rank of 10th dan black belt in judo. Only three other living judokas have reached that level—and they're all men. She became a judo instructor in 1937, and in 2011 was still teaching judo three times a week—at age 98.

SPEARED FOOT

Track and field judge Lia Marie Lourenco receives medical aid after a competitor's javelin speared her foot during the warm up for the Troféu Brasil championship in São Paulo. She was rushed to hospital, where she underwent surgery to remove the javelin tip.

VOLCANO BOARDING

Guests at a hostel in León, Nicaragua, can hike to the top of the Cerro Negro volcano and then board down 1,640 ft (500 m) of its slopes at speeds of more than 50 mph (80 km/h). The volcano is Central America's youngest and also one of its most active.

Fitness Fanatic

At 102 years old, former postman Shi Xiaochun of Xiaoshan, China, still worked out every day, doing pushups on both of his fists and even on one hand.

Longest Jump

In 2011, Algerian-born Taig Khris set a world record for the longest jump on rollerblades when he leaped 95 ft (29 m) in front of the Sacre Coeur Basilica in Paris, France.

Chess Challenge

Israeli grandmaster Alik Gershon played 523 games of chess simultaneously in Tel Aviv on October 21, 2010—and defeated 454 of his opponents.

GRANNY'S SIX-PACK

At 75, grandmother Ernestine Shepherd of Baltimore, Maryland, is the world's oldest competitive female bodybuilder.

She wakes up at 3 a.m. every day to meditate, and then clocks up runs totaling 10 mi (16 km) before lunch. She started working out when she reached the age of 56, but has since won two bodybuilding contests and run nine marathons.

Bodyboard Party

On July 2, 2011 a world record 272 bodyboarders gathered in the water simultaneously at Figueira da Foz, Portugal, known for having some of the biggest waves in Europe.

Juggling Robot

The Czech Technical University has designed a robot that can juggle five pool balls at once. The robot uses a high speed camera to track the balls, if it drops a ball it can pick it up and carry on.

FLYING HOUSE

Inspired by the Disney/Pixar movie *Up*, a house took to the sky near L.A., California, attached to 300 weather balloons, setting a new world record for the largest balloon cluster flight. The 18-ft-high (5.5-m), custom-built, lightweight house was re-created by engineers from National Geographic and, with the balloons on top, stood ten stories high. It flew for about an hour, reaching an altitude of 10,000 ft (3,000 m). To lift an average-sized, normal-weight house off the ground would actually require more than 20 million helium balloons.

Jet-ski Record

Reaching top speeds in excess of 69 mph (110 km/h), Jeremy Burfoot of Auckland, New Zealand, covered a world record 1,421 mi (2,287 km) on a jet ski in 24 hours on Lake Karapiro on February 8, 2011.

Sumo Runner

Weighing 400 lb (180 kg), American sumo wrestler Kelly Gneiting became the heaviest man ever to complete a full marathon when he finished last out of 11,891 men in the 2011 L.A. Marathon in 9 hours 48 minutes 52 seconds. Battling heavy rain and strong winds, he jogged the first 8 mi (12.9 km) and walked the last 18 mi (29 km).

Armless Pitcher

Born without arms, Tom Willis from San Diego, California, has thrown out the ceremonial first pitch at more than a dozen Major League baseball games. He throws the ball with his right foot, and his pitches usually make the entire distance from the mound to home plate (60 ft 6 in/18.4 m) without bouncing.

Extra Large

In June 2011 in Nashville, Tennessee, a manufacturer unveiled a colossal T-shirt measuring 180 x 281 ft (54.8 x 85.6 m). The T-shirt took six weeks to make and weighed more than two tons.

Cheese Remedy

Nursing a badly bruised shin that left her participation in the 2010 Winter Olympics in Vancouver in doubt, U.S. alpine skier Lindsey Vonn tried cream and painkillers to no effect before deciding to smear the wound with soft cheese. The cheesy remedy was so successful that a few days later she won gold in the downhill event.

Super Shirts

Former Welsh international soccer player Robbie Savage managed to wear soccer shirts from all 72 English Football League clubs at the same time.

LIP SERVICE

Natalie Irish of Houston, Texas, paints with her lips.

Wearing colorful lipstick, she presses her lips against a blank canvas to create amazing portraits of celebrities such as Marilyn Monroe and Jimi Hendrix. She varies the pressure of her kisses to achieve different shades and textures, and applies several layers to achieve darker tones.

HAND PAINTED

With their piercing eyes and vivid, colorful markings, Guido Daniele's paintings of animals and birds look incredibly lifelike. Yet they are all painted on human hands. Look closely, and you can see how the different parts of the hand form the animals' features, with the fingers becoming a flamingo's beak, a tiger's head or an elephant's trunk.

Healthy Profit

Leafing through a pile of old textbooks bought at an auction in 2010 for a total of $10, Bill and Cindy Farnsworth of Austin, Texas, found a 25-cent banknote that had been hand-signed in 1843 by the President of the Republic of Texas, Sam Houston. They later sold the note for $63,250.

Miniature Masterpiece

Collector of miniature books Nikunj Vagadia of Rajkot, India, owns a tiny gold-plated copy of Mahatma Gandhi's autobiography that measures a mere 1.3 x 1.8 in (3.25 x 4.5 cm).

Time Keeper

During the making of the 1963 movie *Cleopatra*, Elizabeth Taylor's then husband Eddie Fisher was paid $1,500 a day just to make sure she got to work on time.

Working Model

Fernando Benavides from Madrid, Spain, has built a remote-control LEGO® car in the style of a Porsche 911 Cabriolet. It has all-wheel drive, a working seven-speed dual-clutch transmission, a working retractable hardtop, a retractable spoiler, and three working differentials, and it took him 18 months to build.

Cubist Movement

Josh Chalom of Toronto, Canada, and a team of eight assistants spent more than 400 hours re-creating Michelangelo's masterpiece *The Hand of God* using 12,090 Rubik's Cubes. The finished work measured 29 x 15 ft (8.8 x 4.6 m) and weighed 2,000 lb (907 kg). The individual cubes, which were bought for $1 each, had to be adjusted by hand so that the colors matched those in the original. *The Hand of God* was the first part of a project to copy the entire ceiling of the Sistine Chapel, in Rome, Italy, using 250,000 Rubik's Cubes. Chalom has also created Rubik's Cube versions of Leonardo da Vinci's famous works *The Last Supper* (which Chalom sold for $50,000) and the *Mona Lisa*.

Top Marks

Charlie Kratzer used only $10 worth of black permanent markers to create a magnificent mural that covers every square inch of wall space in the basement of his Lexington, Kentucky, home. His cartoon creation features fictional detectives Hercule Poirot and Sherlock Holmes, artists Pablo Picasso and Claude Monet, British Prime Minister Winston Churchill with author and playwright George Bernard Shaw, and TV squirrel Rocky and his moose pal Bullwinkle.

Death Watch Beetle

Artist Mike Libby from Portland, Oregon, customizes real dead insects, spiders and crabs with antique watch parts and electronic components to create intricate sculptures of new hybrid creatures. He was inspired by finding an intact dead beetle, which he thought looked and worked like a small mechanical device. So, he sought out an old wristwatch, and added its screws, springs and gears to the insect's body to create a mechanical beetle sculpture. Each of his pieces takes up to 40 hours to create and can sell for up to $2,000.

Sushi Soccer

In August 2011, 20 chefs in Bodø, Norway, created a soccer-themed mosaic from 13,000 pieces of sushi over an area of 270 sq ft (25 sq m).

Artificial Animals

Dutch artist Theo Jansen creates giant artificial animals from plastic pipes and rubber tubes that walk around powered by wind and carry sensors that allow them to change direction. One of his kinetic creatures is so sophisticated that it can anchor itself to the ground if it senses a storm approaching.

Marble Mosaic

A team of 15 artists from the U.K. and Bahrain spent four months creating a marble mosaic of the Sultan of Oman using 128,274 individual pieces of marble in 90 different natural shades. The mosaic measured 27.2 ft x 17.4 ft (8.3 x 5.3 m) and had to be created using a photograph of the sultan, as he rarely appears in public and did not sit for the artwork in person. His face alone took 40 days to complete, the beard and mustache being made from the sultan's favorite stone, imported all the way from Italy.

Long Hours

It took more than 800,000 hours to create the computer-generated images for the 1995 movie *Toy Story*, which worked out at more than a week of computer time for every second on screen.

Twist Parade

During the 2011 Mandan Independence Day Parade in Mandan, North Dakota, an amazing 2,158 people lined up on Main Street to dance the Twist, breaking a world record.

Guitar Marathon

On June 17, 2011, Dave Browne from Dublin, Ireland, broke the world record for the longest continuous guitar-playing session after performing a marathon five-day gig lasting 114 hours 20 minutes. He began with Dusty Springfield's "Son of a Preacher Man" and finished 1,372 tracks later with U2's "With or Without You."

Chicken Costume

One of Brad Pitt's first jobs was dressing in a giant chicken costume to lure customers to an El Pollo Loco Mexican fast-food restaurant in California.

WALL OF SOUND

Joined by his band B-Monster, record-breaking musician John Lee from Vancouver, Canada, showcases his 9-ft-high (2.7-m), 40-ft-long (12-m) wall of speakers, which can channel 2,000 watts of power fed through the world's largest guitar amp. Made up of 168 speakers, it has been dubbed the Wailing Wall of Sound.

HOOF BOOTS

To mark the centenary of England's famous Cheltenham horse racing festival, fashion designers created a pair of ladies' fashion boots and shoes in the style of horses' hooves for a well-known betting company. The footwear was made up of carbon-fiber hooves and some 5,000 individual horsehairs, and was sold for around $2,000.

Sweet Music

A Japanese fruit company played Mozart to its ripening bananas for a week in the belief that classical music makes for sweeter fruit.

Food Illustrator

Graphic designer David Meldrum from Essex, England, kept a record of everything he ate for a year between June 15, 2010, and June 14, 2011, by painting every meal. His illustrations, which were exhibited at a London gallery, revealed that in the course of the 12 months he consumed 1,360 cups of coffee, 305 pints of beer and 122 chocolate bars.

Brick Car

Chinese artist Dai Geng spent over a year making a full-sized model of a BMW car by cementing hundreds of bricks together. Only the windows of the car are not made of brick. The bodywork, tires, steering wheel, exhaust pipe and trimmings are all brick and he even managed to build brick hinges so that the doors open and close.

Longest Train

It took more than 3,500 hours of work, for a group of volunteers from Wilmington Railroad Museum, North Carolina, to build a model train comprising 31 locomotives and 1,563 freight cars. The model stretched a record 925 ft (282 m) long, and could move under its own power.

Underwear Exhibit

Yi Ci, a student at China's Hubei Institute of Fine Arts, collected several hundred items of underwear to arrange as a piece of art entitled *Privacy* for her graduation exhibition.

CREATURE FEATURE

Andrew Lancaster is an unusually inventive taxidermist from New Zealand. He has turned the traditional skill on its head with his bizarre mutant creations, stitching different dead animals together to make creepy new creatures. Lancaster, an ex-farmer who has been into taxidermy for 14 years, regularly stops his car to pick up roadkill for his projects. Although his pieces might look outrageous, they are made using traditional techniques, taking a few hours to complete before they are dried out over a period of two weeks.

Young Painter

At age four, Aelita Andre of Melbourne, Australia, had a solo art exhibition at a gallery in New York City—and her paintings sold for up to $9,000 each. Aelita, who has been painting since she was just 11 months old, specializes in large, colorful, abstract works, which often have children's toys and other small objects stuck to them.

Master Forger

For decades, experts believed that *The Procuress*, a painting at the Courtauld Institute of Art in London, England, was a prized 17th-century copy of a work by Dutch master Dirck van Baburen. However, in 2011 it emerged that the painting was instead the work of Dutch master forger Han van Meegeren, who died in 1947. Van Meegeren, who specialized in faking great artworks, swindled his buyers out of the equivalent of $100 million in today's money. One forgery fooled the Rijksmuseum in Amsterdam into parting with the equivalent of $18 million, but that painting now languishes in the museum storeroom.

Toothpick Liner

Wayne Kusy used a million toothpicks to make a model of the liner Queen Mary that was so big it filled his Chicago, Illinois, apartment. The 25-ft-long (7.6-m) model had to be built in six sections so that he could get it out of the building.

GUITAR REVENGE

Japanese artist Yoshihiko Satoh has designed 12-necked guitars that are almost impossible to play. After fretting over his own inability to learn the guitar, he decided to create 72-string monsters that even the most accomplished musician would struggle to play. Each guitar took up to six months to make and some have sold for $90,000.

LIGHT PAINTINGS

Scary skeletons with brightly illuminated bones rising menacingly up through the trees make the snow-covered woods of Finland seem really spooky.

These light-painting photographs are the work of Helsinki artist Janne Parviainen who creates them by using different light sources during varying exposure times, ranging from a few seconds to several hours. While the camera is exposing, his skeletons and other figures are drawn with LED lights.

Bodies appear to lie immobile in the snow with footprints of light walking away into the distance.

Janne places his skeletons in everyday situations as well as scary ones, as this cool guitarist demonstrates.

Toast of Hollywood

Screen legend Marilyn Monroe has been immortalized in Shanghai, China, in the form of a huge toast portrait by New Zealand artist Maurice Bennett, measuring 13 x 12 ft (4 x 3.6 m) and comprising almost 6,000 slices of bread.

Living Paintings

When Washington, D.C., artist Alexa Meade paints her subjects, she really does paint them. Instead of using a canvas, she paints directly on to the bodies of her models with acrylic paints, making the 3-D subjects appear 2-D. Only the eyes and hair are left untouched. She then photographs the result, which looks uncannily like a conventional painting hanging in a gallery.

Cart Trees

For the 2010 holiday season, Anthony Schmitt of Santa Monica, California, built two giant Christmas-tree statues using 86 shopping carts. The trees, which went on display in his home city and in Emeryville, California, had full-sized carts at the base and smaller ones on the top. All the carts were supported by an internal structure.

Freehand Circle

Alex Overwijk, a teacher from Ottawa, Ontario, Canada, can draw a perfect freehand circle about 3 ft (1 m) in diameter in less than a second—and the YouTube clip showing him performing the feat has attracted more than six million hits.

Maggot Art

Rebecca O'Flaherty, an entomologist at the University of California, creates "Maggot Art" from colored trails left by maggots that have been dipped in paint. Using special larval forceps, she dips the squirming maggots in brightly colored, nontoxic, water-based paint, places them on a sheet of paper and watches them crawl.

Sole Signature

Considered to be one of the greatest artists of all time, Italian Renaissance painter and sculptor Michelangelo (1475–1564) signed only one of his many sculptures during his entire artistic career.

Smiley Face

At Continental Soldier's Park in Mahwah, New Jersey, 2,226 people, all wearing yellow ponchos, gathered to create a huge human-made smiley face.

Giant Shoe

A giant shoe measuring 18 ft (5.5 m) long was unveiled in Amsterdam, the Netherlands, in November 2010. The shoe was an exact replica of a Converse Chuck Taylor All Star—and was equivalent to a U.S. size 845.

Paints with Toes

Despite being born without hands, Zohreh Etezad Saltaneh of Tehran, Iran, paints so beautifully with her feet that her artworks have been shown in more than 60 exhibitions around the world. Her mother placed a paintbrush between Zohreh's toes when she was young to encourage her painting. She has also learned to weave intricate Persian carpets using her toes.

Picasso in Wool

A group of 40 women called The Materialistics, from Tyne and Wear, England, spent months knitting copies of famous works of art. They began by drawing the image of the original artwork on graph paper and then applied a yarn finish to pieces such as *The Scream* by Edvard Munch, *Seated Woman in Garden* by Pablo Picasso and *Sunflowers* by Vincent van Gogh.

ALI TRIBUTE

Californian artist Michael Kalish created a giant tribute to boxer Muhammad Ali out of 1,300 punch bags. Viewed close up, the 26 x 23 x 25 ft (7.9 x 7 x 7.6 m) installation, which was unveiled in Nokia Plaza, L.A., in March 2011, looks like a series of punch bags randomly hung from a metal frame. It's only from a distance and looked at head on that the punch bags morph into a portrait of Ali.

HERE'S LOOKING AT YOU, KID

A six-month-old baby has attracted 50,000 hits a month on his Internet blog by posing with props for pictures that re-create classic movie scenes. With the help of his mother Emily and assorted stuffed toys, Arthur Hammond from Oxford, England, conjured up iconic images from movies including *Rambo: First Blood*, *American Beauty*, *The Blair Witch Project*, *Jaws*, *Alien* and *The Godfather*.

American Beauty

Rambo: First Blood

The Blair Witch Project

Rear Window

Young Reporter

As Hurricane Irene battered the U.S. East Coast on August 27, 2011, five-year-old Jane Haubrich from Doylestown, Pennsylvania, became the world's youngest TV reporter by delivering regular weather updates throughout the day via CNN's iReport. Her last report was sent over right before her bedtime.

Famous Pose

In 1928, Mexican actor Emilio Fernández was approached by Hollywood art director Cedric Gibbons to pose naked for a full-length sketch. Fernandez agreed reluctantly, but the moment made him immortal as the drawing was used to create the design for the Oscar statuette.

Cool Movies

A temporary outdoor movie theater in London, England, was built mainly from 150 recycled refrigerators. U.S. design student Lindsey Scannapieco conceived "Films on Fridges," a venue where the screen was surrounded by old fridges, the bar was made of fridge parts and fridge doors were incorporated into the seating.

Antler Statue

Artist Kurt Gordon of Dubois, Wyoming, created a life-sized elk statue made entirely of discarded antlers. Gordon, who has been working with antlers for over 35 years, has also sold antler chandeliers to hotels all over the world.

Organ Recital

Fueled by coffee, vitamins and jelly beans, Jacqueline Sadler of Toronto, Canada, played a church organ continuously for over 40 hours in June 2011.

Labor of Love

Despite losing the sight in her left eye when she was a child, 69-year-old grandmother Heather Hems, of Hampshire, England, spent 12 hours a day for more than 17 years creating an embroidery covering 540 sq ft (50 sq m)—the size of 12 table tennis tables. Her creation features important world figures, as well as major global events, such as the Moon landing. She has devoted more than 70,000 hours to the tapestry, spending thousands of dollars on materials. The work has also been so physically exhausting that she has had to undergo shoulder surgery.

Finger Face

U.S. actress Nikki Reed spent four hours painting the face of her fiancé, former American Idol star Paul McDonald, on each of her gold metallic fingernails for the Teen Choice Awards 2011.

On Tape

Ukrainian-born Mark Khaisman from Philadelphia, Pennsylvania, creates amazing artworks—including his favorite movie scenes—from packing tape. By using layers of translucent brown tape on backlit Plexiglas panels, he is able to depict light and shade and even detailed facial features. The darkest sections of his images require up to ten layers of tape, and he uses around three 330-ft (100-m) rolls on each picture.

Party Pooper

In their teens, the Followill brothers of U.S. rock band Kings of Leon used to throw parties at their father Ivan's house. When Ivan decided it was time for the party to break up, he would put jalapenos in the microwave, and the fumes burned everyone's eyes so that they quickly left the house.

Bruce Springsteen

WEIRDEST BACKSTAGE RIDERS

When singers and rock bands reach the top, they demand some strange things backstage, before and after performing.

Van Halen Van Halen demanded a candy bowl of M&Ms® with the brown sweets picked out and discarded.

AC/DC In 2008, the "Highway To Hell" rockers required the promoter to make sure that three oxygen tanks and three oxygen masks be made available at the U.S. venues they were playing. Additionally, Twinings English Breakfast Tea and a case of bottled beer were two of their less demanding needs.

The Rolling Stones On the Stones' 1997–98 "Bridges To Babylon" tour rider was a request for a full-sized snooker table (a pool table would not be acceptable) and the necessary accessories, such as cues and chalk. Bizarrely, the band's rider also mentioned that the tour organizers would be providing their own balls.

Christina Aguilera A police escort, a large vanity mirror, dressing room plants and flowers, four candles with matches, and the rider staple, honey, are just a few of the demands on Christina Aguilera's four-page tour document from 2000.

Bruce Springsteen Sensibly, "The Boss" likes to have a designated guitar security guard watch over his precious guitar at all times, and practical backstage supplies of protein and energy boosting food and drinks.

50 Cent An all-day supply of peanut-butter-and-jelly sandwiches is what rapper 50 Cent needed to perform at his best. Chewing gum and cough drops were also essentials on his 2005 backstage shopping list, together with shrimps on ice.

Amy Winehouse

27
AN UNLUCKY NUMBER FOR ROCK LEGENDS

They didn't all sell their souls to the devil, as legend has it bluesman Robert Johnson did when just 27. So let's just hope it's nothing more than weird coincidence that links all these top music makers who died at that tragically early age.

1911–1938 **Robert Johnson** died aged 27 years and three months.

1942–1969 **Brian Jones**, The Rolling Stones' guitarist, died aged 27 years and four months.

1942–1970 **Jimi Hendrix** died aged 27 years and nine months.

1943–1970 **Janis Joplin** died aged 27 years and eight months.

1943–1971 **Jim Morrison** lead singer with The Doors, died aged 27 years and seven months.

1967–1994 **Kurt Cobain** lead singer with Nirvana, died aged 27 years and one month.

1983–2011 **Amy Winehouse** died aged 27 years and ten months.

Two Funerals

A month after Michael Jackson died in 2009, a ceremonial funeral was held for him—without the body—in the Ivory Coast village of Krindjabo, where he was crowned a prince of the Agni people while on a visit to the country in 1992.

Top Tour

U2's 360° Tour (2009–11) grossed $736 million in ticket sales, making it the highest-grossing concert tour of all time. With 120 trucks needed to transport each of the three giant claw sets, the tour cost over $750,000 a day to stage.

Comic Collection

Brett Chilman of Henley Brook, Western Australia, has been collecting comic books for over 30 years and now has more than 68,000. His comics are stored in two houses and are worth an estimated $1.3 million.

Delayed Doctorate

Queen guitarist Brian May has a PhD in astrophysics. He completed his thesis on interplanetary dust clouds at Imperial College, London, England, in 2007—36 years after he started, having postponed his doctorate in favor of a career as a rock star.

Before

After

SUPERMAN'S DOUBLE

Superman fanatic Herbert Chavez, from Calamba City in the Philippines, has undergone more than 13 years of cosmetic surgery to turn himself into the comic-book hero. His nose has been reshaped, he has had a chin augmentation to acquire Superman's iconic cleft, silicone injections in his lips to make them fuller, liposuction on his stomach, and thigh implants to make his legs appear more muscular. As he is only 5 ft 6 in (1.67 m) and Superman is 6 ft 2 in (1.88 m), Herbert says: "I wouldn't rule out surgery to make me taller."

Auto Accident

Dutch TV show host Ruben Nicolai was run over while recording a 2011 show designed to find the country's worst driver. The driver was performing a task that involved steering between traffic cones when he lost control and sent the car careering toward a cameraman and Nicolai, who was taken to hospital with a torn lip, shoulder pain and a sore foot.

Shed Gigs

Jon Earl has used his garden shed, which measures 12 × 10 ft (3.6 × 3 m), in Somerset, England, to stage gigs by more than 1,000 musicians from all over the world, including legendary folk–rock band Fairport Convention and a 26-strong gospel choir.

Vivid Dream

Released by The Beatles in 1965, Paul McCartney's "Yesterday" has since been covered more than 1,600 times, making it the most recorded song in modern music history. McCartney claims he composed the entire melody in a dream one night and before writing the final lyrics he gave it the working title "Scrambled Eggs."

Grenade Attack

The band La Excelencia was attacked with guns and a grenade—killing two band members—for refusing to play an encore performance after a set in Guadalajara, Mexico, on January 17, 2011.

Chart Glee

In 2010, the cast of the TV series *Glee* had 80 singles chart on the Billboard Hot 100, the most by any act in a single year in the chart's history.

Queen Dethroned

In January 1976, Queen's song "Bohemian Rhapsody," which contains the famous line "mamma mia, mamma mia, mamma mia, let me go," was knocked off the number one spot in the U.K. chart by Abba's "Mamma Mia."

SQUARE EYES

To mark the 60th anniversary of TV in the Netherlands, six people stayed awake and watched TV nonstop for 87 hours. Fifty-five people started out in the attempt—staged in pods at a studio in Hilversum—but by the fourth evening only six were still glued to their screen.

Total Faith

Hollywood executives were apprehensive about casting Leonardo DiCaprio as the Kid in the 1995 movie *The Quick and the Dead*, but co-star Sharon Stone was so confident in his ability she paid his salary out of her own pocket.

EYELYN+ EVELYN

Dressed identically in connected garments, musical duo Evelyn Evelyn look like conjoined sisters—but in fact they were played by Amanda Palmer and Jason Webley.

They even invented a fictional backstory to their characters, claiming that Eva and Lyn Neville were born as conjoined twins on a Kansas farm, sharing between them three legs, two hearts, two arms, three lungs and a single liver.

Backward Pianist

U.S. student Evan Petrone can play music with his back to the piano. He filmed himself sitting down, facing away from the keyboard, before twisting his arms into a seemingly impossible position to play "Clocks" by Coldplay. He suffers from Ehlers-Danlos Syndrome, which gives him unusually loose joints and ligaments. He said he chose "Clocks" because it was simple and repetitive, but it still took him more than five hours to get his brain to adjust to his unusual playing position.

Kermit Coat

For an interview with a German TV station, eccentric U.S. pop singer Lady Gaga wore a coat made from the bodies of *The Muppet Show* character Kermit the Frog. The green furry creation by designer Jean-Charles de Castelbajac was draped with dozens of Kermits, and Lady Gaga even wore a Kermit head as a matching hair decoration.

Life Imitating Art

While filming his role as t he Greek god Achilles in the 2004 movie *Troy*, Brad Pitt tore his left Achilles tendon, delaying the movie's final scenes for months.

Solo Session

Rajesh Burbure, a professional singer from Nagpur, India, sang continuously for 80 hours—that's more than three days—in 2010, during which time he performed nearly 1,000 songs.

Post-It® Drawings

Artist John Kenn Mortensen of Copenhagen, Denmark, has drawn over 250 illustrations on humble Post-it® Notes. His works, which sell for up to $100 each, often feature spooks and creatures inspired by U.S. horror author Stephen King.

Doing the Macarena

A record-breaking 2,219 staff and students from schools and colleges in Plymouth, England, simultaneously danced the "Macarena" in July 2011.

Bacteria Fashion

Artist Suzanne Lee from the Central Saint Martins School of Fashion and Textiles in London, England, has designed a range of clothes from bacteria. She has developed a technique for creating a cellulose material from a brew of yeast, bacteria and sweetened green tea, which, when dried, can be shaped into thin shirts and jackets. She hopes that we will eventually wear living clothes.

Becoming Vincent

Artist James Birbeck from Edmonton, Canada, turned himself into a Vincent van Gogh portrait. After friends noted his physical resemblance to the Dutch master, Birbeck bought a jacket like Vincent's and applied paints and makeup to his face to complete the transformation.

Foot Carver

Pema Tshering of Thimphu, Bhutan, is a professional artist who carves and paints with his feet. He was born with cerebral palsy and congenital deformities in his spinal column, which have rendered both of his arms useless. He also has only limited use of his legs, but carves beautiful wooden dragons, holding the implements between his toes.

Square Hole

In June 2011, what appeared to be a giant hole opened up in the middle of the main square in Stockholm, Sweden—but it turned out to be an imaginative work of photographic art. The 3-D optical illusion, was just a giant photograph measuring 105 x 59 ft (32 x 18 m), and was created by Swedish artist Erik Johansson.

HAIR DRESS

Dress designer Thelma Madine and hair stylist Ryan Edwards, both from Liverpool, England, teamed up to create a dress made from 820 ft (250 m) of human hair. It took 300 hours to make, weighs 209 lb (95 kg), and uses hair extensions containing more than 10,000 individual hair wefts. The $75,000 dress also features 1,500 crystals and 12 underskirts.

ENCYCLOPEDIA GIGANTICA

Connecticut-based British designer Rob Matthews published a book made from hundreds of articles from the popular Wikipedia website, and it's 19 in (48 cm) thick. Incredibly, Rob used only 437 articles, 0.002 percent of the content available. If all the articles on Wikipedia were made into a book, it would be over 225 million pages long, or 13½ mi (21.6 km) thick—that is the length of Manhattan Island, New York.

Numbers Book

A Million Random Digits with 100,000 Normal Deviates, a book containing nothing but a giant list of randomly generated numbers, sold thousands of copies in the 1950s and 1960s.

Europe Tour

London, England, music journalist Greg Parmley visited 26 live music festivals across Europe in 30 days. Traveling by motorbike, he journeyed 5,500 mi (8,800 km) through 13 countries and saw over 150 bands playing live.

Instant Cameras

Wong Ting Man of Hong Kong, China, owns more than 1,000 instant cameras—including more than 800 Polaroids—at an estimated value of $130,000.

Best Sellers

With combined sales of more than 450 million copies (and translated into 67 languages), J.K. Rowling's series of Harry Potter books is the fourth best seller of all time, behind only the Bible (3 billion copies), the Quran (1.5 billion) and *Quotations from Chairman Mao* (800 million).

Deaf Rapper

Sean Forbes of Detroit, Michigan, has been deaf since childhood—yet he is a professional musician and rapper who uses sign language for each lyric as he speaks it.

Boss Tribute

There are more than 60 Bruce Springsteen tribute acts working in the U.S.A. and Europe, including The B Street Band who played at New Jersey governor Chris Christie's inaugural ball after Springsteen himself declined the invitation.

Rare Find

Members of the St. Laurence Church in the village of Hilmarton in Wiltshire, England, found a 400-year-old original copy of the 1611 King James Bible, of which fewer than 200 exist, sitting unnoticed on a church shelf.

One Title

To boost sales of his book *Martian Summer: Robot Arms, Cowboy Spacemen, and My 90 Days with the Phoenix Mars Mission*, Brooklyn author Andrew Kessler opened a new bookstore in New York City's West Village and stocked it with 3,000 copies of just one book—his own. The store, Ed's Martian Book, had alien artwork on the walls and was divided into sections including "staff favorite," "self-help" and "best seller," although in each case the recommendation was, of course, the same book.

CLOWNING AROUND

A bizarre fashion craze swept Mexico in 2011, with young men sporting flamboyant cowboy-style boots with curled toes, some measuring more than 3 ft (1 m) long. The footwear epidemic originated in the town of Matehuala, where a shoemaker was asked by a mysterious customer if he could make him a pair of boots with elongated toes that curved upward. Dancers at local rodeo nightclubs picked up on the impractical fashion accessory and soon the craze spread.

Elvis Impersonator

Simon Goldsmith of Suffolk, England, sang Elvis Presley hits nonstop for more than 35 hours in 2010.

SMURF ALERT

For the launch of the 2011 Sony Picture movie *The Smurfs*, the traditional white houses, businesses, and even a church in the Spanish village of Júzcar were painted blue, using 1,110 gal (4,200 l) of paint. The locals liked the new color so much they voted to keep it. For the film itself, designers built an exact two-thirds replica of Belvedere Castle in Central Park, New York.

Elvis Festival

Over 4,000 Elvis Presley fans flock to the annual Elvis Festival at Collingwood, Ontario, Canada, which ends with over 120 Elvis impersonators competing to become Grand Champion.

First Novel

A girl with cerebral palsy who can write only by touching a keyboard with her lips has been offered a contract to have her first novel published. Wang Qianjin, 18, of Zhenjiang, China, is virtually completely paralyzed and has never had a day's schooling in her life—but she taught herself Chinese by watching captioned TV dramas and memorizing the pronunciation and structure of the different characters.

Elephant Orchestra

Formed by U.S. composer Dave Soldier and conservationist Richard Lair, the Thai Elephant Orchestra has released three CDs of music, which feature elephants playing giant instruments such as xylophones, drums and harmonicas.

MALLOW MAIDS

Tiffany Tezna, from Virginia, and her best friend sent us these amazing pictures of stylish and vibrant wedding and bridesmaid dresses that they designed and constructed from Marshmallow Peeps candy.

VOMIT ARTIST

Millie Brown creates unique works of art by vomiting. Mastering the ability to regurgitate different colors to order, she has established herself as an international "Vomit Artist," and in 2010 even threw up over Lady Gaga's dress for the singer's Monster Ball Tour interlude.

Millie, from London, England, first performed her "vomit art" live at a 2006 art show in Berlin—a daunting feat as she had never made herself sick before and had no idea whether she could.

Vomiting may seem a random exercise, but Millie has got it down to a fine art. First she does not eat for two days before a performance. Then she mixes soy milk with different color food dyes to create the palette she would like for the piece. She sits down and drinks the milk before approaching the blank canvas. There, she stands up or kneels down and begins to make herself sick by sticking her fingers down her throat, and, almost without noise, vomits on the canvas. She repeats this process for each of the different colors.

Millie uses her fingers to make herself sick and then vomits colored soy milk onto the canvas.

Millie's finished work of art.

213

HARD TO CREDIT

As a protest against what he considers to be the evil of plastic credit cards, L.A.-based artist Cain Motter burns and melts old cards down into creative sculptures, which he then sells for up to $1,200 apiece—to pay off his credit-card bill.

Horse Blood

For a 2011 project in Luxembourg exploring trans-species relationships, artist Marion Laval-Jeantet injected herself with horse blood plasma. In the performance piece, titled *May the Horse Live in Me*, she also wore a set of stilts with hooves on the end.

Chopstick Tree

To raise awareness of the 100 trees that are felled in China each day to make chopsticks, the China Environmental Protection Foundation assembled 30,000 used chopsticks to create a 16-ft-high (5-m) sculpture of a fallen tree in a Shanghai street.

Whale Songs

Mark Fischer, an expert in marine acoustics from San Francisco, California, captured the sounds of whales and dolphins and transformed their songs into beautifully patterned visual artworks by using a mathematical process known as the wavelet transform.

Human Spirograph

Illinois-born visual artist Tony Orrico creates huge Spirograph-like artworks using his body as the cog wheel. Holding drawing materials in his hands, he moves his arms in circles while lying straight, bending his knees, or standing on his toes to create patterns on a blank canvas. Each artwork can take 12 hours of physical effort.

HEADS UP

Designer Taras Lesko from Covington, Washington, made a scale model of his own head entirely from paper. Taras worked by photographing his head from all sides as a visual guide. He then used computer software to design a three-dimensional model, which is printed out on paper and meticulously assembled into the final giant paper head.

215

Unwashed Jeans

Josh Le, a student at the University of Alberta in Edmonton, Canada, wore the same pair of jeans nearly every day for 15 months without washing them. At the end of the experiment, he found that the amount of bacteria on his unwashed jeans was no greater than on a pair that had been worn for only 13 days.

Musical Tie

British Conservative Member of Parliament Nadhim Zahawi apologized to fellow members during a debate in the House of Commons after he was interrupted in the middle of a speech by his own musical tie. The red tie emitted a tinny tune that was amplified by a microphone above his head.

Cruise Control

To film scenes in *Mission: Impossible—Ghost Protocol*, Tom Cruise had to go to the very top of the world's tallest building, the 2,717-ft-high (828-m) Burj Khalifa in Dubai—a journey that required him to take three elevators and then climb more than 443 ft (135 m) of ladders.

Record Run

Actor George Lee Andrews played opera house-manager Monsieur André in the same Broadway production of the musical *Phantom of the Opera* for 23 years and a record 9,382 shows. During his run, 12 different actors played the role of the Phantom.

Too Loud

Finding himself surrounded by a pack of four snarling wolves while on his way home from school in Rakkestad, Norway, 13-year-old Walter Acre scared off the animals by playing them a blast of U.S. heavy metal band Megadeth on his mobile phone.

Popped the Question

For her wedding to Duncan Turner, schoolteacher Rachel Robinson from Lincolnshire, England, wore a dress made from bubble wrap. The dress and train were made out of 13 ft (4 m) of the packing material by pupils and parents from her school. The sheets of bubble wrap were stitched together, attached to an inner lining of cloth, and topped off with white packing foam and candies.

Big Banjo

Richard Ineson of Whitby, England, owns a giant banjo that measures 26½ in (67 cm) across the drum and stands about 5 ft (1.5 m) high. Although the novelty banjo is more than 100 years old, it is still in good working condition.

Floral Shoes

Florist Nikola Mihajlovic of Gornjeg Milanovca, Serbia, provides wedding-day shoes for brides that he painstakingly decorates with real flowers. He travels to every wedding with a small battery-powered refrigerator to keep the flowers fresh until the bride is ready to walk down the aisle.

Copy Case

To mark the 150th anniversary of Louis Vuitton, a gigantic suitcase measuring 100 ft (30 m) long and 30 ft (9 m) high was constructed in Moscow's Red Square in 2013. The suitcase was a copy of a model owned by a Russian noble, Prince Vladimir Orlov.

Sock it to Me!

Each year, factories in Datang, China, produce enough socks to give two pairs to every person on Earth.

NIPPLE DRESS

At the 2011 London Fashion Week, Liverpool designer Rachael Freire unveiled a rose-covered dress made of 3,000 real cow nipples. Created from patches of leather recovered from tanneries, the dress was part of her Nippleocalypse collection, which also featured a bra made from layers of protruding nipples.

DORMANT TALENT

Lee Hadwin of Henllan, Wales, has created about 200 pictures, including one that sold for over $150,000... in his sleep. While sleepwalking, Lee—dubbed "Kipasso"—draws on walls, tablecloths, furniture and newspapers, but the following morning he has no recollection of what he has done. In fact, when awake he displays no artistic talent whatsoever.

LEGO® Frog

Dave Kaleta from Chicago, Illinois, made an anatomically accurate model of a dissected frog from LEGO® bricks. The model took him seven hours to build and used over 1,000 pieces.

Smallest Aquarium

Russian microminiature artist Anatoly Konenko has made the world's smallest aquarium—holding just two teaspoons (10 ml) of water. The miniature glass tank measures 1.2 x 0.9 x 0.6 in (3 x 2.4 x 1.4 cm). Even so, it contains miniature plants, stones and several tiny zebrafish, which had to be added with a tiny net. The water was applied with a syringe in order to avoid disturbing the aquarium.

Interview King

From every U.S. president since Gerald Ford to rap star Snoop Dogg, TV host Larry King has interviewed more than 50,000 people in a career spanning over 50 years. That works out at an average of more than three interviews a day.

TV Watchdogs

Recent research shows that the average dog in the U.K. watches 50 minutes of TV a day, with one in ten watching at least two hours. Labradors are the biggest TV addicts and soaps are dogs' favorite programs.

Valuable Vase

An 18th-century Chinese vase found by a brother and sister during a clearout of their late parents' modest semidetached house in London, England, fetched over £51.6 million ($83.6 million) at an auction in 2010. The auctioneers had given the 16-in-high (40-cm) vase a guide price of only £800,000. When the hammer went down, the owners had to be led from the auction room in shock.

Short Stories

A 2005 anthology of fiction called *Meeting Across the River* comprised 20 short stories by different writers based entirely on a song of the same title from the 1975 Bruce Springsteen album "Born To Run."

Magnetic Statue

Tim Szeto and Denis Saveliev, the founders of Nanodots— small magnetic toy balls— used over 550,000 gold Nanodots to create a replica of the famous Golden Globe award that weighed more than 600 lb (272 kg). The statue was created in Canada before being unveiled in L.A., California.

Filming Erosion

Kane Cunningham bought a clifftop house near Scarborough, England, for a cut-price £3,000 ($4,800) because coastal erosion means that it will soon fall into the sea. He is using it as an art installation, *The Last Post*, rigging rooms with cameras so that he can film its eventual collapse.

MINIATURE MOVIE SCENES

Spanish artist Maya Pixelskaya has carefully re-created scenes from her favorite movies such as *Jaws*, *Amélie* and *The Wicker Man*—on her fingernails. For each miniature painting, she applies a layer of white nail polish and draws over it with a tiny marker pen to create the basic outline. She then applies up to six layers of nail polish, and because she needs to let each layer dry before proceeding to the next, she has to keep her fingers still for hours on end.

FIREWORK ARTIST

Pyro-artist Rosemarie Fiore from the Bronx, New York, creates unique, abstract paintings in her backyard by exploding fireworks onto blank sheets of paper.

She makes eye-catching images with colored smoke bombs, firecrackers and lasers bombing the paper a number of times to create layers. Fiore directs the colorful blasts onto paper with buckets, jars, poles and planks of wood to create a collage effect. The dyes that usually give the aerial explosions their color are then singed across the heavy paper.

Created by fireworks blasting across paper!

HAIR NECKLACE

Artist Kerry Howley from Cambridge, England, makes necklaces from human hair. She spends up to 60 hours creating each necklace, cutting and weaving the strands into abstract shapes. The hair is held in place by tiny specks of glue. Kerry's main source of materials is her mother's Japanese friend, who agreed to have 12 in (30 cm) cut from her waist-length hair.

Changing Colors

Surendra Kumar Verma and a team of helpers from Kharagpur, India, created a 294-sq-ft (27-sq-m) Rangoli sand artwork, which appears as two entirely different portraits depending on whether green or red light is used to illuminate it.

Art Sickness

People with Stendhal Syndrome become so overwhelmed in the presence of fine art that they suffer dizziness, fainting and confusion.

Ballet Lover

French artist Edgar Degas (1834–1917) was so fascinated by ballet dancers that he made more than 1,500 paintings, pastels, prints and drawings of dancers at the Paris-Opera Ballet. Over half of his total works depict dancers.

Trash Hotel

German artist HA Schult built a temporary hotel in Madrid, Spain, from garbage. The five-bedroom Beach Garbage Hotel opened in January 2011.

Bidding War

One of the four versions of Edvard Munch's painting *The Scream* sold at Sotheby's, New York, on May 2, 2012, for $119.9 million—the most ever paid for a work of art at an auction. The iconic picture, painted by the Norwegian artist in 1885, was bought over the phone at the end of a 12-minute bidding war.

Novelty Tree

The Rocks, a shopping district in Sydney, Australia, erected a Christmas tree made from chairs in 2008, another made from bottles in 2009, and one made of bicycles in 2010.

Side View

The skull image embedded in *The Ambassadors*, a 1533 painting by German artist Hans Holbein the Younger, can be seen properly only when viewed from the side.

KNIT WIT

Brooklyn-based, Polish-born artist Olek spends hundreds of hours covering cars and even people in crochet. In 2010, she wrapped Wall Street's famous *Charging Bull* sculpture in crochet. In her most ambitious project yet, she has created an entire crocheted living environment. She covered the floors, walls and all of the furniture in a studio apartment measuring 15 x 14 ft (4.6 x 4.3 m) in bright, acrylic yarn.

LEGO® Yoda

For Christmas 2011, thousands of San Franciscans built a 12-ft-tall (3.6-m) Santa Yoda, with an ear span of 10 ft (3 m), from about 6,000 LEGO® bricks. The giant model of the *Star Wars* character weighed 4,000 lb (1,816 kg).

Mirror Writing

Leonardo da Vinci's personal notes were always written starting from the right side of the page and moving to the left, a technique known as "mirror writing" because anyone who wanted to read his private notebooks had to use a mirror. He only wrote in the standard manner from left to right if he intended his texts to be read by others.

Scrap Dinosaur

Hot air balloon pilot Brian Boland of Post Mills, Vermont, built "Vermontasaurus," a 25-ft-tall (7.6-m), 122-ft-long (37.2-m) dinosaur sculpture made from wood. He cut a huge pine tree into four pieces and sank them into the ground as the bases for the feet. He assembled the body from old planks and discarded junk, including the belly of an old guitar and part of a ladder from a child's bunk bed.

Cable Hat

To brighten up the dull gray electrical junction boxes in Leeds, England, local artists gave them a makeover. One box was put behind red velvet curtains that opened to reveal a painting of acrobatic rabbits and hares, while another was covered by a giant wooly hat, hand-knitted from electric cable by Sheffield artist Tony Broomhead.

Gun Conversion

For his work *Palas por Pistolas*, artist Pedro Reyes collected 1,527 guns in the city of Culiacán, Mexico, and transformed them into shovel heads to be used in a tree-planting project.

Photo Mosaic

In honor of World Sight Day, on October 11, 2012, at Tampa, Florida, eyewear company Transitions Optical created a record-breaking photo mosaic consisting of 176,750 individual photographs and covering an area of 21,479 sq ft (1,995 sq m). People submitted photos of things they would miss seeing if they lost their sight, and the mosaic formed the image of a human eye viewing the world.

CD ART

Fascinated by the way light and color reflect off a compact disk, Sean Avery from Ottawa, Canada, makes sculptures of birds and animals—including a rat and a falcon—from old CDs. He cuts up the disks with scissors, arranges the shards according to size and color, and then attaches them to a wire mesh frame using a hot glue gun. Some of his works use 300 disks and take a month to complete.

extraordinary BODIES

DIME MUSEUMS

Dime museums were a popular form of entertainment in the U.S.A. during the 19th century.

Often for the cost of just a dime, visitors could step into a strange world entirely beyond their imagination, populated by midgets, giants, bearded ladies and other incredible sights.

The first dime museum was opened in New York in 1841 by legendary showman P.T. Barnum.

Rival entrepreneur George B. Bunnell opened his first dime museum in New York in 1876, employing a variety of performers such as the world's tallest couple—Captain Bates and his wife Anna Swan—and celebrated midgets Admiral Dot and Major Atom, and the Wild Men of Borneo (who were actually two brothers from Ohio).

A later establishment was Hubert's Museum that opened in Times Square, New York, in the mid-1920s. Among the acts on display there were sword swallower Lady Estelline, Albert-Alberta the Half-Man Half-Woman, Susie the Elephant Skin Girl, Professor Heckler's Flea Circus, Martha the Armless Wonder and Zip the Pinhead. Hubert's Museum finally closed in 1969.

Martha the Armless Wonder

Martha, one of Hubert's Museum acts in New York in the 1920s, was born in the early 1900s with no arms, and shortened legs protruding from her hips. Her act included eating, writing and typing with her feet.

Zip and Pip

Jennie Lee and Elvira Snow a.k.a. "The Snow Twins," suffered from microcephaly, a condition characterized by abnormally small craniums. They were commonly known as "pinheads."

Percilla Lauther and Emmitt Bejano

Billed as "Monkey Girl" and "Alligator Boy." Percilla had excess hair on the body and two rows of teeth. Emmitt had hard callouses on his skin. They eloped in 1938, but returned several years later to exhibit themselves as the "World's Strangest Married Couple."

STRANGEST MARRIED COUPLE
PERCILLA *Monkey Girl* — EMMITT *Alligator Boy*

BACK LAWN

Chinese performance artist Yang Zhichao had grass from the Suzhou River surgically implanted into his back without anesthesia. The surgeon made two incisions in Yang's shoulder before planting the freshly picked grass into the deep cuts. Owing to his ability to withstand intense pain, Yang has also had objects surgically implanted in his leg and stomach and had his ID number branded on his back with a red-hot iron.

DIY Op

A 63-year-old Californian man was taken to the hospital after he tried unsuccessfully to perform a do-it-yourself operation on his hernia by slicing open his stomach with a 6-in (15-cm) butter knife.

Hole in Jaw

Wu Moude, a worker on a building site in Quanzhou, China, survived a fall in which a half-inch-thick (1.2-cm) steel bar penetrated his jaw and embedded itself 6 in (15 cm) into his skull.

Skeleton Found

Hanged in 1821 for murdering his former girlfriend, John Horwood finally received a proper burial 190 years later after his family tracked down his skeleton to the University of Bristol, England, science laboratory where it had been displayed with the noose still around its neck. Following his execution, Horwood's body had been publicly dissected, and the skin removed and used to bind a book about the case.

Modern Styles

A study of hair samples of mummies showed that Ancient Egyptians used to style their hair using similar products to the ones we use today. They used fat-based products as gels, tried to curl their hair with tongs, and even plaited it in extensions.

New Skills

Before losing half of her brain in a 2008 car crash in St. Petersburg, Russia, Taisia Sidorova was right-handed and displayed no artistic talent—but since the accident she has become a skilled artist who paints with her left hand.

Twins Separated

A team of British doctors at London's Great Ormond Street Hospital for Children successfully separated Sudanese-born twins Rital and Ritag Gaboura who were born joined at the head—a condition where the chances of survival are just one in ten million. Although the twins did not share brain tissue, they did share vital arteries and nerves. The blood flow between their brains made the operation particularly difficult.

Life Saver

Days away from death because of a muscle-wasting disease called Duchenne muscular dystrophy, a 15-year-old Italian boy became the world's first child to be given a permanent artificial heart—an implant that should give him at least another 20 years of normal life. His new heart is powered through a plug positioned behind his left ear and is connected to a battery that he keeps on a belt. The battery is charged during the night like a cell phone.

BLOCKED NOSE

Doctors in Yongkang, China, discovered that a man who had gone to the hospital with breathing difficulties had a tooth growing in his nostril. Feng Fujia, 21, had experienced nasal problems for five years, during which time his nose smelled so bad that his coworkers would stay away from him. When X-rays were finally taken, doctors were stunned to see a tooth in his nose. They think he must have eaten something hard when he was young that pressed one of his upper teeth into his nostril. The tooth then slowly started to grow.

COLORED POOP

Based on medical research, Alexandra Daisy Ginsberg and James King's design piece Scatalog demonstrates how special *E. chromi* bacteria can be used to change the color of a person's poop to indicate the presence of disease in the body. A team of biologists from Cambridge University genetically engineered the bacteria, which, on detecting disease in the human gut, secretes a color signal—red, green, yellow, brown, blue or violet—that is visible in the feces. Each color denotes a different disease.

Pointed Ears

New York City cosmetic surgeon Dr. Lajos Nagy offers patients the opportunity to acquire pointed, Mr. Spock-like ears, which he claims improve the experience of listening to music, as pointed ears focus sounds better.

Giant Cyst

Anne Warren, 60, of Westport, New Zealand, had a 22-lb (10-kg) ovarian cyst—a tumor the size of triplets. The cyst had been growing for years, but it wasn't until it began to affect her organs that Anne realized something was wrong. It was so big that the incision needed to remove it stretched from her groin to past her belly button.

Breaking Glass

American vocal coach Jaime Vendera can shatter a wine glass using only the sound of his voice. He can get his voice box up to an incredible 120 decibels, which is louder than the roar of a motorbike doing 60 mph (96 km/h).

On the Move

U.S. President Abraham Lincoln's coffin was moved 17 times after his funeral and was kept under a pile of lumber to hide it from grave robbers.

Emergency Call

On October 17, 2010, three-year-old Vincent Lamitie of North Ridgeville, Ohio, called the 911 emergency line to help his unconscious father—after remembering the 911 number from a cartoon.

Single Handed

Despite being born with just one hand, Kevin Shields from Fort William, Scotland, is an accomplished rock climber and has even managed to master treacherous ice climbs.

Saved by Tooth

Walter Davis was shot in the face in New Orleans, Louisiana, in February 2011—but escaped serious injury when the small-caliber .22 bullet ricocheted off his gold tooth.

Born Twice

Doctors in Texas performed prenatal surgery at 25 weeks to remove a grapefruit-sized tumor from Macie McCartney while she was still inside her mother's womb. The procedure involved pulling out mother Keri's uterus and then half of Macie's body. Once free of the tumor, Macie was returned to the womb, where she recovered and grew for another ten weeks before being "born" again.

Auto Degree

Mike Needs, a 48-year-old from Canton, Ohio, has been blind for decades, yet is finishing his degree as an auto mechanic.

Missing Years

For almost two months in 2008, 28-year-old Naomi Jacobs of Manchester, England, was convinced that it was 1992 and that she was a 15-year-old schoolgirl about to take her exams. Cell phones and the Internet were a mystery to her, and she had no idea who her 11-year-old son Leo was or any recollection of giving birth to him. She was suffering from Transient Global Amnesia, a form of memory loss brought on by stress. Her memory started to return after eight weeks, but it was another three years before she had fully recovered.

Died Twice

A woman died from shock after waking up to find that she was at her own funeral. Fagilyu Mukhametzyanov, 49, of Kazan, Russia, had been wrongly declared dead by doctors, but she died for real after she realized where she was and had a heart attack.

TOENAIL INSECTS

Rachel Betty Case has created *Human Ivory*, miniature creatures crafted from real human toenails. In 2003, the Pennsylvania artist began collecting the discarded toenails from her art school colleagues and professors, who would leave them in bags outside her door. After gathering two years' worth of clippings, Rachel decided to get creative with her macabre collection. Noticing how people reacted to her work, she was soon "addicted to shocking people, and to making art from the most unconventional materials."

Noisy Eyeballs

For six years, Stephen Mabbutt of Oxfordshire, England, suffered from a rare medical condition that meant he could hear his eyeballs move in their sockets. He first experienced the symptoms in 2005 when he felt a dull ache in the side of his head. He was diagnosed with superior canal dehiscence syndrome, an ear condition in which he could hear sounds inside his body. Until he had an operation to cure it in 2011, as well as hearing his eyeballs move, he could hear his heart beating, and the noise while he chewed food was deafening.

Red Tape

Although he has been living in America for almost a century, 95-year-old Leeland Davidson of Centralia, Washington State, discovered in early 2011 that he wasn't officially an American because his parents did not fill out the proper paperwork.

Sword Extraction

Surgeons in Hunan Province, China, successfully removed a 20-in-long (51-cm) metal sword from the head of a 15-year-old boy. The sword accidentally stabbed Zhang Bin between his eyes, penetrating at least 2 in (5 cm) into his forehead.

Surgical Implants

Marie Kolstad of Santa Ana, California, had $8,000 breast implants at age 83. She kept the surgery a secret from her four children, 13 grandchildren, and 12 great-grandchildren until the day before for fear they might disapprove.

Large Family

After giving birth to two sets of quadruplets (in 2004 and 2005), Dale Chalk from Strathpine in Queensland, Australia, had twins in 2009, giving her a total of 11 children under the age of seven.

SHEAR HORROR

Eighty-six-year-old Leroy Luetscher from Phoenix, Arizona, survived a horrific gardening accident in which he impaled himself through the eye with a pair of pruning shears. After dropping the shears blade-side down in the ground, he lost his balance as he bent to pick them up and fell face-down on the handle, which penetrated his eye socket and went down into his neck, resting on the external carotid artery. Half the shears were stuck in his head; the other half left sticking out. Surgeons removed the shears and saved his eye.

LUCKY FRIED CHICKEN

Extreme chef Kann Trichan retrieves pieces of deep-fried chicken from vats of boiling hot fat that bubble at temperatures of over 400°F (200°C) using his hands! He feels no pain and his hands show no sign of burns. Trichan discovered his strange ability when he emerged unscathed after being sprayed with hot oil. It's possible that Trichan's feat is explained by the Leidenfrost effect, when water on the skin vaporizes on contact with the hot oil, providing a protective layer for a short period of time.

400°F/200°C!

Blood Donor

John Sheppard of Fort Myers, Florida, has given more than 300 pints of blood in 60 years. His 39 gal (150 l) of blood could have saved almost 1,000 lives.

Magnet Boy

Eleven-year-old Paulo David Amorim of Mossoró, Brazil, can stick metal objects such as forks, knives, scissors and cooking pans to his chest, stomach and back.

Incriminating X-ray

A thief who stole a diamond from a woman in Marbella, Spain, and swallowed it, was caught when police gave him an X-ray. The X-ray showed the gem in his stomach, and he was charged with theft.

All's Well...

When four-year-old Deng Rui from Tengchong, China, tripped and fell to the bottom of a 30-ft (9-m) dry well, he found he had company—a cat that had fallen down the well earlier. Two days later Deng was found in the well and was rescued, with nothing worse than a few scratches to his face. The cat was also hauled to safety, but ran off as soon as it reached the surface.

Run over Twice

A woman from Melbourne, Australia, survived after being run over by her own car—twice. After pulling into the driveway of her home, she forgot to put on the handbrake, whereupon the runaway car knocked her to the ground, running over her abdomen and legs. As she lay injured, the car continued rolling down the slope, hit a fence, and rebounded back toward her, running her over for a second time.

Sore Leg

On June 21, 2010, Tracy Durham of Peoria, Illinois, awoke with a sore leg. When he looked, he discovered that he'd received a gunshot wound the night before but hadn't noticed it.

Alien Hand

For nearly 20 years, Karen Byrne of New Jersey has suffered from Alien Hand Syndrome, a rare neurological disorder in which she is frequently attacked by her own hand. It also affects her feet, with one leg going in the opposite direction she wants to go. It started when she had surgery to control her epilepsy, which was cured but she was left with this new, stranger condition.

False Toes

Two artificial big toes dating back over 2,600 years to Ancient Egypt were probably the world's first functional prosthetic body parts. One of the false toes, made from wood and leather, resides at the Egyptian Museum in Cairo while the other, made from a mix of linen, glue and plaster, is on display at the British Museum in London, England. Replicas of the artificial toes were tested on modern volunteers, whose big right toe had been lost, in order to prove that the limbs had a practical use and had not simply been attached to the foot during mummification for religious or ritualistic reasons.

Sum Girl!

A 15-year-old schoolgirl with a love of math was awakened from a medically induced coma when her father began asking her simple sums. Vicki Alex of Northamptonshire, England, had been unconscious for three days and had failed to respond to other attempts to stimulate her brain, but after her father's intervention she soon regained full consciousness.

Knife Blade

After being stabbed in a 2006 robbery, Li Fu of Yuanjiang County, China, lived for the next four years with a 4-in (10-cm) blade buried in his face—and he didn't even know it! Doctors found the knife blade, which had penetrated his tongue root, muscles and brain, only when they carried out an X-ray to investigate Li's complaint of headaches and a nasty taste in his mouth.

Oldest Woman?

Antisa Khvichava, a woman from a remote mountain village in Georgia, claimed to have celebrated her 132nd birthday on July 8, 2012 before dying on 30 September 2012. Although her original birth certificate has been lost, documents and evidence from her family support her age claim. If true, she would be the oldest person in recorded history.

Two Uvulas

Ben Duvall of Missouri was born with not one uvula—the small piece of soft tissue that hangs down from the soft palate over the back of the tongue—but two.

Blue Glow

Angel Glow is a rare battlefield condition where an injured soldier's wound begins to glow blue. It is caused by glowing bacteria that typically inhabit the guts of worms.

CRAZY CARTILAGE

Ricky Nakamura from Seattle, Washington, wrote to tell us about his curious nasal ability. He is able to crack, flatten and fold the cartilage in his nose without feeling any pain.

Missing toe

TOE SWAP

Li Zicheng of Huiyang, China, has a toe on his hand! After the thumb of his right hand was severed beyond repair in a work accident, doctors cut off one of his toes on his left foot and transplanted it onto the hand in place of the thumb.

Metal Muncher

Doctors in Cajamarca, Peru, removed 2 lb (900 g) of metal from a man's stomach, including nails, coins, rusted copper wire, and scrap metal. Requelme Abanto Alvarado said he had been eating metal for months and had once swallowed 17 nails, each 5 in (12.5 cm) long, in one day.

Human Robot

Wang Kang, a telecoms worker from Shanghai, China, enjoyed the 2008 movie *Iron Man* so much that he spent nearly three years building his own 110-lb (50-kg) suit of armor and then wore it to the office— to the amazement of his work colleagues. Some froze as he approached them in his robotic suit, and others screamed.

Pulling her Leg

While fishing on Lake Ida in Alexandria, Minnesota, Beth Krohn caught a prosthetic leg that Pam Riley had lost while swimming in the lake three years earlier. Beth returned the leg to Pam after tracking her down through a local prosthetic limb manufacturer.

Martial Arts

Sixty-year-old Ba Desheng of Kaifeng City, China, uses kung-fu skills to draw giant calligraphy with a brush that is 6 ft 6 in (2 m) long and weighs 11 lb (5 kg).

TINY MEXICAN

Mexican Lucia Zarate (1864–90) stood just 20 in (50 cm) tall, weighed 5 lb (2.3 kg), and had a 14-in (35-cm) waist, making her one of the smallest adults in history. Weighing only 8 oz (225 g) at birth and measuring just 7 in (18 cm) long, she stopped growing when she was one year old.

At the age of 12 she went to the U.S.A. and became a major draw in sideshows, where she appeared as the "Mexican Lilliputian" and earned an average of $700 per week—as much as $20 per hour—a small fortune in those days. With her earnings, Lucia was able to buy her own ranch.

GREATEST WONDER OF THE AGE.

SENORITA
LUCIA ZARATE
THE MEXICAN LILIPUTIAN.

THIS YOUNG LADY IS

15 YEARS OF AGE! 20 INCHES HIGH!

AND

WEIGHS ONLY 5 POUNDS!

IS PERFECT IN FORM AND FEATURE.

Tom Thumb is a giant compared with her—this wonderful Mexican Pigmy. It would be difficult to exaggerate the wonder of this human curiosity. The plain truth makes it strange enough.

You must see, hear and feel, and even then you will leave wondering.

J. WOOD, PHOTO., 208 BOWERY.

Lucia wore tiny jewelry to match her tiny frame and one museum at which she appeared offered a diamond ring to any baby who could fit a ring the same size as one of Lucia's on one of its fingers.

Latex Masks

Two robbers who stole $60 million worth of jewelry in a 2009 raid in London, England, reportedly hired an unsuspecting makeup artist to disguise their faces with liquid latex masks. The artist, who thought the pair were appearing in a music video, also changed their hair color and skin tone during the $700, four-hour session.

Famous Wiggle

The bottom wiggle that became one of Marilyn Monroe's trademarks was the result of her having weak ankles and bow legs. Once she saw the attention her walk was getting, she emphasized it by sawing a quarter of an inch off the right heel of all of her shoes.

Human Skulls

A self-confessed witch from New Zealand, 74-year-old Anna Hoffman has a collection of more than 20 human skulls— and she claims one of them is that of notorious Australian outlaw Ned Kelly who was hanged in 1880. His skeleton was discovered in a mass grave in Melbourne in 2009, but much of his skull was missing.

VAMPIRE WOMAN

Maria José Cristerna is not actually a vampire, but she could probably pass for one after such extensive body modification.

The Mexican tattoo artist has transformed herself with numerous tattoos, titanium implants under the skin, a large number of piercings, stretched earlobe tunnels and permanent fangs. Maria, a mother-of-four who studied to be a lawyer, reinvented herself as a vampire as a sign of strength after troubles in her life.

Toddler Plunge

Two-year-old Zhu Xinping miraculously survived after falling from the 21st floor of a tower block in Jianyang City, Sichuan Province, China. She suffered only a broken leg because she landed on a freshly dug pile of soil that cushioned her fall.

Self-service

After badly cutting his leg in an accident while renovating his kitchen, a 32-year-old man became so frustrated at having to wait an hour at Sundsvall Hospital in northern Sweden that he picked up a needle and thread and sewed up the cut himself.

Baby's Tail

Surgeons in China performed an operation to remove a 5-in-long (13-cm) tail from the body of a four-month-old baby girl. Hong Hong, from China's Anhui Province, was born with the tail, but it quickly doubled in size. X-rays had shown that it was connected to a fatty tumor within her spinal column.

STICKY SKIN

Etibar Elchyev, Georgia's "magnet man," displayed his magnetic powers in December 2011 when 50 metal spoons were stuck to his body. The 40-year-old from Marneuli, Georgia, can also hold a car hood, with a man sitting on it, on his chest without using his hands.

Eight Limbs

Seven-year-old Deepak Paswan of Bihar, India, was born with eight limbs—having the arms, legs and buttocks of a parasitic twin protruding from his chest. Although the parasitic twin's arms were small and withered, its legs grew at the same rate as Deepak, meaning the youngster had to carry a heavy weight around until he had the extra limbs removed in a complex operation in 2010.

Skin Shoes

Following the 1881 public hanging of outlaw George "Big Nose" Parrot in Carbon County, Wyoming, a local doctor had his skin made into a pair of dress shoes and a medical bag. The top of Parrott's skull was also sawn off and the cap was presented to a 15-year-old female medical assistant who used it variously as an ashtray, a pen holder and a doorstop.

Long Lobes

Jian Tianjin, a farmer from Taiwan, has earlobes that stretch 6½ in (16 cm)—so long and flexible that they reach his shoulders and he can wind them around his chin.

LONG IN THE NAILS

Kathy Hayes from L.A., California, has let her toenails grow over a number of years to what is now an incredible length. The anthropologist keeps her 5-in (13-cm) nails in tiptop condition, always polished and painted. Kathy's devotion to her decorated feet means that she is unable to wear regular shoes; she is restricted to open-toed sandals with platform soles in order to protect her nails.

B   e   l   i
l   t   o   r

CURLY CHARACTERS

Mayuko Kanazawa, a design student from Tokyo, Japan, created her own bizarre font by photographing the hair on her friend's leg, arranged to look like letters of the alphabet. Mayuko came up with the idea after her class was challenged to make a font without the aid of a computer, to ensure no digital trickery was involved!

New Language

A 13-year-old Croatian girl woke from a 24-hour coma speaking fluent German, which she had started studying at school only shortly before she fell into the coma. Bizarrely, she could no longer, however, speak Croatian!

e

v

e

N

o

t

Hairy Hands
Since becoming the first American to undergo a double hand transplant, Jeff Kepner from Augusta, Georgia, has noticed that his new hands are considerably hairier than the rest of his body because the donor had more hair than him.

Self-amputation
Trapped by a fallen concrete girder in the rubble of a building that collapsed during a 2009 earthquake in Padang, Indonesia, an 18-year-old construction worker named Ramlan survived by sawing off his own leg.

Legless Acrobat
Although he was born without legs, Lv Li from Dengfeng, China, makes his living as an acrobat. The amazing street performer's act includes handstands, snake charming and fire breathing, drawing huge crowds wherever he goes.

BIGGEST BREASTS

With a bra size of 102ZZZ, American Annie Hawkins-Turner (who goes under the stage name Norma Stitz) has the biggest natural breasts in the world. They weigh a combined 112 lb (51 kg)— a third of her total body weight. Her cleavage is 3 ft 6 in (1.07 m) long... and still growing.

Senior Teacher

Gladys Morris of Oldham, England, was still teaching yoga four times a week at the age of 90. She had three great-grandchildren and had been practicing yoga for nearly 50 years. Making her the world's oldest yoga teacher!

Ovarian Cyst

Jane Alexander from Fife, Scotland, had a 21 lb (9.5 kg) ovarian cyst removed from her body. The cyst, which was so big it made her look pregnant, began growing at a rate of 2 in (5 cm) a week until it had grown to twice the size of a soccer ball.

ACTING DOUBLE

Margaret Clark was an entertainer born with her twin attached by the head to her stomach. That was the backstory proclaimed at her performances at sideshows across the U.S.A., but Margaret did not have a conjoined twin; indeed, Margaret did not actually exist. She was an act played by sideshow operator Billy Logsdon, who ran "Side Show Beautiful" out of Indiana in the 1940s. The unfortunate baby twin was merely a rubber "gaff" taped to Billy's belly. His face was covered because he played another character in his shows, a hermaphrodite, also thought to be a hoax.

Rapid Aging

A young Vietnamese woman looked like she had aged 50 years in just a few days following what she thinks was an allergic reaction to eating seafood. Nguyen Thi Phuong suffered the rapid aging affliction in 2008, leaving her with sagging, wrinkled skin all over her face and body. At age 26, she looked like a woman in her 70s and was so upset by her appearance that she began wearing a mask in public. Doctors are baffled by her sudden aging and have yet to reach a diagnosis.

Youngest Granny

In 2011, 23-year-old Rifca Stanescu of Investi, Romania, became the world's youngest grandmother. She was just 12 years old when she had her first child, Maria, who gave birth to a son, Ion, when she was just 11 years old.

Stranger Delusion

Fregoli delusion, which can be triggered by brain damage, causes a person to suspect that strangers are actually people they already know—just acting in disguise.

Facial Recognition

A Japanese company has invented a vending machine that uses facial recognition to recommend drinks to customers. The machine uses sensors to work out the age and gender of a customer and then suggests items based on that information, while also taking into account factors such as the time of day and the weather. When the first interactive drinks machine was introduced at a Tokyo train station, sales were three times that of its predecessor.

GENE JUNIOR

At just 14 years of age, Michigan's Adrianne Lewis already has a tongue that measures a whopping 3½ in (8.75 cm) long. She is known as the "Mini Gene Simmons" after the Kiss frontman whose tongue is more than 7 in (17.5 cm) long.

Eye Lift

In July 2011, Rakesh Kumar of Ludhiana, India, broke his own world record by lifting a 22-lb (10-kg) weight using a hook placed in one of his eye sockets. He can also lift a 178-lb (81-kg) weight with one ear and pull a school bus with his teeth.

Stomach Grip

China's Wu Zhilong has such powerful stomach muscles he can use them to pull a 2.2-ton car a distance of 65 ft (20 m). He is also able to hold an iron pot so firmly in his abdomen that others cannot pull it off.

Artificial Heart

Charles Okeke became the first person to live outside a hospital with an artificial heart. Fitted at a clinic in Phoenix, Arizona, his mechanical heart was powered by a 13-lb (5.9-kg) backpack that ran on batteries. He wore it at home for 263 days until eventually a suitable donor was found to give him a new human heart.

Top That!

George Linn of Lakewood, Colorado, suffered a heart attack in July 2010 and was saved by a pizza delivery man who applied CPR.

Biggest Tonsils

A tonsillectomy performed on 21-year-old Justin Werner of Topeka, Kansas, revealed that one tonsil was 2.1 in (5.25 cm) long, 1.1 in (2.75 cm) wide, and 0.7 in (1.75 cm) thick, while the other measured 1.9 in (4.75 cm) long, 1 in (2.5 cm) wide, and 0.7 in (1.75 cm) thick, breaking the record for the world's largest tonsils by a total length of 1.4 in (3.5 cm).

Shortest Woman

At just 2 ft 3 in (69 cm) tall, 22-year-old Bridgette Jordan from Sandoval, Illinois, is the world's shortest living woman. She and her 20-year-old brother, Brad, who is 3 ft 2 in (97 cm) tall, have a disorder that affected their growth while they were still in the womb.

Cramped Cell

A Dutch prisoner, serving a two-year sentence for fraud, went to court in 2011 to complain that his cell was too small for him. At 6 ft 9 in (2 m) and 504 lb (229 kg), he claimed he was unable to use the toilet in his cell at Krimpen aan den Ijssel and could not sleep properly for fear of falling out of bed even after guards had added an extra plank. The judge ruled against his claim.

Shaved Beard

Teacher Gary Weddle of East Wenatchee, Washington State, vowed not to shave his face until Osama bin Laden was killed or captured. He kept his promise and left his beard untouched from 2001 until Bin Laden's death on May 2, 2011.

Spat Bullet

A 39-year-old man was shot in the face while walking down a street in Chicago, Illinois. Incredibly, he spat out the bullet and a tooth, suffering only minor injury.

Ate Toes

As 61-year-old diabetic James Little slept in his home at Roseburg, Oregon, his dog ate three of his toes. The dog was thought to have been acting instinctively to help remove diseased flesh, and Mr. Little felt nothing because numbness in the hands or feet is a symptom of diabetes.

Twins Peak

Among the 34 employees on duty at the Bexley Park Pool, South Euclid, Ohio, in the summer of 2011 were four sets of twins (including two identical sets), meaning that nearly a quarter of the staff were twins.

ELEPHANT MAN

Joseph Merrick was born in Leicester, England, in 1862. Despite his severe deformities, he led a remarkable life.

At birth, Merrick did not have any obvious deformities but, by the age of 21 months, his lips had started to swell abnormally. His skin became loose and rough, his right arm ballooned, and a huge bony growth appeared on his forehead. He also suffered a childhood fall, damaging his left hip and leaving him permanently lame. But Merrick was determined to make his way in the world and even tried working as a salesman.

"I AM NOT AN ANIMAL!
I AM A HUMAN BEING!
I...AM...A MAN!"

Poster from the Hollywood
movie *The Elephant Man*
(1980), starring John Hurt.

THE
ELEPHANT
MAN

more...

Despite Merrick's difficult background and problems with communication, visitors to the hospital where he lived would remark on his intelligence and sensitivity. He wrote letters and poems about his condition to friends, and was able to build a detailed model of a church that can still be seen in the hospital museum (replica far right in this picture). He became a popular draw for Victorian high society, even hosting the Princess of Wales in his chambers, a meeting that left him "overjoyed."

By age 20, the growth from his mouth was some 9 in (23 cm) long, making it difficult for him to eat, so he had part of the lump surgically removed. However, his enlarged head was still so heavy that he had to sleep in a sitting position for fear of breaking his neck if he tried to raise his head from a pillow. Unable to earn a conventional living, he decided that the only way to escape the workhouse was to exhibit himself as a human freak. He toured locally and became a regular performer at a shop in the East End of London, where he was billed as the "Elephant Man," complete with posters depicting a monstrous creature, half-man, half-elephant. He was hidden behind a curtain, and when it was pulled back visitors were visibly horrified by the sight before them, even though they were assured that the Elephant Man was "not here to frighten you, but to enlighten you."

When the authorities clamped down on freak shows in England in 1886, Merrick was forced to ply his trade in Europe, but he was robbed by his new manager of his savings and left to make his own way home. Back in London, he was put in touch with surgeon, Dr. Frederick Treves, who took him to The Royal London Hospital where he lived for the rest of his life.

Sadly, Merrick's condition deteriorated. His facial deformities continued to grow and his head became even more enlarged. Finally, on April 11, 1890, he was found dead in his bed. It seems that he had tried to sleep lying down for once, but the sheer weight of his head had, as he had always feared, dislocated his neck causing asphyxia.

Merrick's story was not forgotten, and the 1980 David Lynch movie **The Elephant Man,** *starring John Hurt, recounted the short, sad life of Joseph Merrick to a new generation. Hurt wore a mask and cap identical to that which Merrick used when venturing outside The Royal London Hospital, to avoid shocking the public. He also had to sit for seven hours every day while his makeup was applied. The movie was nominated for eight Academy Awards.*

SLIPPERY PROBLEM

Doctors removed an eel from a man's bladder after it had swum up his penis during an unorthodox beauty treatment. Zhang Nan of Honghu, China, climbed into a bath with ten eels. However, he soon felt a sharp pain and saw one of the eels drilling into his urethra. He went to hospital where the 6-in-long (15-cm) eel was removed in a three-hour operation.

Gun Shot

A Polish man who was hit in the back of the head by a .22-caliber bullet during New Year's Eve celebrations in the German town of Herne took five years to realize he had been shot. It was only when he went to a doctor after feeling a lump on his head that an X-ray revealed the presence of the bullet.

Artificial Teeth

Scientists from Tokyo University of Science, Japan, have grown fully formed teeth from stem cells. The artificial teeth, which were grown in mice, looked realistic, could chew food, and were sensitive to pain.

Ancient Bones

A woman in Marathon, Florida, discovered human bones in her garden in October 2010. On inspection, experts estimated that the bones are in fact 2,400 years old.

TOOTHBRUSH TRAUMA

A woman from Jinan, China, went to a hospital and doctors found a toothbrush lodged in her stomach. It had been there for a month since she arrived home drunk from a party and fell asleep while brushing her teeth, at which time she had swallowed the brush.

Waldo Tattoo

John Mosley of Norwich, England, has a *Where's Waldo?* scene of 150 characters tattooed on his back. He sat patiently for 24 hours while tattooist Rytch Soddy created the body artwork, which features Darth Vader from *Star Wars*, cavemen, pirates, Vikings, cowboys and Waldo himself.

Body Branding

Canadian body modification artist Blair specializes in multiple-strike branding, in which he is able to create intricate designs on people by heating a small piece of metal and applying it repeatedly to a person's skin like a paintbrush. Those who have been branded compare the smell of their skin during the procedure to that of cooking bacon.

Head Turner

A YouTube clip shows a Russian waiter named Alexander turning his head and neck 180 degrees to look behind him. It was during gymnastics training that he first realized he had a spinal abnormality, which made his body extremely flexible. He says he has to concentrate energy from his whole body to perform the feat.

STOMACH GROWTH

Chinese factory worker Wang Yongjun grew a new fingertip... on his stomach. He accidentally cut off the end of his middle finger, and doctors in Liaoyang attached the bony finger to his stomach so that new skin and muscle could grow around it.

Surgical Sponge

Helen O'Hagan of Sydney, Australia, lived for more than 15 years with a surgical sponge the size of a grapefruit sewn inside her following an abdominal operation in 1992. She suffered cramps, fevers and bowel problems until an X-ray detected the sponge in 2007.

Saved by Dentures

When 81-year-old Zacarias Pacheco de Moraes was shot while working in the bar he owns in Alta Floresta, Brazil, his life was saved by his dentures deflecting a bullet that was headed for his brain. The bullet hit his dentures before lodging in his throat.

Severed Foot

In an attempt to save a patient's severed left foot, doctors in Zhengzhou, China, attached it to the calf of his right leg. Ma Jun lost his foot after slipping into a concrete mixer on a building site, and his left leg was too badly damaged for it to be reattached straightaway. So in a 12-hour operation, doctors transplanted the foot onto his right calf so that it could grow new skin, tissue and muscles before being reattached in its rightful place.

ROLY-POLY MAN

Born without arms or legs so that he was just a head and a trunk, William Thomas Goy was billed in the Barnum & Bailey Circus as the "Roly-Poly Man" because when he wanted to get from one side of a room to the other, he tipped over on his side and rolled there.

He was raised in London, England, where, despite being limbless, he was able to write well with his mouth, get up and down stairs unaided, make bead bangles and necklaces with his teeth and lips, and even drive a van. Goy was married to Mary Jane, who stood 5 ft 6 in (1.67 m) tall next to his 2 ft 3 in (68 cm), and they had six children.

Colored Sweat

Exposure to certain dyes, foods, and chemicals can cause chromhidrosis—colored sweat that usually appears on the face and underarms in a variety of bright hues. Cases of red, blue, green, yellow or black sweat have been reported.

Silence on Court!

The grunts and screams that famously accompany every tennis shot hit by Russian player Maria Sharapova regularly reach 101 decibels—that's louder than the roar of a freight train at full speed or a police siren when heard at close-quarters.

Iron Finger

Some Shaolin monks can do one-finger handstands or "iron fingers." To balance the body on just one finger requires immense strength and concentration—yet Hai-tank, a 91-year-old monk from the Sil Lum Templein China, can perform the feat.

Prophetic Tattoo?

When he was arrested in May 2011 on suspicion of assault, Robert Kennedy of Horry County, South Carolina, had a tattoo on his forehead that read: "Please forgive me if I say or do anything stupid. Thank you."

Worker Impaled

Wang Tao from Xian, China, survived after an accident at a concrete factory left him impaled on 13 metal rods. An explosion sent the steel rods spearing into his thigh and hip. Some of them were so long that workmates had to use an angle grinder to sever them so that Tao could fit into the ambulance. After a four-hour operation he soon returned to work.

Believe It or Not!

PARASITES

This tangle of giant roundworms was found in the intestines of a child from Kenya.

The worm begins life when an egg hatches in the host's intestine. The larva then travels to the lungs via the blood vessels, where it continues to develop until it is coughed up and swallowed, ending up in the stomach. The worm, which infects around a billion people worldwide, then travels back into the small intestine where it completes its life cycle.

Giant roundworm

BODY LOUSE

Body lice lay their eggs on clothes, and move on to human skin only to feed on blood, causing intense itching. They excrete on skin and clothing and can occur in large infestations where living conditions are cramped and hygiene is bad.

BEFORE

AFTER

TICKS

Ticks suck up so much blood that their body fills up like a balloon. They can't fly or jump, but they carry many diseases that are deadly to humans.

LEGLESS FOOTBALLER

Although he was born with no legs and stands just 3 ft (90 cm) tall, Bobby Martin of Dayton, Ohio, is a formidable opponent on the football field. Encouraged by coaches, he played as a defensive tackle for his high-school team and has since gone on to play at his local college. Far from being a handicap, the 24-year-old father, who suffers from a rare condition called Caudal Regression Syndrome meaning his body ends at his pelvis, says his size actually helps him play football. He uses a skateboard to get around and is so strong that he can lift three times his body weight—over 330 lb (150 kg).

Hidden Gem

When Calvin Wright of Athens, Georgia, went into the hospital with an acute case of bronchitis, an emergency room nurse discovered a pearl inside his ear. It had been in his ear canal for 41 years, after his mother's necklace had broken and his baby sister had playfully stuffed two of the pearls into his ear. Although doctors had managed to remove one immediately afterward, amazingly the other pearl had gone undetected.

Tattooed Grandpa

Great-grandfather Tommy Wells from Greater Manchester, England, has more than 1,000 tattoos etched across every part of his body. He has spent more than 50 years having tattoos inked not only on his arms, hands, legs, torso, back and head, but also on the soles of his feet, his lips, his butt and even his genitals.

Telltale Tattoos

Grant Dey of Christchurch, New Zealand, has his face covered in flame tattoos—and in September 2011 he was convicted, after pleading guilty, of deliberately burning down his neighbor's house.

Mighty Yawn

College student Holly Thomson of Northampton, England, found a lesson in government and politics so tiresome that she yawned hard enough to dislocate her jaw. She remained with her jaw locked open in a yawning position for five hours until a doctor at the local hospital was able to open it even further and unlock it.

Shortest Man

In 2011, an 18-year-old from the Philippines, Junrey Balawing, was declared the world's shortest man. The son of a blacksmith from Sindangan on Mindanao Island, he stands just 23.6 in (60 cm) tall—5 in (12.5 cm) shorter than the average one-year-old boy—after he stopped growing when he was two years old.

34 Digits

Akshat Saxena of Uttar Pradesh, India, was born with 14 fingers (seven on each hand but no thumbs) and 20 toes (ten on each foot), giving him 34 digits—more than anyone else in the world. He later had the excess digits surgically removed and doctors made him thumbs from the fingers they amputated.

Brain Surgery

Helen Hollis, 47, from Nottinghamshire, England, graduated from the University of Derby in 2011 with a degree in psychology and counseling studies—five years after part of her brain was removed. Part of her right temporal lobe was taken out in a high-risk operation to overcome her repeated epileptic attacks, which used to total around 40 a month.

No Hands

Ten-year-old Nick Maxim of Readfield, Maine, won a national award for penmanship—despite being born without hands. He writes fluently by holding the pencil between his arms, which end just above where his elbows should be.

Twin Curse

Gladys Bulinya of Nzoia, near Kenya's Lake Victoria, has given birth to six sets of non identical twins over a period of 17 years. Sadly, after the sixth set arrived in 2010, her husband decided she was cursed and left her. The rest of her family also shunned her, as many people in her region think twins bring bad luck.

ELF EARS

Kimberleigh Smithbower Roseblade of Vancouver, Canada, underwent complex surgery to acquire a pair of genuine pointy elf ears. Body modification artist Russ Foxx carried out the procedure by removing a piece of Kimberleigh's ear, then folding the ear over and stitching it shut. Kimberleigh had previously worn prosthetic elf ears as a fashion statement, but is now delighted to own the real deal.

King's Head

In 2010, scientists identified the long-lost head of King Henri IV of France, who was assassinated in 1610 and whose head had been stolen during the French Revolution. Scientists used forensics to identify the head, which had passed between collectors, by features visible in portraits, including a lesion near his nose, a pierced ear and a healed facial wound from an assassination attempt.

Body Metal

Rolf Buchholz, a computer expert in his fifties from Dortmund, Germany, has 453 rings and studs pierced into his body.

Made of human hair!

HAIR-RAISING INSECTS

Artist Adrienne Antonson from Asheville, North Carolina, bends and weaves real human hair into remarkably detailed insect artworks. On her praying mantis, moths and flies, she uses glue to mold the hair and to hold it in place. Adrienne collects locks of different-colored hair from close friends and family, and is interested in using her creations for art therapy, working with people who have lost their hair through illness.

Three Generations

Kathryn Crills of Ephrata, Pennsylvania, is the proud matriarch of three generations of identical twins—her own daughters Karen and Sharon (who were born August 7, 1959), her granddaughters Melanie and Michelle (who were born September 22, 1973), and her great-granddaughters Maleah and Makelah (who were born April 16, 2010).

Corpse Display

Cancetto Farmica, a U.S. carnival worker, died in 1911, but when his father failed to collect his son's body, the funeral home at Laurinburg, North Carolina, put him on display until 1972.

Outsize Only

Body Exchange, a fitness gym in Vancouver, British Columbia, admits only plus-size women—and prohibits thin women and men from using its facilities.

DESIGNER SCARS

Instead of tattoos, some people now choose scarification, the technique of cutting or scratching permanent designs into the skin with a sharp surgical scalpel. One of the world's leading scarifiers is Ryan Ouellette from Nashua, New Hampshire, who started out by cutting small patterns into his own leg with a sewing needle. He says that bleeding usually stops five minutes after a line has been cut, and a new layer of skin will form over the finished design within two weeks.

266

Smelly Urine

Thorpe Park theme park in Surrey, England, asked visitors to provide smelly urine samples so that the foulest odor could be re-created for a new horror attraction alongside the smells of burning hair and rotting meat. In order to stand a chance of winning the £500 ($750) first prize for the smelliest pee, participants were advised to drink alcohol or coffee and to eat garlic or asparagus.

Driver Skewered

Andrew Linn of Las Vegas, Nevada, survived being speared through the face with a 2-in-wide (5-cm) metal pole after falling unconscious at the wheel of his car, veering off the road, and plowing into a chain-link fence. The pole tore through his face just below the right side of his nose, ripping out some of his teeth, before exiting through the back of his neck.

Bionic Fingers

After losing fingers on both hands to blood poisoning when she was a toddler, 15-year-old Chloe Holmes from Swindon, England, has been fitted with a full set of bionic digits on her left hand, enabling her to pick up things for the first time. The false fingers are controlled by electronic signals from the nerve endings in her hand.

TOP MOP

Aevin Dugas holds a hair-raising record on top of her head—the world's largest "afro" hairstyle, which has grown to 4 ft 4 in (1.3 m) in circumference and rises to 7 in (18 cm). The 36-year-old social worker from New Orleans has been caring for her curls for 12 years, but doesn't always wear her hair at its biggest, as it restricts her vision when driving and can get too hot in the Louisiana summer.

that's WEIRD!

EXTREME PLANKING

Planking was a worldwide craze that took off dramatically a few years ago after plankers posted their bizarre images on the Internet.

Reuben Wilson planks on Cairns Esplanade, Queensland, Australia, in May 2011.

The phenomenon involved participants lying face down in unusual locations with their hands touching the sides of the body—mimicking a wooden plank—while someone else took a picture of the event.

Several people claimed to have invented planking, including New Zealander Andy Welch, who says he invented the original craze while on vacation in Croatia, after he and his girlfriend became bored with striking the usual poses for holiday photos.

A Russian planker photographed by Tima Sergeev is seen here planking on an advertising sign in St. Petersburg, Russia.

Vincent Migliore demonstrated his planking skills on a tree stump in a city park in Folsom, California, in August 2011.

Taiwan's most famous plankers were the Pujie Girls (meaning "Falling on the Street" in Mandarin).

Andy Welch, Sussex, England, planked face up as well as face down.

Goat Grabbing

Buzkashi is a traditional Central Asian sport—and the national sport in Afghanistan—that uses a headless goat carcass as a ball. Teams on horseback try to grab the carcass from the ground and pitch it into a scoring area. Players usually wear heavy protective clothing, as the sport can be very dangerous. The winning team gets to boil and eat the carcass.

Snowshoe Race

The midwinter La Ciaspolada foot race in Italy has been held annually since 1972, with its contestants wearing snowshoes from start to finish. It is run over a 5-mi (8-km) course in the Dolomite Mountains and attracts up to 6,000 entrants each year.

Fisherman's Friend

Heather, a 40-year-old, 52-lb (23.6-kg) carp living in a pond in Hampshire, England, had been caught and released hundreds of times before she was found dead in 2010.

Monkey Security

Indian authorities used 38 trained gray langur monkeys to frighten away other types of monkeys from the athletes' village during the 2010 Commonwealth Games in Delhi.

Multinational Match

The English Premier League soccer match between Blackburn Rovers and West Bromwich Albion on January 23, 2011, featured players representing an amazing 22 different countries.

Straight Ollies

On July 16, 2011, Eric Carlin, 18, of Mount Laurel, Pennsylvania, strung together a record 247 straight "ollies" on a skateboard without his feet ever touching the ground. An "ollie" is a trick where the rider and skateboard leap into the air without the rider using his or her hands.

Triple Backflip

On May 28, 2011, BMX rider Jed Mildon landed the world's first triple backflip at Unit T3 Mindtricks BMX Jam in his hometown of Taupo, New Zealand. He nailed the record-breaking jump by riding down a 66-ft-high (20-m) ramp carved into a hillside.

3

4

Finished wax figure

Playing with Fire

An enterprising trombone player called Scott, from Jackson, Missouri, has fitted up his trombone with a gas tank so that it also serves as a flamethrower. His YouTube video shows him shooting out 21-ft-long (6.4-m) jets of fire while playing his "Flamebone."

WAX CHAMP

World light–heavyweight boxing champion Bernard Hopkins was cast for a full-size wax figure at Ripley's Believe It or Not! world headquarters in Orlando, Florida, in August 2011. Hopkins became the oldest boxer ever to unify world titles when he defeated Beibut Shumenov on 19th April 2014 at the age of 49.

High Ground

Every year Pakistan stages a polo tournament high up on the Shandur Mountain Pass—12,251 ft (3,734 m) above sea level—in which teams from the towns on either side, Gilgit and Chitral, play each other.

Biker Impaled

During a motorcycle accident in January 2011, a 20-year-old man in Delhi, India, was impaled through his chest by inch-thick (2.5-cm) iron rods. Doctors saved his life in a four-hour operation.

Ashes Tattoo

Brother and sister Andrew and Helen Bird of Stoke-on-Trent, England, created a lasting tribute to their dead grandfather by having his ashes tattooed into their skin. Andrew had an extract from one of grandpa Reginald Alefs' poems etched on to his arm, while Helen had a rose inked onto her back. The tattoo artist mixed some of Mr. Alefs' ashes with ink to create the artworks.

Persistant Caller

In September 2011, police in Rotterdam, the Netherlands, charged a woman with stalking after she had called a man 65,000 times in a year—an average of 178 times a day, or about once every eight minutes.

PINBALL PARK

Skateboarders and BMX riders ride around a giant pinball machine at a park in Auckland, New Zealand, as if they are tiny pinballs. They are given a push down the first hill by a huge "arm" and, just like in a real pinball game, they can build up points by jumping over bleepers and bouncing off flippers.

CHEESY OUTFITS

Students from Bath Spa University, England, spent 1,000 hours making five dresses from a ton of cheese. Their designs included shoes made of cheese, and dresses encrusted with heat-molded, sculpted Cheddar.

Cicada Dessert

In 2011, an ice-cream shop in Columbia, Missouri, prepared cicada ice cream—and sold out of it within hours. Employees at Sparky's Homemade Ice Cream collected the cicadas in their backyards and removed the wings. Then boiled the bugs and coated them in brown sugar and milk chocolate before adding them to the brown sugar and butter ice-cream base.

Costly Kebab

Chef Andy Bates from London, England, served up a £750 ($1,100) kebab, made from expensive purple violet potatoes, coeur de boeuf tomatoes, milk-fed lamb, and a mint yogurt topping infused with luxurious Krug champagne.

Chocolate Tree

French chocolatier Patrick Roger created a chocolate Christmas tree, 33-ft-high (10-m) and weighing more than four tons, in his Paris laboratory.

Bumper B.L.T.

In Kansas City in 2011, volunteers assembled a bacon, lettuce and tomato sandwich that was 209 ft (63.7 m) long. It took 14 people 42 minutes to prepare the sandwich, using 3,300 slices of bacon, seven cases of lettuce, and 750 lb (340 kg) of tomatoes.

Birthday Cake

To celebrate Canada's 144th birthday on July 1, 2011, three bakeries in Toronto, Ontario, joined forces to create a cake more than 5 ft (1.5 m) tall, with 255 layers. The giant confection required 287 lb (130 kg) of sugar and copious amounts of eggs, flour and butter.

Old Cake

In 2010, Justin Agrella of San Leandro, California, discovered a steamer trunk belonging to his grandparents containing a well-preserved piece of their 96-year-old wedding cake.

MEALWORM MORSELS

Mealworm quiches and grasshopper spring rolls are among the edible delights created by Dutch scientist Arnold van Huis who has teamed up with a cooking school in Wageningen, the Netherlands, to produce a cookbook of tasty insect recipes. Van Huis believes that bug-eating is the future of nutrition, and that increased bug consumption will help alleviate global food shortages, as well as reduce carbon emissions created by other foodstuffs.

FACEBOOK FAD

In the Facebook fad of horsemaning, two people would pose for prank pictures to make it look as if one of them had lost their head.

Inspired by Washington Irving's short story, the craze for posing for photos as headless horsemen (hence the name) was actually around in the 1920s—long before the advent of the Internet.

Paul Silviak's head and Robert Mahler's body made up this horsemaning pose with a guillotine, taken by Brent Douglas in Oregon.

CONTAINS ONE ARCHITECTURAL SCALE MODEL

UP

Jeffrey Bautista and Paul Riddle from San Jose, California, horsemaning in formalwear.

L.A. photographer Deney Tuazon took this shot featuring Jade Zivalic's head and Isaiah Castellanos' body in San Francisco, California.

Mini Chopper

U.S. company Vanguard Defense Industries has developed a remote-controlled helicopter that is being used to track pirates off East Africa and tackle crime in the U.S.A. The Shadowhawk UAV is just 7 ft (2.1 m) long and weighs 49 lb (22 kg), but it has a top speed of 70 mph (112 km/h). It can fire tasers, grenades and shotgun shells, and record and broadcast footage in real time.

Lizard Lunch

A lizard commonly eaten in restaurants across southeast Vietnam is an all-female species that was unknown to science until 2010. Scientists came across the creature on a lunch buffet menu, and named it *Leiolepis ngovantrii*.

Squid Bottle

An Ika Tokkuri is a Japanese liquor bottle that has been made from an entire sun-dried squid. The cleaned and dried squid skin is often stuffed with rice or grain to help it form a bottle shape, and when sake (rice wine) is poured into it, the drink absorbs the flavor of the squid. The bottle can be reused up to six times, after which it can be eaten!

Think Bike

Toyota has created a bicycle with gears you can change using your mind. The rider of the Prius X Parlee (PXP) wears a special "neuron helmet" that uses electrodes to pick up cues from the brain and send signals to a thought-controlled gearbox mounted under the seat of the bicycle.

Nasty Shock

Joseph Ferrato of Akron, Ohio, sustained only minor injuries after 23,000 volts of electricity burst through the windshield of his car. The damage was caused by a falling power line that had been cut down by copper thieves.

Soap Eater

A rare and dangerous medical condition left Tempestt Henderson, a teenage girl from Florida, addicted to eating soap. She used to go through five bars of soap a week, as well as devouring washing powder daily, and licking soap bubbles off her skin in the shower. Doctors diagnosed her as suffering from pica, a condition that causes people to eat substances with no nutritional value, such as chalk, metal, sand and soap!

Salad Dressing

To encourage Chinese people to adopt a meat-free diet—meat consumption in the country has quadrupled over the course of the last 40 years—actress Gao Yuanyuan wore a gown made of lettuce and cabbage leaves topped with a necklace fashioned from red chili peppers. Gao herself had stopped eating meat after her pet dog suffered food poisoning two years earlier.

Rusty Bullet

In 2011, doctors finally discovered why a Chinese farmer had been affected by epilepsy for more than two decades—a ¾-in-long (2-cm) rusty bullet had been lodged in his brain since 1988. Wang Tianqing of Zhangjiakou City remembered being knocked unconscious by a blow to the head, but had no idea he had been shot.

Playing Twister

At the age of 80, Chen Daorong from Zhengzhou, Fujian Province, China, is a contortionist. He started contortion in 1999 to cure back pains and can now twist his legs around his neck, do the splits and sleep as he rests his head on one foot as a pillow.

VERTICAL PARKING

Heralding today's multistory parking lots, in the early 1920s cars were hoisted up on individual platforms to form elevator-style parking lots in order to save space.

Low Car

Students from Okayama Sanyo High School in Asakuchi, Japan, built a single-seater electric car that is just 18 in (45 cm) high and runs at speeds of up to 30 mph (50 km/h).

FERRARI TABLE

French furniture designer Charly Molinelli has encased the wreck of a Ferrari F40 supercar in a coffee table. Asked to build a unique piece and knowing that his client was a motor-sports fan, Molinelli approached a friend who worked at a scrapyard that was crushing a Ferrari and managed to procure it.

Perfect Parking

German stunt driver Ronny Wechselberger squeezed his Volkswagen Polo car into a parking space that was just 10¼ in (26 cm) longer than his vehicle. He performed the incredible feat of parallel parking by using the handbrake to flick the car's rear end around.

Traffic Director

Civilian Hugh McManaway spent so much of his spare time directing traffic at a busy intersection that the city of Charlotte, North Carolina, built a statue to commemorate him.

Jeep Record

On August 12, 2011, more than 1,100 Jeeps from across the U.S.A. converged on the Bantam Heritage Jeep Festival at Butler, Pennsylvania, to break the record for the world's largest Jeep parade.

New Roads

Although it already has 2.9 million mi (4.7 million km) of road, placing it third in the world behind the U.S.A. and China, India is building another 15 mi (24 km) of road every day to cater for the nation's increase in cars. However, it still has one of the lowest highway-to-person densities in the world.

DARING STUNT

A daredevil driver in Florida calmly maneuvered his Mazda car under a moving 18-wheel juggernaut traveling at a speed of around 40 mph (65 km/h)... and stayed there for over a minute. His reckless action, captured on film by a shocked motorist, mimics a scene from the 2001 movie *The Fast and the Furious*, where actor Vin Diesel drives underneath a truck that his gang is trying to rob.

Fire Drill

A team of 25 firefighters from London, England, drove 30,000 mi (48,000 km) around the world—in a fire engine named Martha. Their nine-month journey took them through 28 countries, including Russia, China, Australia, New Zealand and the U.S.A.

Mouse Menace

Shopping at a supermarket in Birmingham, England, Liz Wray was horrified to see half a dozen live baby mice fall out of a packet of potato chips she had just picked up.

First Ban

Venezuela issued its first-ever driving ban in 2011—to a bus driver who was speeding in an overladen, six-wheel passenger bus that was missing one of its rear wheels. Drivers have strong rights in Venezuela, where it took until 2008 to introduce a law that allowed a court to ban motorists from driving. This bus driver's ban was suspended for 12 months.

Baby Driver

A seven-year-old Michigan boy, who had to stand up to reach the gas and brake pedals, drove over 20 mi (32 km) in an attempt to see his father. The boy took his stepfather's Pontiac Sunfire and, barefoot and in pajamas, hit speeds of 70 mph (113 km/h) before being stopped by a police patrol.

MARKET RAILWAY

The Maeklong Market Railway in Thailand runs right through the heart of the market, forcing the vendors to pull back their awnings and move their produce out of the way when a train comes along. Passing just inches from the vendors' faces, the train ruthlessly crushes any stray fruit or vegetables left in its path.

1241

A CUT ABOVE

International pop star Lady Gaga is renowned for outrageous style, designed by her own Haus of Gaga fashion house, but nothing has come close to the genuine meat dress she sported at the 2010 MTV Video Music Awards in L.A., California. The layered beef steak number, complete with a meat hat, was designed by Franc Fernandez and Haus of Gaga. The dress was saved from being eaten by being placed in the Rock and Roll Hall of Fame in Cleveland, Ohio.

Milking The Joke

British comedian Milton Jones performed a stand-up routine to a field of cows on a farm in Hertfordshire, England, to see if they have a sense of humor. His set, called "Pull the Udder One," contained jokes tailored specially for his four-legged audience. Cows are believed to produce more milk if they are happy.

Up House

With an asking price of $400,000, U.S. firm Bangerter Homes has built an authentic replica of Carl Fredricksen's flying house from the Disney/Pixar movie Up at Herriman, Utah—complete with 1950s-style décor, but no balloons.

Giant Tumor

A massive tumor, accounting for one-third of his body weight, was removed from the back of a Chinese teenager in 2011. The 41-lb (19-kg) growth had been expanding on the body of 15-year-old Qiu Sheng, from Yunnan Province, since birth. It started as two bean-sized tumors on his waist, before growing first to the size of a peach, then a coconut, then finally a sandbag on his back that grew into his chest cavity and pushed aside his right shoulder blade.

Heavy Cake

A total of 100 workers from Dairy Queen, Canada, spent 14 hours in a Toronto, Ontario, square in May 2011 making an ice-cream cake that weighed more than 10 tons. The cake contained over 20,000 lb (9,070 kg) of ice cream, 200 lb (91 kg) of sponge cake, and 300 lb (136 kg) of icing and crumble. The gigantic dessert was created to celebrate the 30th birthday of Dairy Queen's much-loved ice-cream cake.

Shark Rock

Matt Waller, a shark tour operator in South Australia's Neptune Bay, has found that great white sharks are attracted by the music of Australian rock band AC/DC. Using underwater speakers attached to diving cages, he pumped rock hits through the ocean, but whereas most had little effect, when the great whites heard AC/DC they quickly swam over and rubbed their jaws against the source of the music.

Money To Burn

In 1994, the KLF (a U.K. music duo consisting of Bill Drummond and Jimmy Cauty) burned £1 million ($1.6 million) in cash of their own money and filmed it as an art project.

Psychic Powers

Don Van Vliet, the U.S. rock musician known as Captain Beefheart who died in 2010, could allegedly change TV channels using nothing more than his psychic powers, according to producer Richard Perry. Perry said that Beefheart could do this in unfamiliar environments where he had no opportunity to conceal a remote control beforehand.

Fast Flight

U.S. photographer Nate Bolt posted a video on YouTube showing a flight from San Francisco to Paris, France, in just 124 seconds. Armed with a camera and a time-lapse controller, he took a picture approximately every 20—30 seconds of the 11-hour journey from take-off to landing, a total of 2,459 shots.

Bond Bonanza

While clearing out the home of Marie Veloso's late mother in Saugus, Massachusetts, junk dealer Leo Guarente found an envelope containing 21 U.S. savings bonds that cost $1,000 each when they were bought in 1972, but were worth $114,000 40 years later. He immediately presented the surprise bonds to Mrs. Veloso.

Potter Magic

In July 2011, the opening weekend box-office takings of the movie *Harry Potter and the Deathly Hallows: Part 2* were $169 million in the U.S.A. and $307 million internationally, giving it the then new opening-weekend record in both groups.

Speed Record

On August 22, 2010, Melissa Thompson from Manchester, England, wrote the text message "the razor-toothed piranhas of the genera *Serrasalmus* and *Pygocentrus* are the most ferocious freshwater fish in the world. In reality they seldom attack a human" in a record time of 25.94 seconds.

Time Warp

Forty-six-year-old Michael McTigue of West Yorkshire, England, loves the 1930s so much that all of his clothes and home furnishings are a tribute to Britain on the eve of World War II. He doesn't own a washing machine—preferring to use an old-fashioned tub and mangle—he has a vintage telephone, gramophone and radio, and his Hoover vacuum cleaner dates from 1938.

FOOD COVERS

A Japanese company designed a range of iPhone covers that look like food. The plastic cases mimic such dishes as sushi rolls, chocolate desserts, and bacon and eggs.

Young Designer

At just 13 years of age, Aaron Bond from Devon, England, has designed and produced an iPhone app video game. Aaron, who set up his own web company when he was only six years old, learned how to write a smartphone game by watching online tutorials. The game, "Spud Run," involves navigating a mutant potato through a maze before it is mashed.

Precious Words

The manuscript of an unfinished novel by 19th-century English writer Jane Austen sold for £1 million ($1.6 million) in London in July 2011. Every page of the manuscript—for an 1804 novel entitled *The Watsons*—is filled with crossings out, revisions and additions, and is one of only a handful of Austen's draft works to have survived.

Air Phone

An iPhone app has been designed that blows out air through the phone's speakers. It is powerful enough to extinguish the candles on a birthday cake.

Chute Gown

In 1947, Ruth Hensinger got married in a dress made from the parachute that had saved the life of her husband three years earlier. Major Claude Hensinger was returning from a bombing raid over Yowata, Japan, in August 1944 when his plane caught fire and he had to activate his parachute. Decades after Ruth walked up the aisle at Neffs, Pennsylvania, in her parachute gown, her daughter and her son's bride both wore it at their own weddings.

Bad Maps

In November 2010, a Nicaraguan military commander blamed Google maps for an accidental incursion by Nicaraguan soldiers into Costa Rica.

Great Catch

A YouTube clip showed a spectator at a 2011 baseball game between the Toronto Blue Jays and the Kansas City Royals catching a foul ball—in his popcorn bucket.

Expert Dancer

On August 29, 2010, nine-year-old Ryota Wada from Herndon, Virginia, became the youngest person to achieve a perfect score on the expert level of the video game "Dance Dance Revolution." He mastered all 223 steps and 16 combinations, while dancing to the song "Heavy Eurobeat."

Friends Tribute

A working replica of the *Friends* coffee house, Central Perk, has been created in Beijing, China, because the U.S. TV comedy series is so popular there.

Video Spoofs

Corey Vidal of Oakville, Canada, makes a living from posting videos on YouTube. He specializes in pop culture spoofs and light-hearted instructional videos, and in just four years his videos have been seen more than 50 million times. "YouTube saved my life," he says.

Cutest Dog

After his U.S. owner posted pictures of him on Facebook, Boo, a fluffy eight-year-old Pomeranian dog, has amassed over 15 million "likes," landed four book deals, and been named the cutest dog in the world. He acquired the look of a cuddly teddy bear by accident, his natural long hair having become so knotted it had to be shaved off.

Five Deaths

Hong Kong actor Law Lok Lam died in five different TV soap operas in a 24-hour period in April 2011. One character died in a fight, the second fatally vomited blood, the third succumbed to an illness, and although two more died offscreen, their deaths were discussed by other characters.

SCENT OF BLOOD

Perhaps inspired by the popular appetite for the Twilight vampire movies and the *True Blood* and *Vampire Diaries* TV shows, an Italian company produced a line of perfume based on the four main blood groups, A, B, AB and O. Although not actually filled with human blood, each fragrance has a hint of the smell of blood. Bottles retail at more than $150.

AB

INFLATED EXTRAS

Next time you see a big scene in a Hollywood movie, look a little closer at the people in the background, for they might not be quite as they appear. You might expect a little computer-generated magic, but perhaps not thousands of individually inflated latex dummies.

The Inflatable Crowd Company, started by Joe Biggins in 2002, provides hordes of rubber dummies to the movie industry, dressed to look like real crowds on screen. Joe's dummies have been fallen soldiers in the Battle of Iwo Jima in World War II (*Flags of Our Fathers*, 2006), victims of a deadly virus outbreak (*Contagion*, 2011), 11,000 fans at a 1930s boxing match (*Cinderella Man*, 2005), and a 7,000-strong horse-racing crowd (*Seabiscuit*, 2003).

Joe was working on the movie *Seabiscuit* when he was asked how to fill the grandstands for the horse-racing scenes in an authentic but economical way. After testing cardboard cutouts, which were the usual method, he realized that the fake figures needed to be portable and three-dimensional. He considered the idea of inflatables, but found that nobody in the industry had done this before so there were none available. He created a prototype torso designed to sit in a stadium and the film's director, Gary Ross, agreed to use 7,000 such inflatables for *Seabiscuit*. Joe started his company after filming had ended.

One year later there was such demand for the inflatable bodies that Joe and his business partner Richard McIntosh had increased their stock to 30,000 pump-up extras, complete with clothing, masks and wigs.

A rubber crowd looks on during filming for the college football movie *We Are Marshall* (2006), which used 2,400 dummies. The only real people in the crowd were seen walking up the stadium steps.

The first full-bodied inflatables were created for *Flags of Our Fathers* (2006) to act as fallen soldiers at the Battle of Iwo Jima, shot in Iceland. The bodies were modified according to the scene—some were filled with plaster to emulate the reaction of a solid body when it is run over by a tank. Water corpses were also made, weighted to float or sink the way a human body would.

TRICKY TRIKE

A man in Jaipur, India, was seen transporting the chassis of an old car attached to the frame of his tricycle. He pushed his trike with his head through the open hood of the car so that he could see where he was going.

Shoe Car

A Chinese shoe manufacturer has converted a giant shoe into an electric car. The 10-ft-long (3-m), 3-ft-high (90-cm) shoe car has leather bodywork and took six months to create from the hide of five bulls. It can carry two people 250 mi (400 km) at a top speed of 20 mph (32 km/h) on a single charge of the battery, which is located beneath the driver's seat in the heel.

Dry Run

Battling against extreme heat and sandstorms, Reza Pakravan from London, England, cycled 1,084 mi (1,734 km) across the Sahara Desert in 13 days 5 hours, averaging more than 80 mi (130 km) a day. The heat was so fierce that he had to drink around 15 pints (7 l) of water every day to keep hydrated.

Electric Trike

Four engineers from Hamburg, Germany, have devised a tricycle powered solely by two 18-volt electric screwdrivers. The 44-lb (20-kg) EX trike, which can reach speeds of 18.6 mph (30 km/h), is driven in a headlong position, the driver operating the brake and gas levers with his hands and the rear wheel with his legs.

Exploding Manhole

An exploding manhole caused by flash floods threw an unoccupied parked car several feet into the air in Montreal, Quebec, Canada, in July 2011. The torrent of water turned the manhole into a geyser which tossed the rear half of the vehicle repeatedly into the air.

Smelly Phone

The Japanese-produced F-022 cell phone has a detachable fragrance chip that owners can saturate with perfume, which then infuses the entire phone with the chosen scent.

$1-million Crash

A woman driver in Monte Carlo caused a $1-million car accident when she crashed into some of the most expensive cars in the world as she tried to negotiate her way around the famous Place du Casino. Her $375,000 Bentley Azure scraped the side of a $110,000 Mercedes before hitting a $200,000 Ferrari, a $225,000 Aston Martin Rapide, and a $120,000 Porsche 911.

HEAVY HULK

This sculpture of the Hulk is made entirely out of car parts! Edward Meyer, Ripley's archivist, was in Thailand looking for a transformer in 2011, when he came across the company that created the Hulk, Art from Steel. Ripley's have since commissioned 40 pieces from the company over the last three years, including a Godzilla, a dragon, and a snake. The Hulk is the heaviest piece, weighing more than two tons!

'APPY BIRTHDAY

Mike Cooper from Kent, England, made a spectacular Angry Birds birthday cake for his son Ben when he turned six years old. Not only was it made from chocolate and sponge, it was a fully functioning Angry Birds game in itself, complete with catapult and sugary birds for catapulting. This swiftly led to a demolition and devouring of the cake, which had taken Mike ten hours to make.

One Step Ahead

John and Janys Warren from Somerset, England, live every winter one hour ahead of the rest of the U.K. because they think it is good for their health. Since 2006, they have lived by British Summertime all year round to combat Mr. Warren's cluster headaches, a painful condition that is thought to be triggered by a change in the clocks.

Identical Birthdays

Against odds of 17 million to one, the identical twin daughters of Tracey and Davood Bageban from Gateshead, England, share a birthday with the couple's identical twin sons. The boys, Diego and Armani, were born on February 27, 2008, and daughters Dolcie and Elisia were born on the same date three years later in 2011.

Military Tombstones

Jason Blackburn of Memphis, Tennessee, discovered 20 buried military tombstones, all dating back to the 1970s, while digging in his yard in May 2012.

Guilty Conscience

A barrister who stole 79 cents from a wishing fountain in Queensland, Australia, turned himself in 20 years later. Simon Matters was 19 when he took the coins in 1992 but after entering a career in the law, he finally decided to confess to the theft. The court ordered that no conviction be recorded.

FOODIE FASHION

A model shows off a dress made of nori seaweed with a dead octopus necklace at a fashion food exhibition in Berlin, Germany. After appearing on the catwalk, the designs were eaten. Other outfits included a chocolate dress with a quails' egg necklace and a bacon suit topped with a salad headdress.

Royal Rebuff

In August 2011, the King and Queen of Sweden were turned away by a German restaurant owner who failed to recognize them. King Carl XVI Gustaf and Queen Silvia called at a 16th-century inn in Ladenburg, but proprietor Nadine Schellenberger was preoccupied with a wedding reception and told them there was no table available. The royal couple and their entourage instead went out for a pizza on the market square.

CUSTARD CHAOS!

Competitors from as far away as Canada, Japan, South Africa and Germany travel to Kent, England, to take part in the annual World Custard Pie Throwing Championships. Points are awarded for throwing pies squarely into opponents' faces and also for the most amusing and original throwing techniques. The event was first held in 1967 and was inspired by a Charlie Chaplin movie.

Dream Cars

The interior of a restaurant in Surabaya, Indonesia, allows customers to eat in converted classic cars. Dream Cars features a 1949 Mercedes Benz limo that has been modified into a dining table that seats 20 people, and a 1962 Chevrolet Impala, which has been transformed into a smaller table for four. A 1961 brown Cadillac forms a seating area, a 1959 yellow Lotus houses an organ and the restaurant's audio system, while a 1969 red Chevrolet Corvette has been converted into an aquarium holding 100 fish.

Doughnut Delivery

In 2011, Voodoo Doughnuts of Portland, Oregon, made a record-breaking box of doughnuts, weighing 666 lb (302 kg), measuring 7 x 7 x 5 ft (2 x 2 x 1.5 m), and filled with about 3,880 doughnuts.

Giant Burger

A hamburger and bun grilled at the 2011 Alameda County Fair, California, by Brett Enright and Nick Nicora, weighed a staggering 777 lb (352 kg). It took 13 hours to cook and measured 5 ft (1.5 m) in diameter, and was 3 ft (90 cm) thick, representing a whole cow's worth of beef. The cheese on top of the burger weighed 50 lb (22.7 kg), and was accompanied by 30 lb (13.6 kg) of lettuce, 20 lb (9 kg) of onions, 12 lb (5.4 kg) of pickles, 10 lb (4.5 kg) of mustard, and 10 lb (4.5 kg) of ketchup. The bun, which took six hours to bake, weighed 272 lb (123 kg) and was 28 in (70 cm) thick.

Fast Food

McDonald's restaurants feed more than 64 million people a day—more than the entire population of the U.K.

Fishy Taste

Japanese scientists who conducted tests to determine why red wine should not be drunk with fish found that the greater amount of iron there is in a wine, the more likely it is to leave a fishy aftertaste when consumed with seafood.

Birthday Bash

On September 1, 2011, a 48.6-gal (184-l) bottle of Jack Daniel's Tennessee Whiskey was produced to celebrate what would have been Jack Daniel's 161st birthday. A bottle orchestra played "Happy Birthday" on 475 bottles of Jack Daniel's while fans of the liquor sent Jack a digital birthday card containing 1,075 individual greetings.

Doughnut Burger

The 2011 New York State Fair at Syracuse unveiled the 1,500-calorie Big Kahuna Donut Burger—a quarter-pound burger, with cheese, bacon, lettuce, tomato and onion in between slices of doughnut.

Fully Booked

A wall in Brushstroke, a Japanese restaurant in New York City, is made from 12,000 old paperback books.

MAGIC MOTOR

Toyota created a car that could change its entire appearance at the touch of a button. The body of the hi-tech Fun-Vii was made of touch-screen panels that allowed the driver to alter the pattern on display in an instant, like a smartphone. The car even flashed up a greeting message to the driver on the door.

Justin's Klout

The San Francisco–based social networking index Klout has calculated that Canadian teenage pop star Justin Bieber is more influential online than the Dalai Lama or Barack Obama. Klout adds up tweets, likes, pings, LinkedIn connections, Google mentions, status updates, and other social media data to measure a person's importance online.

Spam Sandwich

An open sandwich weighing 1,652 lb (750 kg)—including about 1,400 lb (635 kg) of Spam—was produced in Fremont, Nebraska, in 2011.

Crowded Trains

India's rail system serves about 8.5 billion passengers every year—that's over a billion more than the entire population of the Earth.

Dog Bites Shark

A video clip of a dog biting a shark in the ocean near Broome, Western Australia, has been viewed 4.5 million times on YouTube. Two dogs were swimming in the sea and appeared to be herding several sharks toward shore, when one suddenly ducked under the water and attacked a shark before emerging unscathed, to the suprise of the cameraman.

Broom Routine

Beijing road sweeper Zhang Xiufang became a Chinese TV celebrity after performing tai chi in the street using her broom as an exercise prop. A passerby filmed a short video of her routine on his mobile phone and posted it online, where it was such a hit that she was invited to star on a national TV show.

Cheated Death

A YouTube clip taken from his helmet camera as he plunged to the ground shows skydiver Michael Holmes somehow surviving a 15,000-ft (4,573-m) fall after both his parachute and reserve chute failed to open on a jump in New Zealand. Remarkably, he escaped with just two broken bones and some bruising.

Human Cloud

A video clip of a cloud formation in Canada that appears to show the face of a Roman god notched up over 300,000 hits on YouTube in just four days. The cloud, shaped in a humanlike side profile complete with mouth, nose and eyes, was filmed as a storm gathered over Grand Falls, New Brunswick.

HANGAR HOME

Joe Pires of Geneva, Florida, has a home with a stunning trick up its sleeve; it doubles as a hangar large enough to fit an airplane. The façade of the building hinges electronically to reveal a large hangar for various flying craft. Joe can jump into a gyrocopter or microlight without leaving his home, and taxi straight out onto the runway, which also doubles as his lawn.

Twins Restaurant

New York City's Twins Restaurant is owned by identical twin sisters Lisa and Debbie Ganz and is staffed by 37 sets of identical twins who work the same shift in the same uniform. Even the restaurant's business cards, doorknobs, light fittings, mirrors and bar stools are doubles.

Bean Barmy

Although baked beans originated in the U.S.A., the British are such fans of the food that each year they eat more than 800 million cans—three times more than the rest of the world combined.

Royal Bean

When Wesley Hosie of Somerset, England, found a mango-flavored jelly bean bearing what looked like an image of Kate Middleton, Duchess of Cambridge—complete with long hair and smile—he put it up for sale on eBay at a price of £515 ($830).

Pineapple Painkiller

Pineapple is a natural painkiller. The fruit contains enzymes that can reduce the inflammation associated with arthritis and in this way bring pain relief.

Cheese Platter

A cheese platter weighing 2,475 lb (1,125 kg) was placed on show at the World Cheese Awards in Birmingham, England. The platter consisted of 139 different wedges, featuring cheeses from every country in Europe, as well as from the Americas, Australasia and Africa.

Mini Bar

As part of a campaign to save their local pub, The Plough, residents of Shepreth in Cambridgeshire, England, opened up a village telephone box to serve beer. The Dog and Bone was open for only one night, but in that time it served about 70 customers.

High Tea

In L.A., California, a giant tea bag made from cheesecloth was unveiled measuring 6 x 4 ft (1.8 x 1.2 m) and weighing 151 lb (68.5 kg).

Super Sushi

A restaurant in Aichi Prefecture, Japan, serves giant sushi rolls that are wrapped in 6 ft 6 in (2 m) of seaweed and rice. The rolls, which contain 20 foods and cost just under $200 each, must be preordered two days in advance.

Prison Bakery

A team of 20 convicts at Rikers Island prison in New York bake 36,000 loaves of bread a week—enough to feed the prison's population of 13,000. The prison bakery covers an area of 11,000 sq ft (1,020 sq m).

Cupcake King

Competitive eater Tim "Eater X" Janus from New York City ate a record 42 cupcakes in 8 minutes at the Isle Waterloo World Cupcake Eating Championship on April 23, 2011. He has also eaten 141 pieces of nigiri sushi in 6 minutes, nearly 12 lb (5.4 kg) of burritos in 10 minutes, and 7 lb 11 oz (3.5 kg) of boneless buffalo wings in 12 minutes.

Chick Rescue

A visitor to Ireland's Dublin Zoo uploaded a clip to YouTube showing a 210-lb (95-kg) orangutan tenderly rescuing a drowning chick by lifting it from the water. Seeing the tiny moorhen chick struggling in the pond of his enclosure, Jorong, a Bornean orangutan, pulled a leaf from a nearby bush and held it out for the bird to cling to. With a second try, he managed to save the chick, then placed it down on the grass and stroked its head.

SEEING RED

Scottish farmer Andrew Jack dyed his flock of sheep red to cheer up people driving past his field! The farmer used non-toxic dye to paint his 54 sheep. They stayed red for a month, until their coats were shorn.

WACKY WEBSITES

Don't like tomatoes? There is a site dedicated to the belief that tomatoes are evil and cannot be trusted.

Loaf of bread cam allows you to watch a loaf of bread slowly going stale.

A toilet paper site enables you to unroll toilet paper for as long as you want without having to go through the process of winding it up again.

The Iowa State University **Entomology Club website** offers a selection of tasty insect recipes.

A dancing cows website shows cows doing ballet, disco and other dances.

Like repetition? Try the site that lets you open doors over and over again.

Would your **cat look good in a wig?** Visit the site catering for all your kitty wig needs.

The University of Virginia has a site that helps you **dissect a frog online.**

If you like watching paint dry, you might also like the site that enables you to **watch paint peel.**

Check out the site that helps you to find **prison pen pals.**

The University of Oklahoma Police Department website has a **Citizen's Self-Arrest Form** that lets you hand yourself over to the cops.

Does your cat look like Hitler? Check out the site that shows pictures of cats that resemble the Nazi leader.

Ian Usher of Perth, Australia, **sold his entire life** for $380,000. The sale price included his home, his car, his motorcycle, a two-week trial in his job and even his friends.

Mary Anderson of Indiana put her **dead husband's metal walking cane** up for sale because his ghost was said to be haunting the house and scaring her grandson. It fetched $65,000.

A ten-year-old **half-eaten grilled cheese sandwich** bearing a likeness of the Virgin Mary was bought for $28,000.

When Melissa Heuschkel from Connecticut couldn't decide what to name her fourth child, she put the rights up for sale on eBay. Online casino Golden Palace paid $15,100 to **name her baby "Golden Palace Benedetto."**

The right to **push a button detonating an explosion** to demolish a building in Charleston, West Virginia, sold for $5,207.

Justin Timberlake's half-eaten French toast (complete with fork and syrup) sold for $3,154.

GOING GOING GONE

(weird items sold on eBay)

A 19th-century **vampire hunting kit**—including a hammer, four stakes, a prayer book and a crucifix—fetched $2,005.50.

305

SINKING FEELING

Love, Love, a boat created by French artist Julien Berthier, floats at a constant 45-degree angle to give the impression that it is sinking. Berthier split an abandoned 21-ft-long (6.5-m) yacht, sealed it with fiberglass, repositioned the keel, built a new seat, and put two electrical motors underneath the vessel to power it. It looks so real that when the boat appeared on a lake the harbormasters were called to tell them a boat was sinking.

High Speed

A Chinese passenger train traveling between Beijing and Shanghai can reach the incredible speed of 302 mph (486 km/h). The new high-speed train has halved travel times between the two cities from ten hours to five.

Pipe Dream

Anthony Smith, an 85-year-old grandfather from London, England, crossed the Atlantic Ocean in 2011 on a 40-ft-long (12-m) raft that was made from lengths of gas and water pipes. He and his three-man crew—all of whom were aged over 55—set sail from the Canary Islands for the 66-day, 2,800-mi (4,506-km) voyage to the Caribbean.

Recycled Boat

Taiwan's Alex Chou designed an eco boat made primarily from 700 plastic bottles. The sailboat *Forever*, built entirely from recycled materials and powered by wind and solar energy, made its maiden voyage in June 2011.

Flattened Snowman

A bus driver lost his job after his bosses saw a YouTube video recorded by students at the University of Illinois of him running over a snowman that had been built in the road at Urbana, Illinois.

Super Mario

Born in 1985, the same year that Nintendo introduced the first Super Mario Bros. game, Mitsugu Kikai from Tokyo, Japan, has since collected more than 5,400 items of Super Mario memorabilia.

SWEET SUCKERS

This sponge giant weighed 200 lb (90 kg) and was created by Karen Portaleo of the Highland Bakery in Atlanta, Georgia. Karen is a former clay sculptor who has applied her creative talents to incredible cake decorations. The body and tentacles of the octopus were built with layers of sponge cake before being shaped, covered with fondant and airbrushed.

ZOMBIE PRANK

Don't be alarmed! The warning of zombies ahead that greeted drivers in southern Ontario, Canada, in May 2011 was not caused by an invasion of the walking dead but by pranksters hacking into electronic road signs.

Fast Fingers

In July 2011, 15-year-old Eduard Saakashvili, son of the President of Georgia, typed the entire English alphabet (A to Z) on an iPad's software keyboard in just 5.26 seconds.

Pets' Pages

One in ten of all U.K. pets have their own Facebook page, Twitter profile, or YouTube channel, and more than half of pet owners in the U.K. post about their animals on Internet social networks.

Totally Batty

When a group of students called the "Batman Boilers," from Purdue University, Indiana, posted a YouTube video of themselves hanging upside down by their feet—like bats—from the tops of walls, gates, fences, statues, and street signs, it led to a new Internet craze. Batmanning was inspired partly by planking, in which people are photographed face down in unusual places, as seen on pages 270–271.

Presidential Prank

"Rickrolling" is an Internet phenomenon in which an unsuspecting user who clicks on a link is directed to the video of Rick Astley's 1987 hit "Never Gonna Give You Up." When David Wiggs from Tennessee complained in July 2011 that the White House Twitter feed on U.S. debt was dull, the White House "rickrolled" him by suggesting he click on the link that led to Astley's video.

Scary Nose

A 2011 YouTube clip of Emerson, a five-and-a-half-month-old baby boy from London, Canada, freaking out at the sound of his mother blowing her nose went viral, racking up over two million views in its first three days online. After just four months, more than 21 million people had watched it.

Stuffed Shirt

On the U.S. TV show *Late Night with Jimmy Fallon* on March 1, 2011, George Booth stuffed a record 185 hot dogs into his T-shirt in 30 seconds.

Boiled Eggs

While on board the U.S.S. *Fitzgerald* on August 13, 2011, Adrian Morgan of Baton Rouge, Louisiana, ate 20 hard-boiled eggs in 84 seconds—one every four seconds.

Perfect Games

Eighty-five-year-old John Bates of Onalaska, Wisconsin, has bowled more than 3,200 perfect games—ones that consist entirely of strikes—in Wii Sports bowling. He plays about 20 games of Wii bowling a day.

Mascot Brawl

The Duck, mascot of the University of Oregon football team, received a one-game suspension after being involved in a brawl with Shasta the cougar, mascot of the University of Houston. The 20-second YouTube video shows the Duck laying into his opposite number with fists and webbed feet.

PEE-CONTROLLED VIDEO GAMES!

トイレで遊べる！
新しいカタチの広告

TOILET GAMES

Male toilet users in Tokyo, Japan, can play urine-controlled video games. The SEGA game, "Toylets," operates via a pressure sensor mounted on the back of the urinal that measures the strength of the user's urine jet. A small L.C.D. screen at eye level then allows him to play games, including measuring the amount of pee, comparing the strength of the pee with the previous user, and analyzing the character of the user from the strength and amount of pee.

Sucked into Pipe

Writer Allan Baillie of Sydney, Australia, survived with just cuts and bruises after being sucked feet-first into a drainage pipe and spat out onto a nearby beach seconds later. He was swimming in a pool while a workman was cleaning it, and when the workman pressed the button to open the water valve, Allan was sucked into the pipe. The circumference of the pipe was smaller than his body, but luckily the tremendous pressure meant that he popped straight out at the other end like a wine cork.

Steady Hand

Performing in Hamburg in 2010, German stuntman Joe Alexander used his elbow to break a record 24 concrete blocks, assembled in three stacks of eight, demonstrating such skill that the egg he was holding in his smashing hand did not break.

Human Blockheads

At the ninth annual Sideshow Gathering at Wilkes-Barre, Pennsylvania, in November 2010, 36 people simultaneously hammered various objects into their noses to create a mass human blockhead.

Junior Teacher

Shruti Pandey was just four years old when she began teaching yoga to adults at a retreat in Uttar Pradesh, India. Her elder brother, Harsh Kumar, had learned all 84 yoga positions by the age of five.

Dextrous Toes

After losing both of his hands at age three in an accident with electricity lines in his native China, Luo Yanbo has learned to eat, write, and brush his teeth with his feet. His grandmother taught him how to use chopsticks with his feet and he has become so adept that he can even use his toes to make phone calls.

Foreign Accent

When Karen Butler of Toledo, Oregon, went for dental surgery to remove several teeth, she came round from the anesthetic with a British accent—even though she has never traveled to Europe or lived outside the U.S.A. She suffers from foreign accent syndrome, a rare neurological disorder caused by an injury to the part of the brain that controls speech. There have been only about 100 known cases since the condition was first reported in the 1940s.

Raised Arm

Sadhu Amar Bharati Urdhavaahu, an Indian holy man, has kept his right arm raised above his head continuously for decades as a sign of his devotion to world peace.

Sumo Splits

Although Matt Alaeddine from Edmonton, Canada, weighs more than 400 lb (180 kg), he is a contortionist. Despite his considerable bulk, he can press the soles of his feet to the cheeks of his face by doing "sumo splits."

Internal Decapitation

The impact of a car accident jolted two-year-old Micah Andrews' head sideways with such force that his skull separated from his spine—a condition called atlanto-occipital dislocation, or internal decapitation. Surgeons in Phoenix, Arizona, kept Micah's head still by placing sandbags on either side before implanting a titanium loop to reattach the base of the boy's skull to his spine. The rod is held in place with a piece of the boy's rib. Two months later, Micah was released from hospital, able to walk and talk again.

CORSET PIERCING

Fashion victims must endure an hour of pain and risk permanent scarring to acquire corset piercing, a recent trend in extreme body modification. Small hoops are stuck into the skin and then threaded with ribbon to give a corset effect. The decoration can be applied only to an area of the body where the skin is loose. The most popular locations are the back, the ribs, and even the throat. It is only temporary—after a few weeks the hooks grow out, leaving scars in their place.

LIGHT FIGHT

One of the world's bloodiest sports has to be fluorescent-light fighting, during which Japanese professional wrestlers batter each other into submission with long glass rods.

After just a few minutes, both fighters are left covered in blood, and broken glass is strewn around the ring. There is a referee, but the general rules of the contest are that anything goes.

Extreme sports fans love the extra violence and bloodshed. The sport has spawned a whole new range of gimmicky contests in Japanese wrestling, using weapons such as barbed wire, weed whackers, TV sets, folding chairs, cheese graters and cacti!

Exploding Toilets

Two workers at a federal building in Washington, D.C., suffered cuts after a plumbing malfunction caused two toilets to explode and send tiny shards of porcelain flying through the air. The 2,500 employees in the building were warned not to use the bathrooms until the problem was fixed.

So Bootiful

A penguin named Bonaparte has fallen for a Wellington boot! The penguin, named after the famous French emperor Napoleon, has developed a romantic attachment to his keeper's black-and-white rubber boots (named in honor of the Duke of Wellington, Napoleon's adversary at the 1815 Battle of Waterloo). He even fights to keep the gumboots away from other penguins at his home in an aquarium in Germany.

Police Vultures

Police chiefs in Germany hired three vultures—named Sherlock, Columbo and Miss Marple— to replace sniffer dogs in the hope that the birds' amazing eyesight, sense of smell, and ability to locate dead prey would help them to find missing bodies. However, the scheme was abandoned after the disinterested vultures managed only to find a cadaver when it was placed immediately in front of their beaks.

Odd Passenger

A 59-year-old woman was arrested in Chesterton, Indiana, after being caught driving a golf cart while drunk and in the company of a large scarecrow.

TOP BANANA

Keisuke Yamada, a 23-year-old Japanese electrician, sculpts ghoulish faces out of bananas, then photographs them and eats them. In 2011, in celebration of the U.K.'s royal wedding, he deviated from his usual grim carvings by attempting to create banana likenesses of the Duke and Duchess of Cambridge. Keisuke said that carving the royal couple was a challenge he relished.

FISH PHONE

A phone booth in Osaka, Japan, was filled with hundreds of goldfish in October 2011. The unusual aquarium was a piece of street art designed to raise awareness of the mass production of such fish in Japan.

Stamp Storage

The U.S. Postal Service Stamp Fulfillment Department maintains an underground vault with nearly $500 million-worth of postage stamps in storage.

Lentil Sprout

A 4,000-year-old lentil seed found during a 2008 archeological excavation in Kütahya Province, Turkey, germinated and sprouted the following year.

Border Crossings

Baarle-Hertog in Belgium and Baarle-Nassau in the Netherlands make up a single town with twisted borders. Walking only a few streets, it is possible to cross national borders half a dozen times!

SEAL SURPRISE

An adventurous fur seal pup gave the occupant of a house in Tauranga, New Zealand, a shock in December 2011. The seal had made its way from the nearby harbor, across a busy road and slipped in through a cat flap, before making itself comfortable on the couch for the night.

Fox's Revenge

A hunter in Belarus was shot in the leg by a fox in January 2011. As the man attempted to kill the fox with his rifle after shooting it, the animal's paw hit the trigger, firing the gun.

Two Funerals

Romania's fattest man, 870-lb (395-kg) Cristian Capatanescu, had postmortem liposuction so that half of him could be buried in a regular-sized coffin and the other half cremated. His family asked doctors to remove some of his bulk because they couldn't afford to buy him an extra-large reinforced coffin.

Pipe Home

Mao Li, 30, lived for a year in a 6-ft-long (1.8-m) concrete flood pipe beside a bridge in Haikou, China. Squeezing feet first into the narrow opening, he installed a wood floor, a door, rugs and cushions.

In Cuffs

A criminal suspect escaped from a police station in Buffalo, New York State, on April 26, 2011... while still wearing handcuffs. When police rearrested him, they added a new charge for stealing the handcuffs in his possession.

Suicide Watch

Don Ritchie lives opposite the Gap—a rocky cliff along Sydney Harbor in Australia. So far, he has saved more than 160 people from committing suicide by convincing them not to jump from the cliff.

Vampire Conference

Three hundred exorcists from all over the world traveled to Poland's Roman Catholic Jasna Góra Monastery in 2011 for a week-long congress to discuss the increase in vampirism in Europe.

Memory Man

Aurelien Hayman of Cardiff, Wales, can remember what he had to eat, what he did, what was in the news, and even what the weather was like on any given day dating back over a decade. He is one of very few people in the world with hyperthymesia, or highly superior autobiographical memory, and noticed his condition when he was 11 years old.

Smelly Siren

A Japanese smoke alarm for deaf people emits such a powerful smell that those asleep wake up within 2½ minutes of the stench hitting them. Instead of a shrill wail, the device releases the chemical compound allyl isothiocyanate, which is what gives horseradish, mustard and wasabi their bite.

Unusual Motive

Jobless Richard Verone, 59, raided a bank in Gastonia, North Carolina, and he demanded just $1—because he wanted to go to prison in order to receive medical treatment. After the robbery, he waited inside the bank for police officers to arrive and arrest him.

SNAKE INVADER

A giant Burmese Python captured in the Florida Everglades was one of the largest ever found in the state. When biologists performed an autopsy on the 15¾-ft-long (4.8-m) reptile, they discovered a recently swallowed 76-lb (34-kg) adult deer, still remarkably intact.

BALLOON MAN

In a million-to-one freak accident, New Zealand truck driver Steven McCormack's body was inflated to three times its original size when a compressed air nozzle pierced his left buttock.

The 48-year-old was working on his truck at Opotiki on the North Island in May 2011 when he slipped between the cab and the trailer, dislodging the compressed air hose that feeds the brakes. The nozzle pierced his left buttock, sending air compressed to 100 lb (45 kg) per square inch rushing into his body. As his neck, feet, and hands swelled up instantly, he began to scream for fear that he was about to explode. "I had no choice but to just lay there, blowing up like a balloon," he said. Workmates hurried to his aid, and he was rushed to the hospital where his lungs were drained and a surgical drill was used to clear the wound in his buttock, leaving a hole about 1 in (2.5 cm) wide and 2 in (5 cm) deep. Doctors later told him they were surprised the compressed air did not make his skin burst.

Family Tradition

Four generations of one family have got married on September 9—in a tradition stretching back more than a century. Angelynn Perchermeier was wed in Cincinnati, Ohio, on September 9, 2011—100 years to the day that her great-great-grandparents had exchanged their vows. Her great-grandparents and her grandparents also chose September 9 for their weddings.

Busy Life

Ancentus Akuku of Kisumu, Kenya, married more than 100 times and sired more than 160 children before his death on October 3, 2010, aged 94.

Complex Chocolate

U.S. scientists have discovered that humans are less genetically complex than chocolate biscuits. Humans have 20–25,000 genes, but cacao, from which we make chocolate, has 35,000.

LEGO® Tower

Over a period of four days in April 2011, 6,000 LEGO® lovers joined forces to build a LEGO tower standing more than 102 ft (31 m) high in São Paulo, Brazil. The tower, which was composed of 500,000 LEGO bricks, was stacked up with the help of a crane and was held in place by wire supports to stop it toppling over in the wind.

SUPER SHOULDERS

Joshua Carter from Leesburg, Georgia, can touch his shoulders together in front of his chest, but don't try this yourself. Joshua was born without collarbones, which means that he has hypermobile, or double-jointed, shoulders. The collarbone normally forms a strut between the shoulder blade and the breastbone, and is the only long bone in the body that lies horizontally. "Having no collarbones is an advantage," says Joshua, "it has allowed me to fit into small spaces and work through a crowd easily!"

Plastic Birds

Keen bird-watchers Ken and Fay Jackson spent an entire day observing two owls on the roof of an apartment block opposite their home in Torquay, England —before realizing that the birds were made of plastic. The couple thought the reason the owls had not moved at all during that time was because they were stalking prey.

Fashion Victim

Accused of shoplifting from a local store, Stephen Kirkbride turned up in court in Kendal, Cumbria, England, wearing the exact coat he denied stealing.

Peak Condition

A 4x4 vehicle was abandoned near the top of 3,560-ft-high (1,085-m) Mount Snowdon in Wales twice in a month in 2011. On the second occasion— September 29—it had a "For Sale" sign attached to the windshield.

Talking Garbage

As part of the war on litter, British councils introduced garbage bins that say "thank you," applaud, or even burp when trash is dropped into them. In Sweden, a talking bin received three times more trash than a silent one nearby.

Wrong Side

A senior citizen from Jena, Germany, who wanted to block off the entrance to his cellar, worked from the wrong side of the new partition and ended up accidentally bricking himself into the cellar for several days.

Lucky Landing

Five-year-old Ye Zixu escaped with just scratches and bruises after falling from the window of a tenth-floor apartment in Chongqing, China. Luckily, her 100-ft (30-m) fall was broken when she landed on a ground-floor awning.

Laughing Fits

Pseudobulbar affect (PBA) is a neurological condition in which patients are unable to control sudden outbursts of crying or laughter. Episodes can last for several minutes, and a patient might laugh uncontrollably even when angry or frustrated.

Tight Spot

Prisoner Juan Ramirez Tijerina tried to escape from a jail in Chetumal, Mexico, by packing himself into his girlfriend's suitcase. When suspicious guards opened her bag, they found Juan curled up in the fetal position wearing only his underpants and socks.

Improper Address

Australian Thomas John Collins was jailed in November 2010 for calling Cheif Magistrate Matthew McLaughlin "mate" twice during a hearing in Ipswich, Queensland.

Longest Earring

U.S.-based Romanian jewelry designer Adrian Haiduc spent eight months creating an earring that is almost a third of a mile (0.5 km) long. The world's longest earring measures 1,550 ft (472 m) in length and is made from crystals, pearls, gemstones and beads, all strung on silk. It features three strings—one worn in the hair, another forming a necklace, and the third hanging as a conventional earring.

Funeral Clown

Clown Gerry Perry, a.k.a. John Brady of Drimnagh, Ireland, runs a funeral clown company with his clown friend Lee Cooke. Dead Happy Ireland was created for people looking to put the "fun" into "funeral." The company ad reads: "We bring squirting flowers, we make balloon animals. We can even fall into the grave if you want us to. Let your loved one go down with a smile."

EYE POPPERS

Brothers Hugh (left) and Antonio Francis from Essex, England, can pop their eyes out of their sockets. Antonio, who has been able to do this since childhood, has demonstrated his eye-boggling skill on *Britain's Got Talent* and in a music video for electropop act Hot Chip.

Hard Labor

An 11-year-old boy in Aachen, Germany, once called the police to complain that his mother kept making him do chores around the house during the school summer holidays.

Wrong Warrant

Police searched the home of Rose and Walter Martin of Brooklyn, New York, more than 50 times in eight years owing to a computer error.

VAST VEIL

For her wedding to Ferdinand Pucci near Naples, Italy, bride Elena De Angelis wore the world's longest wedding veil, measuring an unbelievable 1.8 mi (3 km) long. The white silk veil, which was 6 ft 6 in (2 m) wide, took months to make and needed a staggering 600 people to carry it. The village of Casal di Principe came to a standstill as hundreds of people turned out to help her along the streets to the church. Her veil was so long, it would take Usain Bolt racing at world-record top speed nearly 5 minutes to run its length.

Embarrassing Dad

Every morning for 170 days of the Utah school year, Dale Price wore a different fancy-dress costume to wave off his 16-year-old son on the school bus from their home in American Fork. Rain Price had been embarrassed when Dale had waved goodbye one day, so Dale decided to prolong the agony. But it turned into the highlight of the journey for other children on the bus. He dressed as such characters as Batgirl, the Little Mermaid, Princess Leia, Elvis Presley, Little Red Riding Hood and Wonder Woman. On another occasion, Dale dragged a porcelain toilet onto the porch and sat on it reading a paper.

Scotch Sculpture

University of North Florida art student Cameron Nunez made a sculpture of a group of rock music fans entirely from Scotch tape. He went through 24 rolls of tape and used himself as one of the casting models, wrapping a layer of tape sticky-side up around his head and arms before rewrapping over that, sticky-side down, to create a mold that was then removed with surgical scissors.

Dirt Bath

A retired police officer from Quebec, was arrested for allegedly filling his estranged wife's hot tub with manure after she had served him with divorce papers.

Christmas Gloom

Convicted of assault at Christmas in 2010, Daniel Martz of Livingston, Montana, was sentenced to spend the next five Christmases in jail to stop him getting into trouble during the holidays.

Dorito Tribute

Following his death on September 20, 2011, Arch West, the man who invented Doritos, was buried along with some of his beloved snack chips. Friends and relatives attending the service at a Dallas, Texas, cemetery tossed Doritos around the burial box containing his ashes as a tribute.

Triple Blast

Sgt. Horace Weigart, a U.S. soldier during the Mexican–American War (1846–48), was hit by three cannonballs during the siege of Fort Texas. The first wounded him, the second killed him, and the third later blew apart his grave site.

Telltale Sneeze

Fugitive Darius Olewski dug a 6-ft-deep (1.8-m) hole concealed beneath a table in the hallway of his home in Pruszkow, Poland, and hid there whenever the police came looking for him—until his luck finally ran out when he emitted an involuntary sneeze and officers discovered his secret lair.

Eyeball Licking

Instead of holding hands or kissing, a new practice among some teenagers in the U.S. Virgin Islands is to lick their partner's eyeball as a sign of affection.

Previous Meeting

Married couple Suzanne and Alistair Cotton from Coventry, England, met and fell in love before they discovered that they both suffered from the same rare heart condition. It turned out that 20 years earlier, in 1974, they had been in the same ward at the same hospital, where they had undergone the same operation, performed by the same surgeon, on the same day.

HAIR CAT

Veterinarians operating on a pet cat in Huntingdon, England, were shocked to discover what they thought was a tumor was actually a giant hairball— 5 in (13 cm) long, and the largest they had ever seen. Gemma the cat had swallowed so much hair she could no longer eat, and the furry ball in her stomach would almost certainly have led to death had vets not intervened.

BAT SOUP

Fruit bat soup is a delicacy on the Micronesian island of Palau.

Frozen bats are taken from the freezer and cooked whole—complete with fur, wing membranes, and feet—before being ripped apart by hand and eaten. The fur can be chewed until the musky taste has been sucked out of it. Confronted with the dish, Western visitor Benjamin Brown said: "They brought out the bat on a plate with a bow around its neck to show it to me before they cooked it. I had thought at the time that they would be cutting it up after to make the soup. Clearly I was wrong about that!"

Mystery Death

An Irish coroner ruled that a man who burned to death in his home on December 22, 2010, died of spontaneous human combustion. The totally burned body of Michael Faherty, 76, was found lying face down near an open fire in his living room in Galway, but coroner Dr. Ciaran McLoughlin ruled that the fire was not the cause of the fatal blaze. The only damage was to the body, the ceiling immediately above, and the floor directly beneath.

Stored Bodies

Jean Stevens of Wyalusing, Pennsylvania, kept her deceased husband's body in her home for a decade—and her twin sister's body for a year. When the authorities found out, they agreed she could keep them if she built a separate building to store them in.

Bad Choice

Stopped by traffic police in Great Falls, Montana, a man who had three outstanding warrants for his arrest gave officers a false name—but finished up in custody anyway because the name he gave was also that of a wanted man!

Gummy Heart

In L.A., California, candy creator David Klein invented an unusual new line for Valentine's Day 2011—a 2-lb-8-oz (1.1-kg), throbbing, anatomically correct gummy heart that oozed candy blood in 11 places. He also marketed an edible bleeding nose and a gummy severed foot with a gangrenous toe.

100-mph Couch

A two-seater brown leather couch, fitted with a motorcycle engine, clocked a top speed of 101 mph (163 km/h) at Camden Airport near Sydney, Australia, in September 2011, making it the world's fastest sofa. Designed by Paul McKinnon and driven by Glenn Suter, the superfast sofa came complete with a coffee table to help the contraption's aerodynamics.

Perfect Symmetry

Richard Burton Vail of Ontario, Canada, had birth and death dates that mirrored each other as a palindrome—11-12-20 and 02-21-11.

Washroom Stolen

In March 2011, thieves stole a 198-lb (90-kg) gray-and-white portable washroom from ski trails near Bognor, Canada.

Coffin Bed

Every Friday night since 1988, Zeli Rossi of Minas Gerais, Brazil, has traded his bed for a coffin. Rossi and a friend struck a deal many years ago that whoever died first would have his coffin bought by the other. Rossi's friend bought him a coffin when he mistakenly thought Rossi had died in a 1983 car crash, so when the friend died five years later, Rossi started sleeping in the coffin to honor his memory.

Back from the Dead

A morgue in Malatya Province, Turkey, has been built with a special motion-detecting alarm system—in case "dead" bodies come back to life. If a patient, declared dead by doctors, suddenly wakes up, the movement sets off an alarm in the mortuary's refrigerators, which also have doors that can be opened from the inside.

Mummified Passenger

Unsure what to do when her homeless friend died in her car, a Californian woman drove the partially mummified corpse around for ten months. On investigating the car, police officers were confronted with a foul stench and a leg poking out from under a blanket.

SMALLEST MAN

A 72-year-old Nepalese man, unknown outside his remote village until 2012, has been recognized as the world's smallest man. Chandra Bahadur Dangi is just 21.5 in (54.6 cm) tall and weighs only 32 lb (14.5 kg). He is 5 in (13 cm) shorter than his compatriot and previous record holder, Khagendra Thapa Magar.

DOLPHIN TATTOO

Heine Braeck from Sarpsborg in Norway lost his right arm in an accident on a railway line when he was a teenager, 20 years ago. Now, he has decided to make an unusual feature of his amputation by enlisting the help of tattoo artist Valio Ska to paint over his shortened upper arm so that it looks like a dolphin. Heine had always thought his arm looked like a dolphin's head, which is why he chose this animal for his tattoo.

Parting Shot

Alabama company Holy Smoke offers to ensure that deceased gun-lovers go out with a bang by turning their ashes into ammunition that can be fired by relatives.

Died Twice

In January 2011, Pinnitla Varalakshmi of Andhra Pradesh, India, was declared dead twice in 24 hours. She awoke as she was being prepared for her funeral, but then died for real shortly afterward.

Tax Bill

In 2011, Martine Courtois of Bruyeres, France, received a $16 land inheritance tax bill in the name of her grandfather, Pierre Barotte, who died in 1949.

Wife Duped

To be rid of his wife, a U.K. immigration officer secretly added her name to a list of suspected terrorists while she was in Pakistan visiting her family, meaning that she was unable to fly back to Britain for three years until his deception was uncovered. The truth came out only when he applied for promotion at work and was asked about his wife being a terrorist. He confessed to the deception and was fired for gross misconduct.

Locked in Bathroom

A 69-year-old woman from Paris, France, survived being locked in the bathroom of her second-floor apartment for three weeks after the door lock broke off in her hand. She tried to summon help by banging on the wall with her shoe night and day, but neighbors ignored the noise.

Car Plunge

Austrian teenagers Jürgen Oster and Felix Lemann escaped serious injury when their car plunged over the side of a Swiss mountain pass and crashed 900 ft (274 m) to the valley floor with such force that the vehicle folded in half.

Moon Suit

U.S. patent 3,139,622 was issued in 1964 for an astronaut moon suit. It had a large dish on the helmet to reflect solar radiation away from the astronaut.

T Party

Students at Georgia Tech in Atlanta have been removing the letter "T" from signs all over the campus, a prank that has cost the school over $100,000 in repairs. The tradition of stealing the "T" off Tech Tower began in the 1960s, but has spread to stadium signs and even book bins in front of the library.

Dung Watch

In 2010, a Swiss watchmaking company produced a one-of-a-kind $11,000 wristwatch with a body made from a coprolite—a fossilized piece of dinosaur dung dating back 100 million years. The watch's band is made from the skin of an American black cane toad.

Shelf Life

Charles Jones Jr. lived unnoticed in the basement of the Ocean Township Library, New Jersey, for nearly two weeks in 2010.

FREAK INJURIES

● In an infamous WBA Heavyweight Championship fight on June 28, 1997, *Mike Tyson* bit off a chunk of Evander Holyfield's right ear and spat it on the ring floor.

● Toronto Blue Jays baseball player *Glenallen Hill* badly cut himself after falling out of bed and crashing into a glass table while having a nightmare about being covered in spiders.

● British cyclist *Mark Cavendish* was snowboarding on a Nintendo Wii video game when he fell off the board and injured his calf.

● Chicago Cubs baseball player *Sammy Sosa* strained a ligament in his back after a violent sneeze.

● Scottish golfer *Sam Torrance* cracked his sternum after colliding with a large plant pot in his hotel room while he was sleepwalking.

● Detroit Tigers baseball player *Brandon Inge* strained a muscle while placing a pillow behind his son's head.

● Former Manchester United goalkeeper *Alex Stepney* dislocated his jaw after yelling at his teammates during a match.

● Competing in Rome, Italy, long jumper *Salim Sdiri* was speared in the side by a wayward javelin thrown by Finland's Tero Pitkamaki who had slipped at the end of his run-up. The javelin penetrated 4 in (10 cm) into Salim's flesh.

SPORTING SUPERSTITIONS

- Tennis player *Serena Williams* always bounces the ball five times before her first serve and twice before her second serve.

- The night before every game, basketball player *Jason Terry* goes to bed wearing the shorts of the next day's opposing team. He also plays in five pairs of socks.

- South African golfer *Gary Player* would play only with even-numbered balls; he left the odd-numbered ones in his bag.

- Basketball star *Michael Jordan* wore his lucky University of North Carolina shorts under his Chicago Bulls uniform in every game. To cover them, he started wearing longer shorts, which inspired an NBA trend.

- Between hockey periods, one-time Philadelphia Flyers goaltender *Pelle Lindbergh* would drink only a Swedish beverage called Pripps—and only if it had exactly two ice cubes in the cup and was delivered by the same trainer.

- Baseball player *Wade Boggs* always ate chicken before each game, took batting practice at 5.17, did running sprints at 7.17, and drew the word *Chai* (Hebrew for "Life") in the dirt before coming up to bat.

- U.S. golfer *Jack Nicklaus* always carried three pennies in his pocket for luck.

- Former New York Mets baseball star *Turk Wendell* used to brush his teeth between innings, chew black licorice, and draw three crosses in the dirt then wave at the center fielder before he pitched.

TINY BIKE

This tiny electric bike, called Mooshiqk (which means mouse in Sanskrit), measures only 13 inches in height and weighs just 11 lbs (5 kg). It can be ridden by an adult man and can travel at speeds of up to 12 mph (20 km/h).

Tree Bed

A woman fell fast asleep curled up on the narrow branch of a tree 20 ft (6 m) above the streets of Lanzhou, China. Shoppers realized she was there only when one of her shoes fell off and hit someone on the head.

No Pants

On January 9, 2011, an estimated 3,500 commuters stripped down to their underwear and boarded subway trains across New York City for the tenth annual No Pants Subway Ride. The event has spread across the globe with tens of thousands of people taking part in 50 cities from Adelaide to Zurich. A modest band of 100 people rode the London Underground; and in Johannesburg, South Africa, 34 no-pants riders were arrested for public indecency before being released without charge.

Hidden Lobsters

A shopper from Biloxi, Mississippi, was arrested for having two live lobsters in his shorts. The man was accused of trying to walk out of a grocery store without paying for food items that he had stuffed down his cargo shorts, including two bags of jumbo shrimp, a pork loin, and the lobsters. Police said he had tried to escape by throwing the pork at store employees.

Moving Experience

Since getting married in Yorkshire, England, in 1955, Orina Wyness has lived in 60 different houses—an average of a new house almost every year. She had to move each time her husband Ray, a naval petty officer, was given a new posting. Their globe-trotting took them all over the U.K. as well as to France and Australia, sometimes living in a house for just a few weeks.

Shark Attack

Kaiju Sushi and Rice Balls, a restaurant in New Smyrna Beach—the Florida town dubbed the shark attack capital of the world—offers a free shark sushi roll for anyone who has survived being bitten by a shark… and can prove it. The first customer to take advantage of the deal not only had a scar on his leg but also a YouTube video of himself on the local news in 2008 being taken away to the hospital.

Keen Gardener

Thomas Jefferson (1743–1826), the third U.S. president, grew 170 different fruits and 330 types of herbs and vegetables at his Monticello, Virginia, home.

Mohican Gathering

A total of 109 staff and students gathered in a room at West Cheshire College, England, on September 16, 2011—all sporting Mohican haircuts.

BATMAN COLLECTOR

Chloe Konieczki from Belvidere, Illinois, is a Batman fanatic! She collects anything she can, from shirts to toothbrushes, and has even called her cat Batman. Her bedroom is black and yellow and she wants to be Batman when she grows up!

WORM DELICACY

People in the Philippines eat a saltwater bivalve mollusk that bores into wooden ships, piers and docks. Known as a shipworm, because of its wormlike appearance and taste for wood, it can also be taken with rum as an aphrodisiac—a concoction called tamilok. Filipino Lloyd Lumbania says: "Tamilok is best eaten raw with a dash of lime juice. It tastes like raw oyster, is a bit salty and slimy, and smells like rotten wood."

Dog Lovers

In the course of "Hot Dog Season," from Memorial Day to Labor Day, Americans consume an average of 7 billion hot dogs, which works out at 818 hot dogs being eaten every second.

Very Smelly Fish

Some airlines and Swedish apartment complexes have banned surströmming, a delicacy of fermented herring, owing to its intense, rotten odor that makes it one of the world's worst-smelling foods.

Lettuce Lover

Elsie Campbell of Derby, England, used to eat four whole lettuces a day. She would eat a whole lettuce at work, and then go home and eat more and more, cutting them into chunks like a watermelon.

Butter Sculptures

As a tribute to the space shuttle program's 30-year legacy, the 2011 Ohio State Fair displayed butter sculptures of the shuttle and an astronaut, alongside its traditional butter sculptures of a cow and a calf. The exhibit took 475 hours to create and used 1,550 lb (703 kg) of butter—about 6,200 sticks.

Top Popsicle

The Marquis Los Cabos resort in Baja California Sur, Mexico, has launched a popsicle selling for $1,000. Although served on an ordinary plastic stick, the popsicle is made from premium tequila, which sells for $1,500 a bottle, and also contains 24-carat gold flakes.

Bagelheads

The latest body modification craze in Japan is the "bagelhead," created by injecting a saline solution into the forehead so that it inflates alarmingly. Body inflators feel only a dull headache during the procedure, and their forehead takes about two hours to swell up. Many then prod their lumps to create more interesting shapes, after which the inflation goes down overnight, usually leaving no scars.

Not So Old

In July 2010, Japanese officials went to congratulate Sogen Kato on his 111th birthday for being the oldest man in Tokyo, but instead found his mummified remains lying in bed—where he had died three decades earlier in 1979 at the age of 79.

Hole Sweet Home

For more than 20 years, Miguel Restrepo has lived with his wife Maria in a converted abandoned sewer pipe in Medellin, Colombia. The pipe, which is also home to their pet dog Blackie, is just 10 ft (3 m) wide, 6.6 ft (2 m) deep and 4.5 ft (1.4 m) high, but it has been fitted with a fan, a stove, a bed and even a TV. At night he covers the entrance to the pipe with planks.

Boy Stowaway

A nine-year-old boy flew alone from Minneapolis, Minnesota, to Las Vegas, Nevada, without a ticket or boarding pass. He went through security checkpoints at Minneapolis—St. Paul International Airport without being detected, but once he was on board the plane the flight crew became suspicious and arranged for him to be met by Las Vegas police on landing.

Lite-Brite Mural

Over the course of 365 days, Rob Surette of North Andover, Massachusetts, used 504,000 Lite-Brite toy pegs to create a mural measuring 10 x 20 ft (3 x 6 m) and weighing about 1,750 lb (795 kg).

Ice Ride

Michal Kawolski of Gdansk, Poland, had to be rescued by coastguards after drifting half a mile out to sea on a sheet of ice. He had been testing the strength of the ice next to the shore, when a piece suddenly broke away and strong currents began carrying him out into the Baltic Sea.

Pasta Hat

Austrian atheist Niko Alm has won the right to have his driver's license photo showing him wearing a pasta strainer as "religious headgear." Mr. Alm, who belongs to the Church of the Flying Spaghetti Monster, said the sieve was a requirement of his religion, pastafarianism.

Bad Driver

Gageen Preet Singh of Surrey, England, was paid up to £800 ($1,200) a time by driving-test candidates to take the test on their behalf—yet he himself was such a bad driver that he repeatedly failed the tests. Out of eight tests he was known to have taken for clients, he failed five. To carry out the illegal impersonations, he used an array of disguises, including fake mustaches and wigs.

Arrow Attack

In 2011, New Zealander Matthew Scheurich survived being shot with arrows in a remote jungle area of Papua New Guinea by a tribesman who wanted him dead so that he could marry his French girlfriend. Scheurich sustained an arrow wound to the stomach, which luckily stopped just short of his aorta (the body's most vital artery), and another to his right lung, and was pelted with rocks. He was airlifted to a small hospital where X-rays showed that his chest was half-filled with blood. He underwent an emergency transfusion to prevent him from bleeding to death.

Heat Hypnosis

In December 2010, staff at a small shoe repair shop in Bromsgrove, England, were shivering in temperatures of 8°F (−13°C) until their boss had them hypnotized into thinking they were warm. Martin Connellan always kept the door to the shop open and had tried buying jackets for his workers, but when that failed he brought in hypnotist Jim Kerwin—and after just five minutes under hypnosis some staff were complaining about how hot they were.

Hot Dog Bet

Jim Harrison, a 22-year-old student at McMaster University, Hamilton, Canada, won a $1,500 bet by eating 450 hot dogs in a month—an average of 15 a day.

Buried Fingers

Playing near Paris, France, a seven-year-old schoolboy dug up a glass jar containing several well-preserved human fingers thought to belong to a local carpenter who lost four digits in an accident more than 30 years before. At the time the carpenter's fingers could not be surgically reattached, so he put them in a jar full of alcohol and buried them near his home.

Devil's Tool

In the Middle Ages, the fork was seen as the tool of the Devil. It did not become a popular dining implement until the 17th century, when the French nobility needed something for eating their new favorite food—peas.

Pizza Passion

There are more than 61,000 pizzerias in the U.S.A., and Americans eat about 100 acres (40 ha) of pizza every day, or 350 slices per second.

CABBAGE HEAD

Russian artist Dimitri Tsykalov uses an ax, a saw and an electric drill to carve scary human skulls out of fresh fruit and vegetables, including melons, apples and cabbages. With surgical precision, he then uses a scalpel, pincers and cotton-wool pads to add authentic detail. Finally, he waits for his sculptures to rot before photographing them. "The flies let me know when it's time to take a picture," he says.

THE GREATEST SHOW ON EARTH

The 1903 lineup at Barnum & Bailey's Circus included a classic Bearded Lady, several "Lilliputians" and many other novelty acts.

Founded by showmen P.T. Barnum and James Anthony Bailey in 1881, and billing itself as "The Greatest Show on Earth," the circus enjoyed tremendous success in the U.S.A. and Europe, exhibiting bizarre and unusual performers alongside animal acts such as Jumbo the world's largest elephant, performing geese and musical donkeys.

1 Mohammed Soliman, Whirling Dervish and Fire-eater 2 Ivy Howard, Contortionist 3 John Hayes, Tattooed Man 4 Leah May, Giantess (8 ft 3½ in/2.53 m) 5 Young Herrman, Expansionist (expands chest measurement by 13¾ in/35 cm) 6 Maxey, Needle Eater 7 George Tomasso, Human Pincushion 8 John/James William Coffey, Skeleton Man 9 Edith Clifford, Sword Swallower 10 James Morris, Elastic Skin Man 11 William Doss, Telescope Neck Man 12 Annie Howard 13 Vera Wren, Female Boxer 14 Billy Wells, Hard-headed Man 15 Hovart family of Lilliputians 16 Beautiful Marie, Human Mountain 17 Hovart family of Lilliputians 18 Krao Farini, Missing Link 19 Hovart family of Lilliputians 20 Lionel the Lion-faced Boy 21 Hovart family of Lilliputians 22 Grace Gilbert, Bearded Lady 23 Charles Tripp, Armless Wonder 24 Hovart family of Lilliputians 25 Albino "Rob Roy," Wild Man of Scotland

Card Games

Nintendo was founded in 1889 and it started by manufacturing hand-made playing cards. This explains why "Nintendo" roughly translates from Japanese to English as "leave luck to heaven."

Sewer Ordeal

In October 2010, Daniel Collins of Raymore, Missouri, fell into a sewer and was swept through more than a mile (1.6 km) of pipe before he was rescued. He was working in the sewage system when his safety line unhooked and the water pushed him along the 2-ft-wide (0.6-m) pipe, finally dumping him in a 12-ft-deep (3.6-m) chamber.

Stuck in Chimney

The remains of Joseph Schexnider, who went missing in 1984, were found 27 years later wedged in the chimney of the Abbeville National Bank in Abbeville, Louisiana. Schexnider, who died of dehydration after getting stuck in the chimney, may have been trying to break into the bank at the time. He had been hiding from police after skipping a court hearing over charges of possessing a stolen vehicle.

Flushed Frenchman

A high-speed TGV train traveling between La Rochelle and Paris in France was delayed for two hours after a 26-year-old passenger dropped his cell phone into the onboard toilet. He attempted to retrieve the device, but his arm became jammed in the toilet system and would not budge. The driver stopped the train, but even firefighters could not extricate the man's arm from the toilet bowl. In order for the train to continue its journey, the firefighters were forced to remove the entire toilet from the carriage, with the man still attached.

Ornamental Skull

A dead man's relatives sued Czech police after officers used his skull as an ornament. The skull—wearing a police cap—was used as a bookend by officers at Volary who also took pictures of it and posted them on the Internet.

Mistaken Ashes

Burglars who raided a home in Silver Springs Shores, Florida, thought they had stolen a quantity of cocaine, only later to realize they had actually discovered the cremated remains of a man and two dogs.

Legless Elvis

Danny Frasier, a legless man from Alabama performs as the world's smallest Elvis Presley impersonator. Danny was born without his legs and is hearing impaired, but he still performs in front of crowds of up to 2,000 people and also responds to calls as a volunteer firefighter.

Deadly Revenge

A fighting cock took deadly revenge on its owner for forcing it back into the ring too soon. Birds are usually given an hour's rest before fighting another opponent, but when Singrai Soren of West Bengal, India, repeatedly tried to push the cockerel back into the ring, it attacked him and slit his throat with the metal blades that had been attached to its legs.

Screaming Corpse

A 50-year-old South African man who was thought to be dead suddenly woke up after spending 21 hours in a morgue refrigerator. When the man screamed to be let out of the morgue in Libode, Eastern Cape, two mortuary attendants ran for their lives, believing he was a ghost.

SCARY RIDE

An ultra-light plane hangs 33 ft (10 m) above ground from a Ferris wheel after crashing into it at a fair near Taree, Australia. The pilot and his passenger were trapped in the plane for nearly three hours, but they eventually walked away unhurt, while two children who were trapped on the ride at the time also escaped injury.

LIGHT FANTASTIC

Rashad Alakbarov, an artist from Azerbaijan, installed this unique artwork in the Phillips de Pury gallery in London, England, in 2012. The "painting" is actually white light projected through 90 plexiglass model airplanes suspended from the ceiling. The image depicts Baku, the capital of Azerbaijan, on the Caspian Sea.

Pizza Pickup

David Schuler of Jackson, Mississippi, makes a round trip of more than 2,800 mi (4,500 km)—just for pizza. Unable to find a pizza to his taste in Mississippi, he drives through 16 states to the Town Spa Pizza in Stoughton, Massachusetts. On one trip he bought 150 pizzas at a cost of $1,200.

Edible Table

Using 14 propane grills and 110 tables, volunteers at Crazy Otto's Empire Diner in Herkimer, New York State, cooked a 2,128-sq-ft (197-sq-m) omelet from 41,040 eggs. Using green food coloring, they turned it into an edible pool table with beach-ball billiards and broomstick cues.

Large Fries

Five staff from the Fish and Chip Shop at the Adventure Island fun park in Southend, England, cooked up the world's biggest portion of fries in June 2011, weighing in at 988 lb (448 kg). It took about four hours to peel, cut and fry the potatoes, which were then served in a box measuring 54 x 46 x 30 in (137 x 116 x 75 cm).

Costly Smash

A forklift accident smashed hundreds of bottles of Australian wine worth a total of $1 million. All but one of the 462 cases of Mollydooker Wines' Velvet Glove Shiraz bound for the U.S.A. were destroyed. Each bottle sells for around $200.

Exploding Melons

Thousands of watermelons exploded in China's Jiangsu Province in the spring of 2011 after farmers sprayed their crops too freely with chemicals designed to make the melons grow faster.

Everything Must Go

Yukako Ichikawa, a chef in Sydney, Australia, gives a 30-percent discount to all customers at her restaurant who eat everything on their plate—excluding only lemon slices, ginger and wasabi.

Timely Warning

J.D. Mullane of Middletown, New Jersey, has a grandfather clock that never runs, but has chimed on several occasions— and every time a child was in danger. It also chimes every April, the month of the death of his sister, Mary Beth, from whom he inherited the clock in 2002.

Vintage Wine

A 200-year-old bottle of Château d'Yquem white wine was sold to French private collector Christian Vanneque for over $115,000—the most ever paid for a bottle of white wine. Most white wines do not age well, expiring in the bottle after just a few years, but the 1811 Château d'Yquem is an exception because it is sweet. The buyer plans to drink his expensive purchase in 2017 to celebrate his 50 years as a wine expert.

Hot Dog King

On July 4, 2011, Joey Chestnut of San Jose, California, ate 62 hot dogs and buns in ten minutes to win the Nathan's Hot Dog Eating Contest in New York City for the fifth consecutive year. He trains by fasting and by stretching his stomach with water, milk, and protein supplements.

Snake Blood

After falling down a pit 79 ft (24 m) deep in Changshan County, China, while hunting snakes, Yi Guofang survived for two days by killing one of the snakes he had captured, drinking its blood, and eating the flesh raw.

BOOGER BALL

Over a period of two years, James Ford, an art student in Nottingham, England, collected his own boogers on a daily basis and molded them into a ¾-in-diameter (21-mm) ball—about the size of a Brussels sprout. He collected the boogers in an eggcup and then glued them together to create his mucus mosaic, which has been exhibited in London, England, and Lithuania.

Headshot Hero

Sergeant Paul "Headshot" Boothroyd earned his nickname after surviving a sniper's bullet to the head while serving in Helmand Province, Afghanistan, in March 2011. Just 15 minutes after being shot, he was smoking a cigarette and walking unaided to a military helicopter. Doctors say the survival rate for being shot in the head is only about one in 10,000.

Hotel Fall

Four-year-old Joey Williams fell seven stories from a hotel balcony in Miami, Florida, but landed without breaking a single bone. He hit several palm trees on the way down.

Atomic Kitchen

A man was arrested in 2011 after attempting to split atoms in the kitchen of his home in southern Sweden. He said it was simply a hobby, but after creating a small meltdown on his stove, he was arrested for unauthorized possession of nuclear material—radium, americium and uranium.

Combat Gnomes

Shawn Thorsson of Petaluma, California, has created a range of Combat Garden Gnomes— regular gnomes wielding army rifles—which he sells online. The U.S. Naval Reserve officer claims he came up with the idea because he wanted a military presence in his garden.

"Male" Mom

Jackie Kelly of Blountstown, Florida, was incorrectly listed as a male on her birth certificate and has officially been a male since 1958—even though she has given birth to two children!

Medical Message

To ensure that she does not endure a lingering death, 81-year-old grandmother Joy Tomkins from Norfolk, England, has tattooed the words "Do Not Resuscitate" across her chest. In case she collapses face down and paramedics miss the big blue letters, she has also had "P.T.O." and an arrow inked on her back.

Weight Issues

Suman Khatun from West Bengal, India, weighed a staggering 201 lb (91 kg) when she was just six years old and 3 ft 5 in (1.03 m) tall—more than five times her recommended weight, and the same weight as an adult Great Dane. In an average week, she ate 31 lb (14 kg) of rice, 18 lb (8 kg) of potatoes, 18 lb (8 kg) of fish, and about 180 bananas, as well as assorted cream cakes and her favorite Bengali sweets.

Dog Beer

Brewers in the Netherlands have devised an alcohol-free beer for dogs so that man and his best friend can enjoy a beer together. The Dog Beer is made from a special blend of beef extracts and malt.

Cutting Edge

A $100,000 shaving razor has gone on sale featuring white sapphire blades that last forever and have an edge less than 100 atoms wide—5,000 times thinner than the width of a hair. Designed by a Portland, Oregon, company, the razor has a handle made mainly from iridium, a metal derived almost entirely from meteorites and ten times rarer than the precious metal platinum.

CEMENT IMPLANTS

A fake doctor, Oneal Ron Morris, was arrested in Miami, Florida, on a charge of injecting a woman's buttocks with a mixture of cement, tire sealant and superglue to give her a more curvaceous appearance. According to detectives, Oneal (seen here) performed a similar procedure on herself.

YOUNG ME, NOW ME

Over 1,000 people have re-created childhood pictures for an Internet project titled "Young Me/Now Me." It is the brainchild of web personality Ze Frank, who asks visitors to his site to submit a photo of their younger self along with another one as they are today in roughly the same pose, hence the lack of smiles on the faces of these superhero brothers!

Robot Waiters

Samurai robot waiters serve customers at the Hajime Restaurant in Bangkok, Thailand. Every 30 minutes the robot waiters stop what they are doing and break into a dance.

Large Glass

An enormous wine glass measuring 7 ft 10 in (2.4 m) high and 5 ft 5 in (1.6 m) in diameter was unveiled at a wine festival in Beirut, Lebanon, in October 2010. The giant goblet-shaped container was created by engineers Walid Richa and Moussa Zakharia from Plexiglas, and was only one-quarter full after having 100 bottles of wine emptied into it.

Sardine Cure

Patients in Hyderabad, India, eat live sardines coated in masala, a spice mix, to cure their asthma. The treatment is administered by 200 members of the Goud family one day in June each year, and several hundred thousand people with respiratory problems line up to eat the 2-in-long (5-cm) spicy fish, the recipe for which is said to have been handed down by a Hindu saint.

Reliable Refrigerator

A General Electric refrigerator bought in 1952 has enjoyed some 60 years of continuous use in the Oxford, England, home of Doris Stogdale. The fridge—bought for the equivalent of $200 in today's money—has never needed any maintenance or even a single new part.

Colossal Corgi

As part of the buildup to the 2011 royal wedding between Prince William and Kate Middleton, British cake designer Michelle Wibowo created a giant cake in the shape of a royal corgi dog. The cake measured nearly 6 x 4 ft (1.8 x 1.2 m) and weighed 150 lb (68 kg).

Rare Wine

On sale in Geneva, Switzerland, in November 2010, a rare large Imperial bottle of 1947 French Cheval-Blanc white wine—equal to eight standard bottles—was sold to a private collector for $304,375. Labeled "the greatest wine ever made," it is so coveted that enthusiasts have traveled thousands of miles to taste it and the wine is thought to be the only bottle in existence.

Winning Sequence

After getting engaged on 10/10/10 and registering a court marriage on 11/11/11, Brandon Pereira and Emilia D'Silva maintained the sequence by having a traditional church wedding in Mumbai, India, at noon on 12/12/12.

Stretch Sausage

Chef Alberto Della Pelle created a record-breaking sausage 1,960 ft (597.8 m) long in the main street of Penne, Italy Around 1,300 lb (590 kg) of meat was used to stuff the sausage skin, and the end product was sliced to fill 6,000 sandwiches.

Burger Milestone

In May 2011, Don Gorske of Fond du Lac, Wisconsin, ate his 25,000th Big Mac—39 years after eating his first nine in a single day. He says the burgers make up 90 percent of his solid food intake, adding: "I plan on eating Big Macs till I die."

Pub Crawl

A team of 13 people had a drink in 250 Manhattan bars and restaurants in 24 hours on September 3, 2011. One team member drank a half pint at each stop.

GUM MAN

Chris Antes of Cleveland, Ohio, sent in these pictures of pieces of gum that he has sculpted into more than 250 different shapes—including animals, vegetables, fruit, and body parts—without using his hands. Instead, the Gum Man, as he is known, molds the gum into the desired shape in his mouth, and can complete a new work of art in less than 45 seconds.

King Kebab

Leon Ekery of El Paso, Texas, prepared a lamb kebab that was 28 ft 7 in (8.7 m) long. He used a 31-ft-long (9.4-m), one-piece stainless-steel skewer, a 30-ft (9.1-m) grill, and more than 40 lb (18 kg) of lamb.

Sour Taste

Liu Yuejin of Zhenjiang, China, drank three bottles of vinegar in 28 seconds as part of a competition to promote the health benefits of drinking vinegar. After undergoing medical examinations to check they did not suffer from high blood pressure, heart disease or mental illness, contestants had to drink three 12½-fl-oz (375-ml) bottles of local vinegar, one after the other.

Fast Pizza

Takeout pizza shop owner Alberto Valotta from Hemel Hempstead, England, hired a $225,000 Lamborghini with a top speed of 200 mph (320 km/h) to launch a really fast food service to customers.

Shell Shock

Charlotte Matthews of Rochdale, England, cracked open 29 double-yolked eggs in a row from one carton. Only the 30th and final egg in the box had a single yolk. The odds of cracking open just one double-yolked egg are one in a thousand.

Unusual Drink

A $250-million water-recycling device aboard the International Space Station purifies the astronauts' urine so they can drink it.

Cooking Marathon

In a world-record-breaking cooking marathon, chef Benno Stewart cooked some 50 dishes—including stews, casseroles, lamb shanks and a pig on a spit—for 31 hours 31 minutes 55 seconds at the Bowen Show in Queensland, Australia, in June 2011.

Potato Diet

Chris Voigt, head of the Washington State Potato Commission, ate nothing but potatoes for 60 days in 2010 to prove the nutritional value of the starchy vegetable. He lost 21 lb (9.5 kg) on his potato diet, during the course of which he ate around 1,200 potatoes in various guises—baked, boiled, fried, mashed and shredded.

URINE EGGS

In Dongyang County, China, buckets of boys' urine are collected from local schools—for use in a culinary dish! Cooking eggs in urine to make Tong Zi Dan (small boy eggs) is believed to ward off ailments and promote energy. The eggs are soaked in boiled urine for an entire day before they are ready to eat, and remain popular with locals, despite advice from doctors in the area who say that Tong Zi Dan is potentially toxic.

Distal phalanges

Metacarpal

Proximal phalanges

BONE JEWELRY

Columbine Phoenix from Somerville, Massachusetts, makes jewelry from human bones. Among her creations are an earring with a middle finger bone, a necklace from five fingertip bones and a necklace from a hand bone. She obtains the bones from universities and medical schools, and always uses hand bones because they are the only ones small enough for jewelry.

EXPENSIVE CRASH

The Chugoku Expressway in Shimonoseki, Japan, was the scene of one of the most expensive and exclusive car wrecks in recent years. A total of 14 sports cars, including eight Ferraris, a Lamborghini, and a Mercedes—worth something in the region of $1.3 million—were caught out on a drive to a supercar meeting in Hiroshima. It is thought the Ferrari owners may have been driving too close to one another when one driver lost control, leaving them little time to react before smashing into each other and careening into the road barrier.

Human Parcel

Reluctant to pay the train fare, the parents of four-year-old May Pierstorff mailed her instead by U.S. Mail to her grandparents' home in Lewiston, Idaho. As her 48½-lb (22-kg) weight was just below the 50-lb (22.7-kg) limit, on February 19, 1914, they attached 53 cents in parcel post stamps to May's coat and she traveled the entire journey in the train's mail compartment before being delivered to her grandparents' home by the mail clerk.

index

index

index

index

index

acknowledgments

15 (b/l) Courtesy of The Fairmont Hotel, (b/r) Tim Stewart News/Rex Features; 18 WENN.com; 19 Sinopix/Rex Features; 20–21 (b) Rusty Haight, The Collision Safety Institute; 21 (t) Miller & Maclean; 22–23 Justin Quinnell; 24 Quirky China News/Rex Features; 25 Matthew Holzmann; 26 Imagine China; 28–29 PA Archive/Press Association Images; 30 Library of Congress; 32 Les Wilson/Rex Features; 32–33 (dp) © Ralph White/Corbis; 34 Reuters/Enny Nuraheni; 36 © Europics; 37 Franklin Reyes/AP/Press Association Image; 38–39 Danny Lawson/PA Archive/Press Association Images; 41 Courtesy of The Fairmont Hotel; 42 Kevin Grennan; 43 Quirky China News/Rex Features; 44 good.kz/Rex Features; 46 Reuters/Kham; 47 Reuters/Paul Yeung; 48–49 Caters News; 50 © Picture Alliance/Photoshot; 51 Zilvinas Abaravicius; 52–53 Reuters/Sukree Sukplang; 54 Quirky China News/Rex Features; 55 Tim Stewart News/Rex Features; 57 Imagine China; 58 Sunshine Serpents/Rex Features; 59 (b/l) Jennifer Showalter, (b/r) James Holmdahl; 60–61 Steven Senne/AP/Press Association Images; 62 Katrina Bridgeford/Rex Features; 63 Bay Ismoyo/AFP/Getty Images; 64 Ian Butler/Solent News/Rex Features; 65 Reuters; 66 KeystoneUSA-ZUMA/Rex Features; 68 Andrew Forsyth/Solent News/Rex Features; 69 www.sell-my-photo.co.uk; 70–71 Reuters; 72 Quirky China News/Rex Features; 73 ABC TV; 74–75 Time & Life Pictures/Getty Images; 77 Sunshine Serpents/Rex Features; 78 SWNS.com; 79 Pisces Sportfishing Fleet/Rex Features; 80 Jennifer Showalter; 81 Alex Coppel/Newspix/Rex Features; 83 Tim Green; 84 Mohamed Babu/Solent News/Rex Features; 85 Ren Netherland/Barcroft Media; 87 Gerry Robichaud/Caters News; 88 AP/Press Association Images; 89 © Photoshot; 90 Charlie Hamilton James/naturepl.com; 92 Laurentiu Garofeanu/Barcroft USA; 94 UPPA/Photoshot; 95 © Thomas Marent/ardea.com; 96 James Holmdahl; 97 The Canadian Press/Press Association Images; 98 Scottish SPCA; 100 Reuters/Romeo Ranoco; 101 (b/l) Nancy Sathre-Vogel/Family on Bikes, (b/r) Nigel Hewitt-Cooper; 102–103 Richard Grange/Barcroft India; 104 © Europics; 105 www.sell-my-photo.co.uk; 106–107 Fernando Bustamante/AP/Press Association Images; 108–109 Reuters/Romeo Ranoco; 110 Imagine China; 111 © Chris Hellier/Corbis; 112–113 Courtesy of Lockheed Martin; 114 Amos Chapple/Rex Features; 115 Reuters; 117 Vyacheslav Oseledko/AFP/Getty Images; 118 (t) SWNS.com, (b) KPA/Zuma/Rex Features; 119 (t) UPPA/Photoshot, (b) Quirky China News/Rex Features; 121 Nancy Sathre-Vogel/Family on Bikes, (bgd) © Anton Balazh/Fotolia.com; 122 Nigel Hewitt-Cooper; 123 ChinaFotoPress/Photocome/Press Association Images; 124–125 Quirky China News/Rex Features; 126 Bruce Lewis; 127 Dee Allen; 128 (b) Karin Strandås; 128–129 (dp) Dominik Schwarz; 129 (t/c) Karin Strandås, (t/r) © Julie Dermansky/Corbis, (b/r) Rex Features; 130 seawhisper/yaymicro.com; 131 Picture courtesy of Duane and Sally Arnold; 132–133 Reuters/Desmond Boylan; 136–137 (dp) AFP/Getty Images; 137 (r) Stephen Morton/Getty Images; 138 Peter Bardsley/Fotolibra; 141 Mister Jo; 142 Dinesh Upadhyaya; 144–145 Courtesy of Food For Louis; 146–147 Dinesh Upadhyaya; 148–149 (b) © Jörg Mitter/Red Bull Content Pool; 149 (t) © Europics; 150 Erik Sprague; 152 Quirky China News/Rex Features; 153 Barbara Lindberg/Rex Features; 154–155 Sipa Press/Rex Features; 156–157 Bruce Airhead; 160 Sky News; 161 Brian Bielmann/Solent; 162–165 Bradford Bohonus; 166–167 Nazare Qualifica, E.E.M.; 168–169 Quirky China News/Rex Features; 170 © Europics; 171 Courtesy of Katalin Williams; 174 © Photoshot; 175 Darryl Learie; 176–177 Quirky China News/Rex Features; 178 Reuters/Jonne Roriz-Agencia Estado; 179 Bigfoot Hostel, Nicaragua; 183 WENN.com; 184 Photographer: Nathan Gallagher; 185 (b/l) Janne Parviainen, www.jannepaint.com, (b/r) Natalie Irish; 186–187 Natalie Irish; 188 Sipa Press/Rex Features; 190–191 Sian Williams; 191 (t) Betfair/Solent News; 192 Andrew Lancaster/Rex Features; 193 © Hideto Nagatsuka/Solent News; 194–195 Janne Parviainen, www.jannepaint.com; 197 Gabriel Bouys/AFP/Getty Images; 198 Tim Stewart News/Rex Features; 200 Startraks Photo/Rex Features; 201 Brian Rasic/Rex Features; 202 (c) Reuters/Cheryl Ravelo, (r) Rex Features; 203 Rob Huibers/Hollandse Hoogte/eyevine; 204 Scott Irvine; 205 Burns!; 207 Courtesy of Voodou, Liverpool; 208 Rob Matthews; 209 Dario Lopez-Mills/AP/Press Association Images; 210 Reuters/Jon Nazca; 211 (b) Photographer: M2k Photo model: pink dress: Tiffany Tezna, (c) Julie Clopper - Shutterstock.com; 214 DC Image Photography; 215 Taras Lesko (www.visualspicer.com); 217 Photographer: Nathan Gallagher; 218 Lee Hadwin; 219 (b/l) Maya Pixelskaya/Rex Features, (b/r) Everett Collection/Rex Features; 220–221 Courtesy of Priska C. Juschka Fine Art, New York; 222 Kerry Howley/Rex Features; 223 Courtesy of Olek; 224–225 Sean E. Avery; 227 (b/l) Rachel Betty Case, (b/r) Courtesy of Kimberleigh Smithbower Roseblade; 228–229 Circus World Museum, Baraboo, Wisconsin; 230 Yang Zhichao; 231 Quirky China News/Rex Features; 232 Alexandra Daisy Ginsberg & James King, with the University of Cambridge IGEM team 2009; 234 Rachel Betty Case; 235 (sp) WENN.com, (c/l) University of Arizona Medical Center, Tucson; 236 Bronek Kaminski/Barcroft India; 238 Ricky Nakamura; 239 Quirky China News/Rex Features; 240–241 Circus World Museum, Baraboo, Wisconsin; 244 Reuters/David Mdzinarishvili; 245 Tolu Solanke & Kathy Hayes; 246–247 Mayuko Kanazawa; 248 Steve Meddle/Rex Features; 250 Adrianne Lewis; 253 c.Paramount/Everett/Rex Features; 255 c.Paramount/Everett/Rex Features; 256–257 Quirky China News/Rex Features; 259 © Bettmann/Corbis; 260 CDC/Science Photo Library; 261 (t) Darlyne A. Murawski/Getty Images, (b/l) © Dwight Davis-Fotolia.com, (b/r) © Heinz Waldukat-Fotolia.com; 262 James Ambler/Barcroft USA; 264 Courtesy of Kimberleigh Smithbower Roseblade; 265 Adrienne Antonson; 266 Ashley/Bizarrearchive.com; 267 Steve Meddle/Rex Features; 268 Startraks Photo/Rex Features; 269 (b/l) Vincent T. Migliore, (b/r) Phyllis Keating; 270 (t) Newspix/Rex Features, (b) Tima Sergeev; 271 (t) Vincent T. Migliore, (c) Reuters/Nicky Loh, (b) Rex Features; 274–275 Sam Minnell/Caters News; 276 SWNS.com; 277 Reuters/Jerry Lampen; 278 (t) Brent Douglas, (b) Jeffrey Bautista; 279 Deney Tuazon; 281 FPG/Hulton Archive/Getty Images; 282 Charly Molinelli/Rex Features; 283 SWNS.com; 284 (t) http://www.stanley.sg; 284–285 (dp) Albert Tan; 285 (t) http://www.stanley.sg/; 286 Startraks Photo/Rex Features; 288 Strapya/Rex Features; 289 Rex Features; 291 Courtesy of the Inflatable Crowd Company; 292 © Photoshot/TIPS; 294 Mike Cooper/Electricpig.co.uk; 295 © Picture Alliance/Photoshot; 296 (sp) Gareth Fuller/PA Wire, (b) Chris Radburn/PA Wire; 297 W.C.P.C. Championship; 298–299 Reuters/Kim Kyung-Hoon; 300 Courtesy of Joe Pires; 302–303 Carol McCabe/Rex Features; 304 Jill Johnson; 306 www.julienberthier.org courtesy galerie GP&N Vallois, Paris; 307 Karen Portaleo/Highland Bakery/Caters News; 308 Phyllis Keating; 309 © 2012 Sega Corporation; 311 (t/l) Solent News/Rex Features, (r) Dragstrip/Solent News/Rex Features; 312 Joshua Carter; 313 (b/l) Courtesy of Ugly Models, (b/r) Phillips de Pury & Company; 314–315 Nippon News; 316 Keisuke Yamada/Rex Features; 317 Nippon News; 318 Crown Copyright: Department of Conservation Te Papa Atawhai (11 December 2011), Photographer: Christopher Clark; 319 USA National Parks Service; 320 New Zealand Herald; 321 Joshua Carter; 323 Courtesy of Ugly Models; 324 Sipa Press/Rex Features; 325 Geoffrey Robinson/Rex Features; 326 (b) Benjamin Brown; 326–327 Anthonioo; 329 Reuters/Navesh Chitrakar; 330 SWNS.com; 332 Jed Jacobsohn/Getty Images; 333 Reuters/Toby Melville; 334 Mooshikq - the world's smallest e-bike - Made in India by Santhosh, Mysore http://santhoshbikes.blogspot.in; 335 Chloe Konieczki; 336 (t) Craig Sullivan, (b) John Luther Garcia; 338 Dimitri Tsykalov/Landov/Press Association Images; 340–341 Circus World Museum, Baraboo, Wisconsin; 343 AAP Image/Press Association Images; 344 Phillips de Pury & Company; 346 James R. Ford; 347 © Polaris/eyevine; 348 Ze Frank/Rex Features; 350 Chris Antes; 351 Quirky China News/Rex Features; 352 Columbine Phoenix; 353 Toshiro Kubo/AP/Press Association Images

Key: t = top, b = bottom, c = center, l = left, r = right, sp = single page, dp = double page, bgd = background

All other photos are from Ripley Entertainment Inc.

Every attempt has been made to acknowledge correctly and contact copyright holders and we apologize in advance for any unintentional errors or omissions, which will be corrected in future editions.